The Enlightenment

The Enlightenment

A Genealogy

DAN EDELSTEIN

The University of Chicago Press ❋ *Chicago and London*

DAN EDELSTEIN is assistant professor of French at Stanford University. He is the author of *The Terror of Natural Right* (2009), also published by the University of Chicago Press.

The University of Chicago Press, Chicago 60637
The University of Chicago Press, Ltd., London
© 2010 by The University of Chicago
All rights reserved. Published 2010
Printed in the United States of America
19 18 17 16 15 14 13 12 11 10   1 2 3 4 5
ISBN-13: 978-0-226-18447-0 (cloth)
ISBN-10: 0-226-18447-1 (cloth)
ISBN-13: 978-0-226-18449-4 (paper)
ISBN-10: 0-226-18449-8 (paper)

Library of Congress Cataloging-in-Publication Data
Edelstein, Dan.
    The Enlightenment: a genealogy / Dan Edelstein.
       p. cm.
    Includes bibliographical references and index.
    ISBN-13: 978-0-226-18447-0 (cloth: alk. paper)
      ISBN-10: 0-226-18447-1 (cloth: alk. paper)
       ISBN-13: 978-0-226-18449-4 (pbk.: alk. paper)
       ISBN-10: 0-226-18449-8 (pbk.: alk. paper)
    1. Enlightenment—France. 2. Philosophy—France—
History—18th century. 3. Ancients and moderns,
Quarrel of. 4. France—Intellectual life—18th
century. 5. Philosophy—Europe—History—18th
century. I. Title.
    B802.E34   2010
    944′.034—dc22   2010007668

They order . . . this matter better in France.

LAURENCE STERNE, *A Sentimental Journey* (1768)

Contents

Acknowledgments

This book was written during a one-year fellowship at the Stanford Humanities Center: my first thanks go to the staff and to the director of the center, Aron Rodrigue, for their unparalleled support. I was also most fortunate to have a wonderful group of fellows with whom to debate this book's contents, mostly in heated discussions punctuated by forkloads of Indian food: special thanks to Jonathan Kramnick, Caroline Winterer, Terry Castle, Yair Mintzker, John Hatcher, Dina Moyal, Ken Taylor, and my comrade-in-arms, Josh Landy.

It was David Bell who first whispered the seductive words "short book" with respect to a long paper I had written on the Enlightenment; but my debt to him extends far beyond this tantalizing suggestion, as his comments, criticisms, and saving arguments guided the revision of said paper into its present shape. Many thanks as well to the participants of the Johns Hopkins history seminar: I benefited greatly from remarks by John Pocock, John Marshall, Orest Ranum, Robert Forster, and Eddie Kolla. I am also deeply obliged to Elena Russo for her advice and incessant inspiration. I presented some material from this book at the University of Minnesota as well: my thanks to Dan Brewer, J. B. Shank, Juliette Cherbouliez, and the participants of the TEMS seminar. Thanks also to the participants of the Interdisciplinary Colloquium in the Humanities at Stanford University and, in particular, to Grisha Freidin.

If these pages have any shine, however, it is due to the invaluable polishing skills of Keith Baker. Page by page, and argument by argument, he queried, corrected, challenged, and recast this manuscript to produce a far more coherent and fluid narrative. I have signaled in the text only some of the many ideas he shared with me: so many more originated from other conversations that I am no longer sure which are his and which are mine. No doubt the better ones are his.

This book gestated alongside a number of other works, which have only recently or have still to see the light of day. In a most unbiological fashion, it was influenced by their development and now reflects many of their traits. Larry Norman generously shared his manuscript for *The Shock of the Ancient* with me and provided a stream of crucial comments on the Quarrel of the Ancients and the Moderns. Antoine Lilti and I debated Spinoza on the boulevard Saint-Michel; his article "Comment écrit-on l'histoire intellectuelle des Lumières?" (then still in draft form) was a major influence. Céline Spector sent me her article on "Les lumières avant les Lumières" and laughed when she discovered that we had both stumbled upon the same thesis. I had the great pleasure of discussing J. B. Shank's recent book, *The Newton Wars and the Beginning of the French Enlightenment*, with him over Vietnamese food in Minneapolis: his comments and bibliographic suggestions were invaluable. David Bates and I meet up at regular intervals in a Stanford "Biergarten"; reading and talking about his forthcoming *States of War* has been deeply illuminating. Finally, my knowledge of all things French was constantly enriched by an IV drip of phone and e-mail conversations with Jake Soll, then in the process of finishing *The Information Master: Jean-Baptiste Colbert's Secret State Intelligence System*. Thankfully, on a few occasions we were able to switch out the IV for a bottle of Bordeaux.

I benefit on a daily basis from a most fruitful collaboration with the ARTFL Project at the University of Chicago: my greatest thanks to Robert Morrissey, who has also provided precious criticism on this project; to Mark Olsen, the wizard of Hyde Park; and to Glenn Roe, Clovis Gladstone, and Tim Allen.

My chair, Robert Harrison, continues to be the most persuasive advocate any assistant professor could dream of: *mille grazie, maestro*. Still in my department, thanks also to Sepp Gumbrecht for his most helpful comments on this manuscript and for family dinners; to Jean-Marie Apostolidès for sharing his unrivaled knowledge of Old Regime France; and to Michel Serres *pour l'exemple*. Sarah Sussman, as always, provided precious aid in ordering and tracking down books. My understanding of the Enlightenment has been greatly broadened by our "Mapping the Republics of Letters" project at Stanford: thanks to Stephen Hinton and John Bender for supporting this project with a Presidential Fund for Innovation in the Humanities grant; to the Stanford Humanities Center for its ongoing assistance; and to Paula Findlen, Caroline Winterer, Jessica Riskin, Giovanna Ceserani, Keith Baker, and our wonderful team of graduate students for getting this project off the ground. Without Nicole Coleman, however, it would never have gone anywhere: she is truly the *anima mundi* of our venture.

I am deeply grateful to have received guidance and comments from a number of other colleagues, at Stanford and elsewhere: thanks in particular to Ann Blair, J. P. Daughton, Denise Gigante, Dena Goodman, Anthony Grafton, Peter N. Miller, Pierre Saint-Amand, James Swenson, Liana Vardi, and Kent Wright. I would also like to thank Clifford Siskin and William Warner for allowing me to read, while still in manuscript, their edited volume *This Is Enlightenment*, now published by the University of Chicago Press, as well as the press's two anonymous readers for their careful and insightful reports. I owe a special thanks to my editor at the press, Alan Thomas, for his help in shaping this project and for his generous and loyal support; thanks as well to Randy Petilos, Erin DeWitt, and Stephanie Hlywak for their assistance. As always, thanks to my parents for reading and commenting on this manuscript as well as to my father-in-law, Paul Michael Bower.

This book was finished as another gestational period came to term: I dedicate it to our daughter Anaïs and to my wife, Zoë, at whose strength and love I incessantly marvel.

Introduction

metanarrative

Every age needs its story. In the story we tell ourselves about our values, our government, and our religions, the Enlightenment plays a starring role. Countless books inform us that the Enlightenment was the founding moment of modernity. We are "children of the Enlightenment," particularly in the United States, where the heroes of our national-origin tale double as enlightened scholars. Even critics of the Enlightenment share the belief that modern ills can be traced back to that decisive period.

It is doubtful, however, that many of the players in the Enlightenment drama would have recognized themselves in these contemporary reenactments. For they had their own story about their values, their government, their knowledge, and their religion. And theirs was just as much a story about antiquity as it was about modernity.

To be sure, they were very proud of their present moment, of *their* modernity. The great scientific and philosophical accomplishments of the seventeenth century—of what would become known as the Scientific Revolution—featured prominently in their defining narrative. By the turn of the eighteenth century, observers could proudly point to the dissemination of the "new philosophy" among the upper reaches of society and government, as well as in key institutions, such as the universities and academies. But they never lost sight of that other glorious age, when scholars contemplated nature for the first time, philosophers freely debated the purpose of life, and citizens determined their own political fates. This admiration of both past and present achievements—as opposed to the perceived mediocrity of the Middle Ages—combined to produce the historical and conceptual framework of the Enlightenment.

If the Enlightenment *philosophes* had a hand in shaping the institutions and views that we now associate with our modernity, we cannot begin to understand their motives, doubts, and beliefs without paying greater attention to their story and setting aside our own. That is the prime objective of this book: to reconstruct how the narrative of "the Enlightenment" emerged as a self-reflexive understanding of the historical importance and specificity of eighteenth-century Europe. Without wishing to rekindle nationalist debates over the genealogy of this narrative, I argue that it was in fact devised by French scholars and writers, in the context of an intellectual quarrel over the relative merits of the Ancients and the Moderns. This thesis thus departs from most other current genealogies of the Enlightenment, which trace its history back to political and philosophical developments in England and the Dutch Republic.

The key contribution made by these French scholars, writing between 1680 and 1720, was less epistemological than narratological. In other words, they did not propose a new method of reasoning or advocate a new philosophical understanding of the world. Rather, they offered a seductive account of the events and discoveries of the past century, in conjunction with a more overarching history of human civilization. This account took the form of a story: the present age (*siècle*) was "enlightened" (*éclairé*) because the "philosophical spirit" of the Scientific Revolution had spread to the educated classes, institutions of learning, and even parts of the government. More generally, they argued, changes in science had led to changes in society. While this story depended on a number of important keywords, its ultimate strength and defining feature lay in its historical framework more than in its vocabulary. It was for this reason that antiquity could occupy such an important place in the Enlightenment narrative: after many centuries of "darkness," contemporary observers believed that they were finally rivaling the glorious heights of ancient Greece and Rome. Accordingly, while recognizing their own scientific and philosophical achievements, they sought to reap the benefits of past learning as well.

Over the course of the eighteenth century, this narrative underwent a number of changes. New characters, such as Newton, replaced older ones, such as Descartes, and the meaning of "social transformation" was interpreted differently in different regions. In this regard, the Enlightenment was a heterogeneous phenomenon, to the extent that some historians insist on speaking of it only in the plural. The more fundamental question, however, is whether these varying regional or confessional Enlightenments were entirely the result of homegrown social and intellectual movements or instead stemmed from a process of diffusion through which a singular concept of the Enlightenment was made available to different cultures, which in turn adapted it. The former case appears unlikely: there is no obvious historical explanation for the synchronous appearance, in separate countries, of such a complex narrative and similar social movements. As for the alternative case, it is fairly straightforward to imagine how an important cultural development in one country could trigger a series of related, if not identical, developments elsewhere. This scenario is all the more plausible when the country in question, France, was the recognized trendsetter of the age.

Throughout this essay, "the Enlightenment" is employed in two primary senses. First and foremost, it designates the idea, and more specifically the narrative, of the Enlightenment, a narrative that gave members of the educated elite a new kind of self-awareness before becoming a discursive centerpiece of the *philosophes*. Second, I also use it to designate the loose collection of enlightened texts, institutions, debates, individuals, and reforms that appeared in eighteenth-century Europe. My primary concern lies with the former, yet to establish that the narrative of the Enlightenment that was developed in the French academies (first meaning) truly informed the works and practices of the Enlightenment as experienced throughout Europe (second meaning), it is necessary to discuss the latter as well. Many of the examples that I provide to this end are taken from France, and my specialization in this field undoubtedly tilts the overall picture of the Enlightenment presented here too much toward Paris. Scholars specializing in other national cultures will need to touch up this portrait, but let us not forget that onward from the 1750s (if not earlier), Paris was the universally acknowledged capital of the Enlightenment, and the French texts and figures to whom I refer were known throughout Europe.[1] Although some foreign readers interpreted the ideas of the *philosophes* in a selective or occasionally hostile manner, in many cases their views were welcomed, to an extent, by educated elites across the border. Their positive reception in these circles was further facilitated by the fact that it was largely in works by French authors that the concept of the Enlightenment itself was diffused.

Scholars of the Enlightenment have produced over the years an extensive range of research, stretching from modest articles to eight-hundred-page summits; this range, moreover, crosses numerous disciplines and linguistic borders. As there are few maps of this diverse and difficult terrain, a secondary objective of this book is to provide one, by offering an overview and assessment of recent, as well as classic, scholarship. To this end, the length of this study was deliberately kept short, and discussions of secondary sources were organized thematically, in the order that students are most likely to encounter them. The space devoted to defending my own thesis is accordingly rather limited: the arguments found in the pages that follow should thus primarily be read as suggestions for further inquiry rather than as an attempt to impose cloture in the Enlightenment debates (a dubious proposition in any event). The thesis presented here draws heavily on a wide array of the sources discussed but owes a particular debt to an argument advanced decades ago by Peter Gay. In his monumental study of the Enlightenment, Gay stressed the importance of classical learning and ancient philosophy for the *philosophes*, to the point of defining the Enlightenment as a kind of "modern paganism."[2] The focus of the present study is far narrower than Gay's sweeping panorama of Western intellectual history; his spirit nonetheless informs these pages.

One key difference between my work and Gay's opus concerns the role played by the Quarrel of the Ancients and the Moderns. Readers will find a detailed description of (and bibliography for) this Quarrel in chapter 5, but those unfamiliar with this episode may benefit from a brief summary of its stakes and principal participants. The Quarrel had its roots in earlier debates over the respective worth of ancient versus modern writers but flared up in late-seventeenth-century France, where it raged off and on for roughly forty years. From a predominantly literary quarrel, it evolved into a more general debate about the historical importance of the scientific and philosophical innovations of the "new science." In France (as opposed to, say, England or Germany, where the Quarrel simmered but never attracted widespread interest), almost every intellectual figure of the age joined in the fray. The Ancients were championed by writers such as Boileau, Racine, and La Fontaine; humanist scholars such as Pierre-Daniel Huet and Anne Dacier (who translated the *Odyssey* and *Iliad*); and critics such as the abbé Jean-Baptiste Dubos, one of the main protagonists of this book. On the side of the Moderns, we find the author and architectural administrator Charles Perrault (one of Colbert's close collaborators), the *académicien* Fontenelle, and scholars such as Houdar de la Motte and the abbé Jean Terrasson. But even authors who did not take sides—notably François Fénelon—adopted the language and argumentative framework of the Quarrel in their comments on the current state of knowledge and the arts. Therein lies the critical importance of the Quarrel: it opened up a period of intense self-reflection in which the present was thoroughly studied and contrasted with the past. It was through this process of comparison that the narrative of Enlightenment was fashioned.

[handwritten margin note: sounds postmodern]

In the course of writing this book, some colleagues and

friends wondered why I bothered to try and reclaim "the Enlightenment" as a historicized concept. Has it not come to mean
too much and, thus, too little? A similar question was posed ten
years ago regarding the Renaissance, which was also seen as having become void of specific signification. Yet as Paula Findlen
and Kenneth Gouwens pointed out, the term never went away
and is indeed still with us.[3] We cannot do without the Renaissance, and we will not make do without the Enlightenment. All
the more reason, then, to strive to understand this concept both
historically and philologically. This is tantamount to suggesting,
not that there is only one correct definition or meaning of the
Enlightenment, but rather that the meanings of "the Enlightenment" have their own history, which must be reconstructed. I
seek to advance that process of reconstruction here.

1

Interpreting the Enlightenment: On Methods

Scholars, philosophers, churchmen, journalists, officials, teachers, and scores of others have been discussing the Enlightenment for nearly three hundred years, yet there is still remarkably little agreement on what, precisely, the Enlightenment was. Language is part of the problem: the expression "the Enlightenment," for instance, appeared in English only around the mid–nineteenth century. Of course, there were plenty of other words, especially in other languages, available to designate a phenomenon that, on the surface of things at least, resembled what we would today identify as the Enlightenment. But what was the nature of this beast? What is it we are referring to when we speak of "the Enlightenment"? The contemporary historian is faced with an array of variegated facts, events, practices, and ideas that bear no clear relationship to one another. What unites a popularizing scientific dialogue published in Paris, a Scottish treatise on political economy, a Masonic lodge in Prussia, and the abolition of convents by the Austrian government? Rather than a neatly ordered *Encyclopédie*, we are confronted with a corpus resembling Borges's Chinese encyclopedia: an apparent jumble, missing a coherent classificatory system.

Historians have long sought to palliate this lack of an organizing principle by ingenious theoretical innovations. From Carl Becker's 1932 *Heavenly City of the Eighteenth-Century Philosophers* to Jürgen Habermas's 1962 study *The Structural Transformation of the Public Sphere*, and, more recently, from the volume of essays *The Darnton Debate* to Jonathan Israel's latest defense of intellectual history, the centrality of methodological reflection to Enlightenment studies has made this field a particularly dynamic one.[1] Despite this continuous attention, however, there remain a number of outstanding problems with the approach that many scholars take to the topic. While it would be pointless to search for a methodological silver bullet, we can at least aim not to shoot ourselves in the foot.

These metaphors are perhaps inappropriate, as Enlightenment studies are too often derailed by the search for a smoking gun. To a greater or lesser degree, most historians end up privileging a particular author, intellectual current, form of sociability, or political revolution as the fountainhead and direct source of much, if not all, that the Enlightenment produced. Given that these productions varied so tremendously, one rarely, if ever, finds a snug fit. Yet still we seem unable to resist the siren song of a "key to all philosophies," to paraphrase the learned doctor of *Middlemarch*. The first methodological challenge for Enlightenment scholars, particularly intellectual historians, is therefore to imagine a different model of causation, one that allows a number of nonrelated parts—texts and events—to combine into a greater whole: the Enlightenment.

The second major stumbling block for intellectual and cultural studies of the Enlightenment is that they often rest on a very inadequate model of reading and interpretation. Indeed, most scholars still assume that ideas do not undergo significant (if any) transformation as they are passed on, and that, as Anthony Grafton bemoans, "transmission [is] a simple, one-directional process rather like high-fidelity broadcasting of classical music."[2] Jonathan Israel, for instance, would have us believe that Spinozism constituted a coherent set of necessarily connected beliefs, which remained intact throughout the eighteenth century.[3] Yet Antoine Lilti has pointed out that there is virtually no evidence that this was how Spinoza was read.[4] Intellectual historians cannot assume that their subjects share with them the same interpretation of a text; no deconstructionist faith is required to recognize that, as a simple empirical matter, authors are read in wildly different ways. Anthropologists remind us that each time ideas are transmitted, particularly in literate, historically minded societies, they are likely to be appropriated for new, sometimes contradictory means.[5] It is precisely this instability that explains some of the more ironic twists in the intellectual history of the Enlightenment: as Robert Palmer and Alan Kors have both shown, for instance, some of the most "dangerous" Enlightenment ideas were first formulated, for very different purposes, by Catholic theologians.[6]

The probability of transformation is particularly high when ideas circulate from one culture to another. Much of the debate over the Enlightenment in recent years has hinged on retracing cultural transmission across national borders.[7] These geographical histories have primarily been concerned with the genealogy of Enlightenment ideas: while most historians acknowledge that France, and especially Paris, eventually became the headquarters of the Enlightenment, many argue that the intellectual origins of the Enlightenment lay elsewhere, notably in England or Holland or both.[8] I will return in later chapters to the historical merits of these claims; for now, suffice it to recall that the contents of a text may shift during travel. The case of Newton is paradigmatic: often hailed as a founding father of the Enlightenment, his reception in France, as J. B. Shank has analyzed, was a protracted and complex affair.[9] It was only in the 1730s that his physical description of the universe was accepted by leading figures in the Académie des sciences. Given that, as we will see, there was already by this time a coherent and established theory of the Enlightenment in French intellectual circles, Newtonianism cannot be made into the spark that enlightened Europe.

Social and cultural histories of the Enlightenment are not

immune to interpretive troubles either. In the wake of Habermas's influential study, and of Marxist theory more generally, historians sought to link shifts in public opinion to the emergence
of new forms of sociability.[10] In some instances, such "egalitarian"
models as Masonic lodges seem to have encouraged "republican"
political views, as in the Dutch cases analyzed by Margaret Jacob.[11] Yet this apparent correspondence may have had more to do
with Dutch political culture than with any intrinsic properties
of Masonic sociability.[12] Across the border in France, there is far
less evidence that these same (or similar) practices produced a
comparable republican outlook: one of the most engaged Ma-
sons of the late eighteenth century, Antoine Court de Gébelin,
perceived the order in strictly monarchic terms.[13] Despite their
egalitarian pretensions, lodges could equally well be associated
with hierarchic and conservative ideologies. Rather than infuse
elite Enlightenment sociability with a republican ethos, the salons similarly seem to have perpetuated a "curial," aristocratic
mentality.[14] As David Bell warned, "It is a fallacy to assume
any direct, automatic, relation between social and technological
change and changes in consciousness."[15]

Definitions of "the Enlightenment" in terms of media and mediation confront similar challenges.[16] In a recent volume entitled
This Is Enlightenment, Clifford Siskin and William Warner have
gathered essays that underscore the central role played by media
and other forms of mediation in the creation and operation of
the Enlightenment. Their emphasis lies in particular with jour-
nalistic genres, communication infrastructure (such as development of postal services), and new information technologies (e.g.,
telegraphy), in addition to the new social practices mentioned
above. They subsequently define the Enlightenment in terms of
the overall "proliferation" of these new mediations.[17]

The considerable achievement of this volume is to remind us
of the extent to which mediating technologies were a necessary
condition for the Enlightenment to occur. It was, after all, in and
through books, pamphlets, encyclopedias, journals, Masonic societies, and academies that the ideals and even the notion of the

Enlightenment were transmitted. But is mediation a sufficient condition as well? We must also recognize that the *philosophes* and their allies were not alone in making use of these media. The Jesuits had a far more sophisticated system of global correspondence: does this mean they were more enlightened? As Robert Darnton has shown, the whole of eighteenth-century France can effectively be described as an "early information society."[18] But how can we distinguish works of the Enlightenment from the rumormongering of Darnton's libelers if they are both primarily defined in terms of media? Not all red trucks are fire engines. Moreover, it is difficult to identify any genres or technologies that originated or were even uniquely associated with the Enlightenment: as Ann Blair and Peter Stallybrass note in their contribution to *This Is Enlightenment*, many of the information technologies—including those famously put to use in the *Encyclopédie*—derive from early-modern humanist practices.[19] To locate the singularity of the Enlightenment, we must also consider *what* was mediated, not just *how* it was.

When we survey the content of Enlightenment works, the fact that so many are literary texts further highlights the need for careful interpretive attention. The most influential work of political thought in eighteenth-century France was Fénelon's *Les aventures de Télémaque*, a pastoral novel; the fictional dialogue was the preferred essayistic form of Voltaire and Hume; Diderot, Lessing, and Beaumarchais turned to the theater to stage their philosophical principles; epistolary novels from the *Persian Letters* to *Dangerous Liaisons* voiced arguments for and against enlightened practices; even didactic works on pedagogy, such as Rousseau's *Emile*, were framed by fictional narratives. Where philosophical and scholarly works sought in general to limit as much as possible the different interpretations of their content, fictional texts, particularly in an age of censorship, used vagueness and innuendo for powerful effect.[20] Voltaire did not spell out what he meant, exactly, by the famous conclusion of *Candide*, "*il faut cultiver notre jardin*," leaving it instead for the reader to decide. At face value, statements such as these did not directly challenge traditional beliefs. How one read a deeply ironic author like Voltaire depended largely on what one expected (or wanted) to find there: he could be interpreted as a dangerous radical or as an entertaining *bel esprit*.[21]

One strategy that historians have devised to account for the philosophical divergences between Enlightenment figures and periods has been to divide them into groups: we now have the "radical Enlightenment," as opposed to a "mainstream Enlightenment"; and the last twenty years have seen a flurry of studies dedicated to resituating the Enlightenment in a "national context." This growing attention paid to local and smaller currents has even led some historians, such as John Pocock, to insist that we speak only of "Enlightenments" in the plural.[22] This recalibration of Enlightenment studies presents a formidable challenge to the earlier view that, in Peter Gay's words, "there was only one Enlightenment."[23] But it also rests on a fundamental misunderstanding about the epistemological status of "the Enlightenment."

From an empirical perspective, it may seem justified to group authors and projects into different "Enlightenments." After all, a number of features appear to distinguish Prussian, Tuscan, Austrian, Scottish, Catholic, Protestant, and other Enlightenment currents. One anecdote reveals the divide separating, for instance, the French and German Enlightenments: upon learning that Voltaire had died, Mozart, who was staying with Friedrich Melchior Grimm in France at the time, rejoiced, much to the horror of his host.[24] And Margaret Jacob and Jonathan Israel, among others, have brought to light the existence of shadowy networks of writers, publishers, and philosophers who embraced and disseminated highly heterodox religious and political ideas.

Apart from a few small, tightly knit groups or secret societies, however, these micro-Enlightenments could be equally heterogeneous. Israel portrays Diderot as a principal representative of the "Radical Enlightenment" in mid-eighteenth-century France but does not mention that Diderot authored an entire book rebutting the "radical" proposals of his fellow "radical" *philosophe*

Helvétius.[25] Similarly, as Lilti notes in his review of Israel's two
volumes, not all of those involved in the dissemination of "Spinozist" texts adhered to his doctrine.[26] The works produced by
Enlightenment authors in a single national context exhibited
considerable differences as well: Ian Hunter has argued that
there were no fewer than "three rival Enlightenment movements
at the University of Halle in Brandenburg" alone.[27] If we choose
to speak of "the French Enlightenment," we must ignore the obvious disagreements between, say, Rousseau and Diderot, Morellet and Galiani, or d'Holbach and Voltaire.

This shattering of the Enlightenment into a thousand little
pieces, however, seems to be the product of a basic misunderstanding. The Enlightenment was never just the sum of its parts:
instead of an aggregate of ideas, actions, and events, it provided
a matrix in which ideas, actions, and events acquired new meaning.[28] To partake in the Enlightenment, it was not enough simply to pen a materialist treatise or frequent a salon: it took the
awareness, by oneself or others, that a particular action belonged
to a set of practices considered "enlightened." The Enlightenment constituted a *prise*, not a *crise de conscience*.[29] Or in the terms
of the sociologist Niklas Luhmann, the Enlightenment can be
described as a "second-order observation": it was not so much
a change in the way people thought but a change in the way
people thought about the way people thought.[30]

Complicating matters is the fact that this new self-
consciousness was not a post facto interpretation invented by
historians to make sense of these diverse social or philosophical
changes, as in the case, for instance, of the Scientific Revolution.[31] On the contrary, as I will argue, there was an idea of the
Enlightenment present and readily available from the very onset
of the period we now call "the Enlightenment."[32] Readers, authors, scholars, and officials could thus identify—or contrast—
themselves, their works, and their actions with this idea, which
I suggest was really a historical narrative. To be sure, the books
and beliefs that eighteenth-century observers deemed enlightened may not correspond to our current definition. But there was

not always an agreement at the time either as to what qualified as an enlightened work. Then as now, the narrative of Enlightenment was open to different and evolving interpretations. What all these versions did share, if nothing else, was an assumption that the Enlightenment was nonetheless a singular entity. For this reason, even though there was not in fact "one Enlightenment," it still makes sense for historians to speak of "the Enlightenment," as the plural-only rule contradicts the lived experience that *Aufklärer* and *philosophes* were made of the same wood—a slightly less crooked timber. The alternative would have surprised (the Prussian) Kant, who idolized (the Genevan) Rousseau, just as it would have surprised the (Neuchâtelois) jurist Emmerich de Vattel, who worshipped the (Silesian) philosopher Christian Wolff. Though the Enlightenment differed in key respects from early-modern conceptions of the Republic of Letters (as I discuss below), its members did share similar values of cosmopolitanism and intellectual fraternity.[33] If they disagreed on many other points, there was nonetheless a "thin coherence" to their understanding of their community and philosophical agenda, a coherence that (as Josiah Ober, building on the work of William Sewell, has argued) may be all we can expect from cultural groups of a certain size.[34]

Merely stating that the Enlightenment, by the early eighteenth century, was already a recognizable and theorized category into which a set of cultural activities could be classed does not resolve the methodological difficulty of how we gain access to and define it. A first, straightforward step would be to return to the commentaries of the day in order to piece together how contemporaries understood this category. Such a philological approach has been standard procedure in French and German scholarship for decades: French literary historians have analyzed the meaning and evolution of such keywords as "*lumières*" and "*philosophes*"; the German *Begriffsgeschichte* (conceptual history) school has similarly produced studies of central Enlightenment concepts.[35] These investigations provide a very helpful sketch of how and when the Enlightenment became a self-reflexive object;

they also serve as a strong rebuttal to the commonplace still found in Enlightenment studies that it was only in "the second half of the eighteenth century," with the publication of the *Encyclopédie* and the ensuing disputes it caused, that "Europeans began to reflect on the epochal significance of the intellectual transition of the preceding century."[36]

In the form undertaken so far, however, philological approaches still present two drawbacks. They assume, first, that despite a certain semantic variation over time, a relatively stable, "core" meaning can nonetheless be affixed to terms. As we will see with the expression *esprit philosophique*, such stability cannot always be counted on: sometimes the signification of keywords varies so considerably that it is unclear whether it remains the same concept. This variability is no doubt what makes some keywords more effective than others, but it also presents a challenge to *Begriffsgeschichte* studies. The second problem with these approaches is that they restrict, by necessity, their scope to a very narrow target, usually a single word. But not all concepts can be felicitously grasped by means of one word. No single term or syntagma, for instance, expressed the concept of the Enlightenment in eighteenth-century French: "*le siècle des Lumières*" did not become a generic tag until the time of the French Revolution; before then, a variety of expressions, each with different connotations, were employed seemingly interchangeably.[37] What neither strictly semantic nor conceptual histories provide is a robust explanation of how we might interpret such terminological constellations.

There is another school of intellectual history, the so-called Cambridge school, that does offer a method for tackling these clusters. In an explicit parallel with Saussurean linguistics, these historians suggest that it is possible to reconstruct the "grammar," or *langue*, of a given theory from the body of claims, or *paroles*, made on its behalf.[38] Combining this linguistic approach with the Foucauldian notion of "discourse," Keith Baker applied this method to the study of French eighteenth-century political culture to reveal how a range of distinct political theories could be grouped into three major categories (the discourses of reason, will, and justice).[39] While granting particular importance to certain key terms, historians influenced by the linguistic turn are ultimately able to transcend the "atomistic" perspective of conceptual and semantic history in order to highlight the "molecular" relations between groups of words and ideas. Since the strength of structural linguistics lies precisely in its ability to subsume diachronic utterances (i.e., which occur in and over time) within synchronic structures (i.e., which are not affected by time), it is not surprising that a major shortcoming of this methodology is its treatment of objects that unfold in time, such as fictional or historical narratives.[40] But it is precisely a sense of historical development that lies at the heart of eighteenth-century definitions of the Enlightenment.[41]

To assist us in describing this historical sense and to explain how it might organize and order the keywords of "Enlightenment talk," we may thus turn to a different scholarly tradition, which harks back to Hannah Arendt and Reinhart Koselleck.[42] These scholars explored historical consciousness as an almost existential condition produced by our imaginary projections of how the present relates to the past and future. François Hartog has more recently described this relation as a "*régime d'historicité*," or what one might call a historical horizon.[43] Regardless of how one chooses to define this sense of history, the primary point to remember is that it takes the form of a narrative. Past, present, and future do not coexist as concurrent states but stand in a particular chronological relation to one another—even if, as we will see, the distant past was often brandished as a model for the near future. More importantly, their narrative structure does more than simply group distinct events into a linear whole: as the philosopher David Velleman has suggested, narratives provide a kind of explanation, and it is indeed through narratives that we commonly reach an understanding of events.[44]

The narrative of the Enlightenment that began to circulate in the 1720s would be modified over the course of the century and in many respects may appear strikingly dissimilar to current textbook definitions. There are nonetheless four major reasons to select this narrative as a point of departure for defining and studying the Enlightenment in all its diversity. To begin with, when we do not take historically situated and philologically precise definitions as our point of departure, we are more likely to confuse the Enlightenment with "the vague, and still unfolding, process of 'modernity,'" as Darrin McMahon aptly noted.[45] Accounts of the Enlightenment accordingly end up being something else entirely: thinly veiled ideological manifestos or pale reflections of current trends. Second, narratives possess inherent properties that allow us to deal with the variety of, even contradictions in, Enlightenment thought in a nonreductive manner. As with myths, they can support a range of variants without losing their core identity.[46] A narrative approach thus offers the "thin coherence" that in turn enables us to account for the many interpretations of the Enlightenment by different authors in different cultures without needing to invoke a whole set of rival Enlightenment concepts. Third, exploring the context in which this narrative emerged can help uncover the "conditions of possibility" (as Kant would phrase it) for the Enlightenment. What cultural transformations had to occur beforehand for this narrative to be possible? How did the definition of the Enlightenment relate to earlier philosophical developments? Scholars who study the intellectual roots of the Enlightenment tend to emphasize their long reach into the practices and programs of the Scientific Revolution. But when do we stop talking about the Scientific Revolution and start speaking about the Enlightenment?[47] Finally, adopting a historicized standard to define the Enlightenment—as elastically as possible—will assist us in formulating criteria for determining what the limits of the Enlightenment might be. There is a tendency today to give everyone and anyone their own private Enlightenment: even the Hasidic Jews, apparently, qualify.[48] As one scholar recently pointed out, however, there is a considerable disadvantage to stretching the

Enlightenment blanket so that it covers every square inch of Europe: "'Enlightenment' is in danger of becoming synonymous . . . with 'eighteenth century' and losing any distinctive intellectual features."[49] The following chapters seek to restore to the Enlightenment its distinctive features, through a genealogy of how, when, and where its concept and narrative were first developed.

2

A Map of the Enlightenment: Whither France?

Forty years ago, it was deemed redundant to bother qualifying the Enlightenment as French. "The proper noun in *Greek* philosophy is only an inessential tag, as it is in *French* Enlightenment," intoned one critic.[1] This assumption that the *philosophes*—only the French word would do—embodied and to an extent owned the Enlightenment was enshrined in countless histories of the age, perhaps most notably in Peter Gay's monumental study. While occasionally glancing westward to the American colonies, north to England and the United Provinces, south to Tuscany, and east to Prussia, Sweden, and Russia, Gay's focus was firmly on the "little flock" of French thinkers who resided, for the most part, in Paris. Even the dates he chose to demarcate this era were French, from the birth of Montesquieu (1689) to the French Revolution, a century later.[2]

Today the place of France has greatly dwindled on the scholarly map of the Enlightenment. In its place, three main narratives vie for attention. The first still holds that "the European Enlightenment begins in 1689"—but in England, in the context of the Glorious Revolution.[3] The second narrative, not incompatible with the first, emphasizes the role played by the Dutch provinces and the Anglo-Dutch Republic of Letters;[4] whereas the third narrative, defended most prominently by Jonathan Israel, largely ignores the English and focuses instead on a single Dutch philosopher, Spinoza.[5]

Each of these narratives ultimately concludes in France, which remains the *terminus ad quem* of Enlightenment studies. But the new scholarship locates the cultural and intellectual legwork that made the Enlightenment possible elsewhere. In so doing, it has geographically shifted the way in which we think about the Enlightenment. The key figures are no longer Bayle, Montesquieu, and Voltaire but rather Spinoza, Newton, and Locke. Moreover, even the later French Enlightenment no longer enjoys anything like the privilege it once had: scholars have turned their attention to other national Enlightenments, ranging from England to Russia. In his *Case for the Enlightenment*, John Robertson skips over France entirely, jumping from Scotland to Naples.[6] Interest in the French *philosophes* has not disappeared completely: Israel's second volume deals predominantly with the politics and philosophies of Gay's little flock.[7] But France features as only a latecomer in this and most other accounts. The *philosophes* may have been the loudest champions of Enlightenment in the eighteenth century, but they were not, apparently, the first—or even the most important.

While most of these revisions have been driven by scholarly inquiry, a certain degree of nationalist pride still lingers around the issue of who "owns" the Enlightenment. Such nationalist concerns were more fully on display in the earlier literature: in his study of the origins of *l'esprit philosophique*, Gustave Lanson happily reassured his readers that they need not look to perfidious Albion to discover the intellectual sources of the Enlightenment.[8] This pride of place is not entirely absent from recent works on the subject either, such as Roy Porter's *Enlightenment: Britain and the Creation of the Modern World*, whose title alone is, as they say on the other side of the Channel, *tout un programme*. The *philosophes*' fall from favor, finally, may also be due to certain geopolitical reasons, as well as academic politics: France is no longer perceived as strategically (or even culturally) all that central, a fact that often translates into fewer students studying French and thus going on to study French history; fewer Francophone students in turn means fewer hires for faculty specializing in French studies. Anglo-American studies, in the meantime, continue to reign triumphant on U.S. campuses.[9]

While I have no sentimental or personal ties to France (beyond my professional affiliation), the objective of this book is to suggest that the genealogy of the Enlightenment narrative is primarily a French one. My argument does not rest on any specifically French ideas, events, or great men: the Orléaniste regency does not take the place of the Glorious Revolution, and Malebranche does not replace Newton. Although I focus on a similar period as the earlier historiography—roughly 1675–1730—my protagonists are not, for the most part, canonical *philosophes*. Instead, I argue that it was within the confines of the French royal academies (primarily the Académie des sciences, the Académie française, and the Académie des inscriptions et belles-lettres) and in the context of a very specific academic debate—the Quarrel of the Ancients and the Moderns—that the terms, but also the narrative, used to identify and define what we now call "the Enlightenment" were first put into circulation.[10] By emphasizing the role played by the French academies, I do not mean to downplay the importance of Dutch or English writers in the history of ideas, even in the history of Enlightenment ideas. My claim is simply that the narrative of the Enlightenment developed independently from these intellectual currents.

In addition to the specific stakes of the Quarrel, these French authors were reacting to what they perceived to be a dramatic change in society: increasingly, they found, scholars, professors, writers, aristocrats, ministers, educated women, and even some priests were thinking, conversing, writing, and behaving in novel ways. The Enlightenment might thus appear, in this reading, to be essentially a social phenomenon, since only the social dimension of this change was considered truly new.[11] In fact, what was truly novel at the time was less these social transformations per *how did people conceive of society?*

se than the new *idea* of society that was emerging. As we will see below, the most original feature of the Enlightenment narrative was to be found in its dramatis personae rather than its plot: where earlier historical narratives had focused on the deeds of heroes and sages, it celebrated instead the achievements of civil society. In this regard, it offered a fully secularized narrative of human history.

The chronological outlines of this narrative are fairly clear. The present age appeared when the "philosophical spirit" of the early seventeenth century (which itself dispelled the "darkness" of Scholasticism) had been so successfully assimilated that the face of society had changed. This process of dissemination, moreover, would—barring catastrophe—accelerate over time, thus promising an even more "philosophical" future. What this narrative highlights is how the first theories of the Enlightenment started out as celebratory histories of (what would become known as) the Scientific Revolution.[12] Not only was the Enlightenment a development of the anti-Scholastic principles of Bacon, Descartes, and others, but it was first and foremost a historical interpretation of the meaning and influence of these principles.

To complicate matters, however, this great esteem for the recent breakthroughs in science and philosophy was combined with an equally high regard for another exceptional moment: antiquity.[13] From the first embryonic theories of the Enlightenment to its best-known midcentury celebrations (such as the *Encyclopédie*), the Ancients were consistently presented as worthy models and even, in some cases, masters. While appropriating the Moderns' celebration of the new science, the *philosophes* may have ultimately been more indebted to the party of the Ancients, who demonstrated how faith in progress was not incompatible with admiration for the philosophers of old. I will show how, in a number of other subjects as well, the *philosophes* took their lead from the Ancients.

But how can we know that it was precisely at this particular moment and in this particular context that the defining narrative and concept of the Enlightenment were devised?[14] There are plenty of texts in other traditions that employ many of the same terms as the French. *"Lumière"* has a long history as a metaphor for the intellect (and for religious grace), and there were *philosophes* before *les philosophes*.[15] A variety of works produced independently or even before the moment I am privileging may appear or sound equally "enlightened" to us. Pointing to the presence of similar keywords or philosophical content as proof of a clear and distinct idea of Enlightenment, however, is to presume that the Enlightenment was first and foremost grounded in an epistemological shift. Not only does it then become difficult to draw any line between Enlightenment and pre-Enlightenment texts (Bacon, Descartes, Gassendi, and others can sound enlightened too), but this assumption rests on questionable methodological grounds. Indeed, there is much evidence to suggest that the Enlightenment started out as an interpretation—an intellectual activity, to be sure—but of *social* changes, not of philosophical innovations. As noted in the previous chapter, the defining feature of the Enlightenment was not so much a new outlook on the world as a new outlook on the way in which people—in particular the educated elite—looked at the world. Accordingly, we may even retrospectively project back onto certain individuals, actions, or statements the label "enlightened" when they share these assumptions about the changing nature of society. To paraphrase Molière, one can thus imagine a *philosophe malgré lui*; Bayle might be a good candidate.[16] But the existence of such forerunners and forward-looking texts does not entail that the Enlightenment emerged fully armed, say, from the arsenal of Bayle's mind. It took a complex interpretive operation to arrive at this understanding of society as becoming enlightened; it is the history of this operation that I recount in the following chapters.

The Spirit of the Moderns: From the New Science to the Enlightenment

In 1719 the abbé Jean-Baptiste Dubos, who would be elected to the Académie française the following year and would subsequently serve as its perpetual secretary, surveyed the current state of artistic and intellectual life in France (and beyond) in what would become one of the most influential eighteenth-century treatises on aesthetics, the *Réflexions critiques sur la poésie et la peinture*.[1] Voltaire would later call this work "the most useful book ever written on such subjects in any European nation."[2] The *encyclopédistes* must have agreed, as they excerpted passages from this work in close to eighty articles.[3] It is also one of the first works to define the contemporary arts and sciences according to their *esprit philosophique*, an expression that appears seven times in the text.

Dubos's usage suggests that he did not coin this term but that it was already in circulation at this time: on one occasion, he speaks of "this superiority of reason, which we call philosophical spirit."[4] The term indeed crops up in other works composed around this time, notably Bernard Le Bovier de Fontenelle's

Eloge de monsieur Leibnitz (1717) and Nicolas Fréret's *Réflexion générale sur l'étude des anciennes histoires* (1724).[5] In Dubos's work, however, it forms part of a whole constellation of keywords, which taken together come very close to designating what we would now identify as "the Enlightenment." In a typical passage, for example, Dubos remarks on "the enlightenment [*les lumières*] that the philosophical spirit has spread [*répandu*] throughout our century."[6] While terms such as "light," "reason," and "philosophy" all had a history of being employed to characterize the innovations brought about by the "new science," with Dubos these (and other) keywords produced a network and a narrative that would remain surprisingly stable for the following seventy years. As we will see, Dubos had many reservations about the effects of what he designated *l'esprit philosophique* on art and culture: "the philosophical spirit that makes men so reasonable, and, so to speak, *consequential* [*conséquents*], will soon turn a large part of Europe into what the Goths and Vandals once made of it."[7] But like it or not, this *esprit* was the spirit of the age.[8]

Fontenelle, Dubos, and Fréret were writing at a time traditionally associated with the birth of the Enlightenment: Regency France (1715–23). This period of looser governmental censure is often seen as providing the necessary political and social conditions for such seminal Enlightenment texts as Montesquieu's *Lettres persanes* (1721) and Voltaire's slightly later *Lettres philosophiques* (1734).[9] This last text, in particular, is singled out to validate *translatio studii*–like histories of the Enlightenment, as it imported, wholesale, English (more importantly, Newtonian and Lockean) ideas into France.

But none of the initial trio of writers discussed above, nor Montesquieu for that matter, fit neatly within this genealogy. To begin with, they were not "Newtonians" in any meaningful sense of the term. As J. B. Shank argues in a remarkable study, Newton's *Principia* was read and understood almost immediately in France (no small feat), yet while his *mechanical* findings were roundly praised, his *physics* was found lacking.[10] The problem lay not in "any blind adherence to Descartes or his vortical system," Shank explains, but rather to "the radically idiosyncratic scientific epistemology used in the *Principia*."[11] It was only in the 1720s that Newton*ianism* emerged (in France, at least) as a coherent physical and metaphysical philosophy, and only in the 1730s that one began to find self-identifying French "Newtonians."[12] But none of them were to be found among our *académiciens*: Fontenelle remained throughout his long life the most famous defender of Cartesian physics in France; Fréret was one of Newton's chief antagonists in the discipline of universal chronology; whereas for Dubos, Newton was simply the product of his age.[13] Given that Montesquieu seems to have mentioned Newton only once in his early work, and not a single time in the *Persian Letters*, it is hard to see how he can be dubbed "a representative of the Newtonian Enlightenment," at least before his visit to England (in 1729).[14] He was, however, friends with Fréret by at least 1716, as well as with Fontenelle (to whom he pays tribute in the *Persian Letters*).[15] Dubos could have been a prime conduit for English and Dutch ideas into France, having traveled in both countries and corresponded with John Locke, Pierre Bayle, and Jean Le Clerc; he is even considered to have been "one of the first French to learn English."[16] But if his *Réflexions critiques* do exhibit a sensationalist epistemology, perhaps in part inspired by the *Essay concerning Human Understanding* (which Dubos was instrumental in having published in French translation), his aesthetics can equally well be defined by a "rediscovery of the principles of the ancients," as Ross Hutchinson observed.[17] More proximately, his definition of "sentiment" owes a great deal to Malebranche's theory of a "*sentiment intérieur*."[18]

It is equally difficult to identify any strong Dutch influence on the French writers of this period. With the exception of Fontenelle's *Histoire des oracles* (1687), few writings by the academic trio appear particularly indebted to Bayle,[19] and Montesquieu's trip to the Low Countries seems to have turned him *against* republican politics and radical philosophy.[20] Dubos would pen one of the most unconditional defenses of the *thèse royale* (justifying absolutism), in reaction to Henri de Boulainvilliers's aristocratic-republican *thèse nobiliaire* on the origins of the French monarchy.[21] Indeed, none of these writers can readily be associated with the "Radical Enlightenment." Though Jonathan Israel would have us believe that Fontenelle "was more radical privately than he could disclose publicly," he presents no evidence that compels us to revise Leonard Marsak's conclusion that "Fontenelle had more than a measure of belief" and simply "hoped that theology could keep abreast of civilization."[22] Fontenelle's best biographer noted many years ago that, although Fontenelle probably read Spinoza's *Tractatus*, his freethinking spirit (which was much more influenced by such French *libertins* as Charles de Saint-Evremond) was balanced by a penchant for Jesuit theology.[23] Israel similarly places far too much credit in the attribution of the *Lettre de Thrasybule à Leucippe*, a materialist pamphlet, to Nicolas Fréret.[24] As for Dubos, he does not figure in either of Israel's two volumes.

Who are the philosophical stars, then, in the firmament of these *académiciens*? These authors confound linear intellectual history by peering well behind them into the seventeenth century. The *esprit philosophique* was not a recent development, according to Dubos: it was "born sixty years ago," he affirmed in 1719, revising this date to "eighty years," in the second edition of 1733.[25] He would in fact always remain vague about the exact date (1650s or 1660s), noting for instance that it had been about "fifty or sixty years" since "*les lumières* resulting from these prior inventions, having made a certain progress separately, began to combine."[26] In other words, although this date may reference the foundation of the Royal Society or the Académie des sciences (in 1660 and 1666, respectively), it is ultimately pointless to try and identify any particular event or intellectual shift that occurred at this time, given that it did not mark the beginning of a new process but rather a climax in the history of scientific and philosophical discoveries. The real impetus for these discoveries came earlier: in a move that turned out to be already canonical, Dubos credits two philosophers in particular, the "chancellor Bacon," whose insistence on the need to "see experiments [*voir les expériences*] ... as they are" had determined the procedures of the new scientific academies; and Descartes, "who is considered to be the father of the new philosophy."[27] This last assessment was indeed already commonplace among French scholars at the time: Fontenelle had similarly asserted that it was Descartes who had introduced "this new method of reasoning," a method that was "much more considerable than his actual Philosophy";[28] and Fréret, though even more critical of Descartes's philosophy, recognized "the extent of our obligation to this great man, for having led us away from the dark road along which we walked, by showing us, through his method, the path of truth."[29] This exact same image would later be recycled by Voltaire, who in his unfavorable comparison of Descartes with Newton, acknowledged, "The road that [Descartes] opened has since become immense."[30] For all of these commentators, Descartes's great achievement was to have destroyed "the absurd chimera with which youth was stuffed for two thousand years," in other words, Scholasticism, which was closely linked to Aristotle.[31] With Voltaire, Bacon would be fully associated with Descartes as a presiding deity of the *esprit philosophique*,[32] a position of prestige that would be sealed with the adaptation of his Tree of Learning in the *Encyclopédie*.[33]

This hero worship is of course well known, and the relationship between the Enlightenment and the Scientific Revolution is one of the few topoi on which scholars usually agree. The precise nature of this relationship, however, has proved more difficult to define. What the above citations clearly show is that the key French contribution to the genealogy of the Enlightenment was not epistemological but rather narratological: it simply happened that it was in France that the ramifications of the Scientific Revolution were interpreted as having introduced a philosophical age, defined by a particular *esprit*, and as having a particular impact on society. Given that this interpretation was unrelated to any epistemological change, we ought to stop searching for some intellectual revolution that made, in Paul Hazard's unfortunately catchy image, the French go to sleep one night thinking like Bossuet and wake up the next day thinking like Voltaire.[34] A slightly more accurate version of this sound bite might state instead that the French who went to bed thinking like Bossuet woke up thinking like Descartes, yet even this revision masks the critical point.[35] The *esprit philosophique* designated not just a philosophical innovation but a whole range of medical, astronomical, and physical discoveries: Dubos, for instance, points to the gradual acceptance of Harvey's theory of the circulation of blood, as well as of the Copernican system.[36] The *esprit philosophique* allowed scholars both to identify a unity among the variegated scientific and technological breakthroughs of the seventeenth century (a unity that we would come to call the Scientific Revolution) and to describe the transformation caused by the reception and effects of these breakthroughs in contemporary society—a transformation that led them to characterize their own age as enlightened. The intellectual source—and it was in many respects a "mythical" source—of the Enlightenment for these French scholars lay far back in the break with Scholastic philosophy. To paraphrase another "night thought": if the owl of Minerva waits long enough, she can announce a new day.

But why give such weight to these French accounts? After all, the French were certainly not alone in celebrating the great men who had overturned the long-held beliefs of the past. Bacon's compatriots were equally prone to aggrandizing their age and its discoveries. The Royal Society in particular was active in promoting this sort of discourse: Thomas Sprat's 1667 history of this body (published a mere seven years after its foundation) rhapsodized about how "From these and all long Errors of the Way . . . *Bacon*, like *Moses*, led us forth at last, / The barren Wilderness he past, / Did on the very Border stand / Of the blest promis'd Land."[37] Such encomia no doubt informed the histories of science later narrated by the French *académiciens*; Sprat's work was in fact quickly translated into French. But while this account of the Scientific Revolution shares certain qualities with subsequent French descriptions of the Enlightenment (both are historically situated and highlight the learnedness of their time), the former looks only to philosophers and scientists for signs of present excellence: Sprat in fact laments the absence of "experimental philosophy" in the general instruction of natural philosophy.[38] Fifty years later, it was the progress of the new science among the educated, not the scholarly, elites that had become the sign of the times. As I argue in the following chapter, from a discourse about science, this narrative became a discourse about society. It is with this shift that the possibility of an Enlightenment narrative arose.

4

Society, the Subject
of the Modern Story

Celebratory accounts of great rulers and achievements are as old
as history—indeed, for a long time they *were* history. These heroic
stories were often just as much about the gods (or God) as they
were about men: *Gilgamesh*, the *Aeneid*, the *Chanson de Roland*,
and Jacques-Bénigne Bossuet's *Discours sur l'histoire universelle*
all inscribe human events within a divine master narrative.[1] To
be sure, since Thucydides, historians had also sought to extricate
the realm of human activity from that of religion. Throughout
the early-modern period, however, *universal* histories tended at
least to begin with "first principles" and move on from there.[2]

The Enlightenment narrative broke with both of these conventions. First, where English accounts of the new science
maintained a theological frame (Sprat exclaims how "God with
Design has pickt out you [great Champions of learning] / To
do these noble Wonders by a few"),[3] Dubos's history of ancient
and recent scientific developments makes no mention of divine
will. His is a merely human story, from which even the advent of
Christianity is excluded. This silence should be taken as a sign,
not that Dubos was an irreligious unbeliever, but only that human history, in this and other similar works of the time, was

perceived to unfold in a self-contained sphere. Second, rather than commemorate the "great Champions of learning" *alone* (for they were of course prominently featured), the Enlightenment narrative celebrated another protagonist: society. For Dubos, the *esprit philosophique* defined not only scientific institutions and the state but more particularly the public (at least its educated part).[4] Similarly, the reign of Louis XIV marked the apogee of human civilization for Voltaire not merely because it gave birth to unparalleled statesmen and writers but because "a general revolution has taken place in our arts, in our minds [*esprits*], in our culture [*mœurs*], as in our government."[5] This focus would characterize later canonical Enlightenment narratives as well: for instance, in the "Preliminary Discourse" of the *Encyclopédie*, d'Alembert speaks of "the general enlightenment [*les lumières générales*] that has spread throughout society."[6]

The starring role played by society in the enlightened narrative comes as little surprise: historians in recent years have drawn attention to how society during the Enlightenment became "the ontological frame of our human existence," or, in César Dumarsais's oft-cited words, "a divinity . . . on Earth."[7] The growing importance granted to, and cultural work done by, society can be traced through dictionary definitions and word use, as Keith Baker, Daniel Gordon, and more recently Yair Mintzker have shown.[8] From a term connoting voluntary human associations (e.g., "the Royal Society"), "society" came to designate the world of all human interaction. Céline Spector has examined how this concept of society, which was fully independent from government, emerged in the works of Hobbes, Pufendorf, Locke, and other political philosophers of the period.[9] One can in fact pursue this genealogy even further afield: earlier works addressing natural right theory, such as Etienne de La Boétie's *Discours de la servitude volontaire* (1549), had already employed "society" in this ontological, nonvoluntaristic sense.[10]

Although this concept of society can be traced back to the sixteenth century, writers and philosophers in the late seventeenth century put it to new uses. Bayle famously proposed his "conjecture" of a society of atheists to argue that virtue was independent from religion and depended on the existence of laws.[11] Fréret later elaborated on this conjecture, remarking, "It is not surprising to find atheists behaving morally and submitting themselves for social reasons [*par des motifs de société*] to laws they do not consider obligatory."[12] As John Robertson has noted, such arguments transferred "the confidence of Galileo and Newton that nature was governed by observable laws . . . to the study of society," thereby opening the doors to the political economy programs of the Enlightenment.[13]

By the early eighteenth century, social usefulness had become a standard by which to determine the value of all things. This normative function was on display in Dubos's *Réflexions critiques*: the virtue of comedy, for instance, lies in the fact that "by making us laugh at ridiculous characters, [it seeks] to correct in us the flaws on display, so that we become better for society [*afin que nous devenions meilleurs pour la société*]."[14] Aristotle's cathartic purpose of tragedy is similarly aimed only at those passions that "vitiate and harm society."[15] This utilitarian principle led Dubos to challenge Plato's banishment of poets in his *Republic* on the grounds that "a necessary or simply useful art for society should not be banished because, in the wrong hands, it might become pernicious."[16] In these and other instances, society was consistently presented as an entity that was independent from the state and even, in an anthropological vein, as preceding (and possibly transcending) the state: Dubos writes, for instance, about how "the Greeks had the same origins as other peoples and constituted a burgeoning society before becoming a polished nation."[17] The whole of humanity, he suggests elsewhere, constitutes a "society of nations."[18]

The newfound importance of "society" in the narrative of the Enlightenment was symptomatic of underlying changes in the philosophical, religious, cultural, and political climates of the age. Philosophically, as skepticism and empirical observation challenged the reigning Scholastic doctrines, society emerged as one area of human inquiry in which certainty might be obtainable and knowledge could be useful: "This learning," Locke wrote in reference to Scholastic philosophy, "very little benefits society."[19] Focusing on the needs and requirements of society offered an alternative to what were seen as interminable and unproductive quarrels over religious issues. "Why so much philosophy?" Montesquieu's Usbek asked, contemplating the metaphysical uncertainties surrounding God.[20] Skepticism toward unanswerable questions would indeed be a hallmark of Enlightenment thought: as Diderot cautioned in the *Encyclopédie*, "We must teach people to doubt."[21] Keith Baker even suggested that a more fitting adage for the Enlightenment would be *aude* non *sapere*; that is, dare *not* to know what lies beyond the limits of human understanding.[22]

This insistence on a modest epistemology was in large part triggered by the devastating memory of the Wars of Religion.[23] Not only did metaphysical disputes drag on endlessly, but they were the source of hideously violent conflicts. But the religious wars left behind more than a legacy of destruction: the theological challenges presented by Protestant reformers also transformed the ways in which Christians of all denominations perceived the place of God in the world. More specifically, Calvinism introduced such a breach between this world and the next that even Catholics (and particularly Jansenists) came to consider the realm of the divine as inherently separate from the world of humans.[24] Society, in other words, was all that was left once God has departed from the scene.

More mundane affairs also gave this worldly notion of society new prominence. Salon life and court culture in the seventeenth century had introduced sophisticated notions of social etiquette, which revolved around the concepts of *politesse*, gallantry, and *honnêteté*.[25] Through their strict definitions of proper and polite *mœurs*, these behavioral codes characterized what was starting to be known as *la bonne société*.[26] While limited to the social and cultural elite (hence, not *all* of society), these social norms nonetheless shaped some of the earliest representations of enlightened philosophers. Fontenelle staged his 1687 *Entretiens sur la pluralité des mondes* in a "gallant" setting, a series of nighttime promenades with the "marquise de G."; he would later be hailed by Montesquieu as a "most gallant philosopher" in the *Persian Letters*.[27] This same "polite" ideal lay at the heart of *Le philosophe*, an anonymous treatise (in fact, the work of Dumarsais) that provided one of the most influential descriptions of its title subject: the philosopher, Dumarsais wrote, is "an *honnête homme* who always acts reasonably and combines a thoughtful and just mind with social graces [*mœurs*] and qualities."[28] This ideal, Alain Viala commented, implied a "humanist" theory of society, namely, "a sociability founded on the sentiment of reciprocity."[29]

This development of new norms of politeness in the seventeenth century took place against the backdrop of a political turn toward absolutist governance.[30] As Reinhart Koselleck suggested, however, the state's attempt to monopolize the political sphere opened up a private space, which developed its own set of (moral) laws, determined by society.[31] Society, in this regard, could emerge as an independent entity from the state. This was even true of state institutions such as the Académie des sciences, which were created with the greater glory and power of the state in mind, as the minister Louvois reminded wayward *académiciens* in 1685: "I understand by useful research that which could relate to the service of the King and the State."[32] But the "useful research" conducted by the academy, along with a host of other "useful" institutions sponsored by the Crown, also became an end in itself rather than a mere means to an end. These two objectives were not necessarily at odds. When the academy was reformed in 1699, it was both placed more directly under royal supervision and granted a much more visible role: henceforth, it would publish a yearly *Histoire de l'Académie royale des sciences*, which Fontenelle authored until 1740, in an attempt to further public instruction and the advancement of scientific learning.[33] But these two objectives were not necessarily linked either. Where the state initially sought to transform society in order to further its political and military ambitions, society (duly "transformed") subsequently sought to influence those very ambitions, until the state was obliged to acknowledge the force of public opinion at the end of the Old Regime.[34]

To be sure, one cannot deduce all these later developments from the initial focus by writers such as Fontenelle, Fréret, and Dubos on the transformation of society brought about by the widespread interest in, and dissemination of, the new science. Religious toleration and freedom of expression, for instance, were clearly not distinctive features of French society between 1685 (the year of the revocation of the Edict of Nantes) and, say, 1717 (when Voltaire was *embastillé* for libeling the regent).[35] By making society the subject of their historical narrative, however, these earlier writers nonetheless left a lasting mark on Enlightenment philosophy, in that they introduced the yardstick with which progress, utility, and greatness would henceforth be measured. Their insistence that knowledge be pragmatic was not tantamount to raising a cult to "instrumental reason," as Max Horkheimer and Theodor Adorno have claimed: the abbé Pluche's rhapsodic praise of man as "the Master and Monarch of all the Earth," placed here to profit from "what was made for our Enjoyment," drew mostly mockery.[36] Identifying social improvement as the benchmark for national glory expressed instead a wish that the new science serve to transform human conduct, beliefs, and relations, not to bring about a greater domination of nature.

But why did this interpretation happen to take place in France at this time? There was nothing in the recent French past on which Dubos, Fontenelle, and others focused in particular: for Dubos, there were just as many, if not more, foreign contributors to the general *esprit philosophique* of the seventeenth century as French ones. Contemporary events, such as the Glorious Revolution or the death of Louis XIV, did not factor into their narrative of Enlightenment. The new definition of society was readily available in other languages as well. That the fabrication of an Enlightenment narrative took place in France may ultimately have more to do with a domestic academic dispute: the Quarrel of the Ancients and the Moderns. And as it turned out, defenders of the Ancients had just as much to do with defining the Enlightenment as their Modern opponents.

5

Quarrel in the Academy:
The Ancients Strike Back

One of the first clues pointing toward the so-called Quarrel of
the Ancients and the Moderns can be found in Dubos's *Réflexions critiques*.[1] Almost the entire discussion of, and references to,
the *esprit philosophique* occur in a section of his work arguing
that "the good authors of antiquity will always be venerated" and
casting doubt on the belief that "we reason better than the ancients."[2] Dubos sided with the Ancients, but he was a most measured detractor, who has been called "an 'Ancient' with a modern
mind."[3] In fact, this affiliation with the party of the Ancients
adds an important twist to the interpretation of the Enlightenment as an age idolizing only modern progress. As we will see,
the *philosophes* themselves ultimately owed more to the party
of the Ancients, who could accommodate modern scientific
achievements into their platform, than to that of the Moderns,
who could not find any place for antiquity. This distinction becomes clear when we compare Dubos's arguments with those of
his chief antagonist in the *Réflexions critiques*, the Modern responsible for transforming the Quarrel into a full-blown culture
war: Charles Perrault.[4]

Perrault launched his frontal assault on the Ancients on January 27, 1687, when his poem *Le siècle de Louis le Grand* was read before the Académie française. Its disparaging attitude toward the Ancients and unlimited praise of the Moderns caused a ruckus (Boileau could not contain his rage).[5] The poem was published later that year and was followed by Perrault's multivolume *Parallèle des Anciens et des Modernes en ce qui regards les arts et les sciences.*[6] While the tone of the poem was triumphant, it came at a particularly difficult moment for its author. Perrault had been a protégé of Jean-Baptiste Colbert and enjoyed great power as the architectural supervisor of the kingdom, until the death of his patron in 1683.[7] Defenders of the Ancients were then on the ascendant: favored by the king, their "party" leaders, Boileau and Racine, had been named royal historiographers in 1677, a year after the death of the writer Jean Desmarets de Saint-Sorlin, one of the most vocal Moderns. Perrault had been forced out of the *petite académie* (the forerunner to the Académie des inscriptions) and lost his position overseeing architectural decisions. Rather than mark a moment of Modern triumph, then, Perrault's outburst came at a time when the Moderns were seeing their achievements, power, and ideologies weakened, if not rejected. As Jacob Soll argues in a recent work, Colbert had constructed an unrivaled information system that privileged technical knowledge over traditional humanism, *savoir-faire* over *savoir.*[8] Unfortunately, only he seemed capable of mastering his complex system. It accordingly fell apart with frightening speed, a "catastrophe" that may explain Perrault's curious insistence that the greatness of the present age may already have peaked.[9]

The persistence of a Colbertian agenda is evident in Perrault's argumentation. While much of the Quarrel focused on the comparative strengths of ancient and modern authors (with a nodding Homer as the main polarizing figure), Perrault made clear in the *Siècle* that it was primarily on another terrain that he sought to do battle: "We may challenge it [antiquity] for the prize of science" (*Siècle*, 257). Evidence of the modern superiority in science, he argued, could be found in the technical developments of the preceding decades. The Moderns had, for instance, invented "this admirable glass / Through which nothing on earth or high in the sky / Far as it may be is too far for our eye" (258), in other words, the telescope, as well as a host of other useful devices: "this useful heap of things we invent, / Is incessantly sorted or augmented each day" (271). Thanks to this steady stream of scientific innovations, the modern observer could now enter "into the heart of the smallest beings, / To see the springs of wise Nature, / And glancing into her sanctuary, / Admire the art with which she secretly works" (259). Since the Ancients never had a microscope for exploring the microcosm, they were necessarily at a disadvantage: even Aristotle, "In this dark night / Where secretive Nature hides from us, / Though he may be the wisest of men / He could only see vain ghosts" (258). Perrault's discourse was profoundly marked by a Baconian epistemology: the modern philosopher ought not to remain in the "anterooms of nature" but must gain admittance to "her inner chambers," Bacon had declared in his *Novum Organum*.[10]

Though Perrault played the modern superiority in science as his trump card, it was in fact a bit of a red herring. As admiring of the classics as they may have been, the Ancients were no Luddites. Larry Norman draws attention to how Boileau himself mocked the universities for resisting Harvey's new theory and how Hilaire-Bernard de Longepierre (one of the first to respond to Perrault's attack) showered praise on the new sciences of physics and astronomy.[11] The battle lines between Ancients and Moderns are not easily drawn; even the names given to the warring sides are misleading. In an elegant study of the Quarrel, Levent Yilmaz argues that it was not so much "a debate or conflict between Ancients and Moderns, but a public spat between two Modern factions."[12] Both sides admitted the beneficial effects of progress: the only real difference was that, where Perrault took the thesis that "time perfects everything"[13] to include the arts, the Ancients considered the achievements of Homer and other "classics" to be incomparable.

Beyond this artistic debate, what the Moderns brought to the

Quarrel was an unabashed celebration of present greatness, in none-too-sly attempts to flatter the greatest of all monarchs, the Sun King Louis XIV. Perrault tirelessly returns to the exceptionality of his century, "*ce siècle où nous sommes,*" or "*nostre siècle,*" tracing the moment of present glory back to Richelieu's ministry and the establishment of the Académie française.[14] This genesis would become commonplace and serve to date the mythical founding of the "modern": Dubos, Voltaire, and countless others would similarly extend "modernity" only back to the early to mid-seventeenth century. The same cast of characters populate these accounts: Perrault singles out Bacon and, more importantly in his mind, Descartes as the initiators of the modern age, while also surveying the field of scholarly and scientific developments more broadly to support his claims (he points, for instance, to advances in medical knowledge).[15] Without using the expression, his analysis thus highlights a similar *esprit philosophique* uniting these diverse phenomena. Dubos's adoption of this phrase appears in hindsight as a kind of shorthand by which to designate Perrault's "useful heap of things we invent," that is, his body of evidence for the precedence of the Moderns over the Ancients. In this regard, the *Réflexions critiques* absorbed much of the Modern position, even crystallizing some of Perrault's arguments into a more concise form.

It was precisely this capacity to absorb the Modern narrative that made the Ancient argument all the more powerful. As expressed by Dubos, the so-called Ancient position was in fact a dialectical synthesis between two only apparently opposed claims. Indeed, Dubos had no qualms about adopting most of the Modern *régime d'historicité*, readily granting that "our century is already more enlightened than the centuries of Plato, Augustus, and Leo X"—the same three "happy ages," incidentally, that Voltaire would later place alongside the *Siècle de Louis XIV.*[16] And Dubos likewise accepted the Modern theory of progress: "The unique cause of perfection in the natural sciences . . . is that we know more facts than we used to."[17] But there was more to knowledge than the accumulation of facts. Bacon and Descartes were not simply dwarves standing on the shoulders of giants: their new method, the vaunted *esprit philosophique*, introduced a radical discontinuity in the history of human knowledge. In this respect, their greatness, which Dubos happily acknowledged, had nothing to do with progress:[18] theirs was an almost Kuhnian revolution. But they could not, accordingly, lay claim on a categorical advantage over the Ancients: as Dubos argued, "Did not the Ancients also know as well as us that this superiority of reason, which we call philosophical spirit, must preside over all sciences and arts?"[19] Our natural propensity to reason does not vary over time: Perrault himself recognized that "Nature makes the same effort at all times."[20] The Moderns could simply not have a monopoly on reason. The *esprit philosophique* was present at every epoch: Machiavelli's histories may predate the break with Scholasticism but were still logically sound.[21] (In a related vein, Fréret argued that *before* Aristotle the Greeks had been more knowledgeable: "Aristotle made the Greeks abandon the study of nature and stopped their progress of philosophical discovery.")[22] More than a simple catchword summarizing Modern achievements, the concept of an *esprit philosophique* allowed Dubos to perform a kind of intellectual jujitsu on Perrault, using his forceful arguments in favor of the Moderns against him.

Though the Quarrel resonated throughout the eighteenth century, with Dubos's *Réflexions critiques* its more polemical phase came to an end. The Quarrel had flickered out before, when other resolutions had been reached: Perrault and Boileau famously made peace at a session of the Académie française in 1694.[23] More critically, the unification of the Ancients and Moderns had been realized in practice by a number of individuals. In his 1714 *Lettre à l'Académie*, for instance, Fénelon had traced a *via media* between Ancient and Modern positions, expressing his hope that "the Moderns will surpass the Ancients" and his belief that it was silly to judge a book by the date on its cover.[24] While espousing a number of Modern tenets—yes, he acknowledges, Homer nods—he nonetheless expressed his great admiration for the Ancients, even asserting that the path to potential Modern superiority led straight through the study of the Ancients: "If you [the Moderns] are ever able to defeat the Ancients, you will owe the glory of your victory to them."[25]

The argument of the *Réflexions critiques* seems significantly indebted to the median position outlined in this short text by Fénelon, with whom Dubos corresponded. This position—which in a slightly different form had been the "Ancient" position all along—would ultimately become the defining attitude of the Enlightenment. When Voltaire revisited the Quarrel in the dictionary entry "Ancients and Moderns," he matter-of-factly delivered his Solomonic judgment: "Happy is he who, without prejudice, can recognize the merits of Ancients and Moderns, appreciate their beauties, and acknowledge and forgive their mistakes."[26] Yet a sense of insecurity often accompanied the *philosophes'* relation to the past. As Elena Russo acutely observed, "The philosophes became somewhat schizophrenic in their perception of themselves and of their function as writers."[27] On the one hand, their writings often exhibited the style and spirit of the Moderns while, on the other, they had a "fetishistic cult of ancient taste."[28] They were in fact openly hostile to self-proclaimed Moderns, dismissing Marivaux as a mere *bel esprit* and teasing Fontenelle.[29] Even works that presented themselves as more favorable to Moderns revealed Ancient preferences. In his *Persian Letters*, for instance, Montesquieu indulges in many of the common Modern critiques of their opponents: he has a self-proclaimed "scholar" (*sçavant*) write to Rica, one of his two Persian travelers, to complain that he cannot bury his uncle according to "the ceremonials observed by the ancient Greeks and Romans," having neither "lacrymatories, nor urns, nor ancient lamps."[30] And yet on cultural matters, Montesquieu's attitude toward antiquity could not have been more different: in a direct criticism of contemporary France, he has "a man of good sense" argue that "the sanctuary of honor, reputation, and virtue seems to be in republics, and in countries where there is a deep sense of patriotism. In Rome, in Athens, in Sparta, honor was the sole reward for the most signal services."[31]

As the Quarrel faded into the past, the partisan distinction between defenders of the Ancients and their Modern opponents became increasingly imperceptible. Perhaps because the *philosophes* no longer felt obliged to take sides, however, we tend to forget the considerable impact that the Quarrel had on the Enlightenment. In particular, faced with their praise for the modern *siècle*, we overlook that the *philosophes* could be equally celebratory of—and even dependent on—the Ancients. Voltaire's famous quip "Si Dieu n'existait pas, il faudrait l'inventer" was in fact preceded by a very unjoking passage urging the reader to "Consult Zoroaster, and Minos, and Solon, / And the martyr Socrates, and the great Cicero. / They all adored one master, one judge, one father. / This sublime system is necessary to man."[32] As we will see in the following chapters, consulting the Ancients was not an unusual step for the *philosophes*: in the "Preliminary Discourse" to the *Encyclopédie*, d'Alembert asserted that "we are now almost all agreed that the Ancients were right [about sensationalism], and this is not the only point on which we are moving closer to them."[33] As did Dubos before him, d'Alembert subscribed to the intellectual history of the Moderns, all the while extolling the Ancients, even describing antiquity as the first enlightened centuries, or "*siècles de lumière*."[34] The Ancients could accordingly be trusted, not because of their timeless authority, but because they had carefully reflected, without theological prejudices, on the order of nature.

Humanism and Enlightenment: The Classical Style of the *Philosophes*

Though it began as an argument over the literary value of Christian versus pagan epic poems, the Quarrel of the Ancients and the Moderns thus quickly snowballed into a wide-ranging debate over the importance of the new science, the meaning of history, and the mechanisms of cultural transformation. Any topic could be grist for its mill, and almost every scholar or writer of the time contributed, in some way or another, to this national, and to some degree European, conversation. The preeminence of its participants alone ensured that it would receive wide coverage and set the terms for intellectual discussion. Indeed, Ancients and Moderns were more than rhetorical figures: they were umbrella classifications that played an essential taxonomic role in how people thought about knowledge, history, politics, religion, and society.

At the same time, we must recognize that the Quarrel bore the hallmark traces of being just that: a literary quarrel, of the sort that could occupy the members of the Académie française just as well as the guests at Madame de Lambert's salon (indeed, not a few attended both gatherings.) The Quarrel, in other words, was not an intellectual crisis that ushered in "modernity." It may even be considered as more of an epiphenomenon, a symptom of greater underlying shifts in Western European attitudes toward religion and political authority (which I will address below). The Quarrel, simply put, was not to any degree the *cause* of the Enlightenment: to borrow a chemical metaphor, it was the catalyst that precipitated the Enlightenment narrative. By obliging its participants to consider how the present compared with the distant past, the Quarrel provided both an opportunity for self-reflection (hence making it a "second-order observation") and a conceptual framework (Ancient versus Modern) around which to structure their comparisons. These conditions, in turn, enabled writers such as Dubos to offer new accounts of recent intellectual history in which the defining traits of the Enlightenment could emerge.

Tracing a genealogy of the Enlightenment back to the Quarrel is ultimately most rewarding if it affords us a better understanding of the Enlightenment itself. To what extent did this Enlightenment narrative shape the arguments, rhetorical strategies, representations, beliefs, and even identities of the *philosophes* and their enlightened associates? Can this genealogy improve our understanding of the varied, sometimes contradictory, answers of Enlightenment authors to the polemical questions of their time? In this chapter and the following two, I will examine, with respect to learning, politics, and religion, how the narrative that emerged from the Quarrel allowed Enlightenment actors to imagine a future that drew heavily on the ancient past.

Let us begin with knowledge itself. It has become almost commonplace today to assume that the *philosophes* broke irreversibly with their learned predecessors, and that the Enlightenment had little but scorn for humanism, erudition, and traditional authority.[1] No doubt this opinion is a needed corrective to the earlier view, presented most forcefully by Peter Gay, that the Enlightenment picked right up where antiquity had left off.[2] While there are undeniable instances of explicit emulation between modern *philosophes* and ancient philosophers—Diderot's *Essai sur la vie de Sénèque* comes to mind—in most cases the former were more likely to revise, than to repeat, ancient opinions.[3] As classical reception studies have taught us, antiquity is always mediated by editors and commentators, whose own views change over time.

By the late seventeenth century, in particular, the Ancients no longer stood for the same values that they had only a century before. As an interest in philosophical questions spread to the educated classes, the fear of appearing "pedantic" imposed a new intellectual style.[4] Faced with a frontal challenge by Modern apologists, admirers of the Ancients were obliged to desist from overt *anticomanie*, a transformation that Blandine Barret-Kriegel has described as a *"défaite de l'érudition."*[5] Even a defender of erudition like Jean de La Bruyère had to warn against the sort of "pedantry" that consists of "enlarging rather than enriching libraries, by burying the text under the weight of commentaries."[6] It was no longer socially acceptable for antiquarians to model themselves on Joseph Scaliger or Athanasius Kircher: Nicolas Fréret, who eventually rose to become the perpetual secretary of the Académie des inscriptions et belles-lettres, sparred with Newton and read Bayle.[7]

But was classical erudition truly defeated?[8] Fréret, after all, was a model of scholarly learning in the eyes of the *philosophes*.[9] The famous opposition between an *esprit philosophique* and an *esprit de système*, which Etienne Bonnot de Condillac developed and Jean Le Rond d'Alembert popularized, can be traced back to a paper that Fréret presented at the Académie des inscriptions et belles-lettres.[10] Granted, like many worldly and literary figures in the seventeenth century, the *philosophes* did not have much patience for certain kinds of erudite practices, pretensions, or simply individuals. Jean Seznec relates how visitors to Paris were often obliged to choose between frequenting the salon of the comte de Caylus, a leading antiquarian, and that of Baron d'Holbach.[11] Caylus himself was not on good terms with Diderot, Jean-François Marmontel, or many of their friends (in the 1760s, at least), even though they cited him as an authority in the *Encyclopédie* on more than ninety occasions. But personal animus does not translate so easily into epistemological division. Although Marmontel penned an unflattering portrait of Caylus in his *Mémoires*, another member of the *coterie holbachique*, François-Jean de Chastellux, composed the following moving elegy of past great humanist scholars:

> The Scaligers, Estiennes, Saumaises, Rhodomans, Gronoviuses, Casaubons are ridiculed only by so-called scholars [*prétendus lettrés*] who . . . claim to know Latin because they understand a few things in a few authors. . . . I only enjoy studying the Ancients in their precious *Variorum* editions, which can still be found among enlightened amateurs [*curieux éclairés*]; and I cannot read them without admiring the astonishing wisdom with which these scholarly commentators [*savants scoliastes*] established and explained texts through their knowledge of morals [*mœurs*] and customs.[12]

Unsurprisingly, this high esteem for erudite editors carried over to their ancient subjects as well. When Simon-Nicolas-Henri Linguet published a work *praising* Tiberius, Caligula, Nero, and Claudius, it was his dismissal of the great Roman historians that truly irked antiquarians and *philosophes* alike.[13]

The principal text usually invoked to justify the Enlightenment's alleged hostility to erudition is the *Encyclopédie*. Under continuous threat from the *dévôt* party until its eventual condemnation in 1759, this monument of the Enlightenment is best known for its daring statements on politics (see notably the articles "Autorité politique," "Etat de nature," and "Economie politique"), religion (on display in "Ame"), philosophy (most famously in "Philosophe"), and economics (with the Physiocratic articles "Fermiers" and "Grains").[14] Often perceived, at the time and still today, as a manifesto of the Enlightenment, it became a flashpoint in the conflict between the *philosophes* and their opponents. As such, it is usually heralded as a decisively modern, even postmodern, scholarly and publishing venture.[15]

Its editors and contributors, however, were also appreciative of the work performed by earlier scholars. D'Alembert may have

criticized the "vain display of erudition" that at times characterized humanist studies, as well as their "often ridiculous, and
sometimes barbaric," arguments, but in no way "claimed not to
need" erudite learning, as Pocock has asserted.[16] In fact, if one
reads the "Preliminary Discourse" closely, along with a string of
relevant *Encyclopédie* articles, it becomes evident that the *encyclopédistes* greatly admired their erudite predecessors and insisted
on the importance of classical learning. Memory, after all, constituted one of the three pillars of knowledge in the Baconian
epistemology enshrined by the *encyclopédistes*: "Neither philosophers nor poets realize how much they are indebted to memory,"
d'Alembert asserted, whereas in truth "the studies of the Scholar
[*l'Erudit*] have often provided the Philosopher and Poet with
their own objects of attention."[17] So "indebted" did d'Alembert
feel toward humanists that in his retracing of the history of
Western culture at the end of his "Preliminary Discourse," he
bestowed the title of "*premier siècle de lumière*" (first century of
Enlightenment) on the Renaissance.[18] This history is echoed
in the article "Critique," by Marmontel, who perceived in the
sçavant correcting ancient texts the forerunner to the *philosophe*
unraveling moral and historical problems.[19] Voltaire also acknowledged this genealogy in his article "Gens de Lettres,"
where he describes the contemporary "*esprit philosophique*" as the
successor of an earlier form of learned "critique."[20]

The *Encyclopédie* itself, in some respects, may be regarded as
the greatest book the seventeenth century ever produced.[21] Based
on a rough citation index of over 1,200 "figures of authority," and
adjusting for a few statistical anomalies, there are more than
twice as many references to seventeenth-century authors as there
are to eighteenth-century ones in the *Encyclopédie*. Contributors
were not just citing the usual suspects either (e.g., Bacon, Descartes, Leibniz, Newton): the erudite scholar Jean Hardouin, for
instance, is referenced as many times as Spinoza (199). Overall,
humanists, jurisconsults, philologists, and theologians predominate by a large majority over astronomers, physicians, mathema-
ticians, and naturalists.[22] Despite grand claims about a new *siècle*

de lumière, the *encyclopédistes* remained largely enthralled with the *grand siècle* that preceded them and that had recently been celebrated by Voltaire.

At the very top of this citation index, however, are the Ancients (see table 1). Once the dictionaries (Chambers and Trévoux) are omitted, there are only five "moderns" among the top thirty authors cited, and none from the eighteenth century: Joseph Pitton de Tournefort (a botanist), Newton, Descartes, Herman Boerhaave (a physiologist), and Charles du Fresne du Cange (a philologist).[23] The score for the lowest ranking of these, Du Cange (341), is more than eight times lower than that for the highest-ranking figure, Pliny (2,893). It is fairly unsurprising that Pliny, whose *Natural History* was itself encyclopedic in scope, should top this index, but his prominence is part of a much larger pattern: everywhere the Ancients outnumber the Moderns. Even in areas where the Moderns had made indisputable progress, they remained in the shadow of antiquity: in medicine, for instance, Hippocrates (1,016) outscores Boerhaave (487), René-Antoine Ferchault de Réaumur (246), and Robert Boyle (196) combined; whereas in astronomy, Galileo (188) is cited nearly ten times less often than Ptolemy (1,664). The Swedish eighteenth-century astronomer Celsius, whose name graces temperature degrees in metric countries, is cited ten times less often than his near homonym Celsus (or Celse, in French), who penned a polemic against Christianity in the second century C.E. (21 vs. 213). All told, nearly half of the citations in the *Encyclopédie* are to Ancient writers. This overwhelming number of references strongly suggests that the Ancients were perceived as authorities on a vast number of topics.

One can, of course, question whether citation is a reliable indicator of content, but for the most part it seems that the *encyclopédistes* cited their sources approvingly: in a sample of one hundred Pliny citations, for instance, the vast majority are positive (83 percent), as opposed to a fraction of critical ones (10 percent; an additional 7 percent are slightly qualified).[24] These citation patterns thus largely fit with the editorial guidelines announced

TABLE I Top thirty figures of authority in the *Encyclopédie*, based on the
ARTFL edition

Name	No. of hits	Period
Pline	2,893	Ancient
Ptolomée	1,664	Ancient
Cicéron	1,446	Ancient
Tournefort	1,304	17th c.
Strabon	1,267	Ancient
Chambers	1,154	18th c.
Aristote	1,044	Ancient
Virgile	1,039	Ancient
Hippocrate	1,016	Ancient
Homere	809	Ancient
Horace	795	Ancient
Galien	786	Ancient
Newton	783	17th c.
Pausanias	767	Ancient
Plutarque	760	Ancient
Platon	669	Ancient
[S.] Augustin	663	Church
Tite-Live	661	Ancient
Moy[i]se	645	Church
Tacite	620	Ancient
S. Paul	571	Church
Descartes	506	17th c.
Ovide	506	Ancient
Boerhaave	487	17th c.
Trévoux	485	18th c.
Herodote	436	Ancient
Diodore [de Sicile]	419	Ancient
Vitruve	358	Ancient
Du[ ]cange	341	17th c.
Py[i]thagore	328	Ancient

by d'Alembert in the "Avertissement" to the third volume: "The
Encyclopédie is and should only be for the most part an anthology
of the best Authors [*un Ouvrage recueilli des meilleurs Auteurs*]. . . .
Would that it were indeed but a collection of the best other books
had to offer, with only quotation marks missing!"[25] It was this
absence of quotation marks that most angered the *Encyclopédie*'s
jealous Jesuit critics. All the same, at the heart of Diderot and
d'Alembert's understanding of their encyclopedic mission lay
the basic idea that their greatest intellectual contribution was to
extract and gather existing (and not per se "new") knowledge and
information.[26] Rearranged alphabetically, the *Encyclopédie* was

not that dissimilar to the early-modern commonplace book.[27] The chief model that d'Alembert invoked in his defense against the plagiarism charge was the humanist Charles Rollin (historian, antiquarian, rector of the University of Paris, and member of the Académie des inscriptions): "The late M. Rollin . . . found it fitting to insert into his writings in full the most beautiful passages from ancient and modern authors."[28] "Good extracts" would not only save us time ("How much useless reading will be spared?" asked d'Alembert) but also prevent us from becoming submerged beneath superfluous texts, both past and present.[29] Even when adopting a Modern style and disparaging pedants, the *philosophes* thus perpetuated practices of learning that had been pioneered by their humanist predecessors.

The Philosophical Spirit of the Laws: Politics and Antiquity

For the Ancients, the route to modern superiority passed through the careful study of classical writers, a *passage obligé* that the *philosophes* largely accepted. With respect to political matters, antiquity had, of course, been a reference point long before the Quarrel of the Ancients and the Moderns; one need but think of Machiavelli's *Discourses on Livy* (1531). Where Machiavelli sought to resurrect the culture of republican Rome, however, most defenders of the Ancients during the Quarrel vied instead to celebrate Louis XIV as a new Augustus. Dubos's *Histoire critique de l'établissement de la monarchie française dans les Gaules* (1734), for instance, put classical learning to the service of absolutism, arguing that since the Franks had been "invited" into Gaul, the French Crown could lay claim to the Roman imperial mantle.[1] That said, the Ancients never reached the same level of hyperbolic praise as the Moderns, for whom Louis surpassed Augustus, Alexander, and all other ancient rulers. And alongside the flattering representations of Louis as a Roman *imperator*, one continued to find more critical accounts of absolute monarchy that reflected a long acquaintance with classical authors.[2] Indeed, as we will see, an unintended consequence of the Quarrel may have been to strengthen the memory of ancient political forms in modern minds. As a result, the most lasting and innovative concepts of Enlightenment thinkers represented less of a departure from than a revision of Ancient arguments about the state.

It is usually assumed that the foundations of Enlightenment political theory can be traced back to the events and philosophical ruptures of the late seventeenth century.[3] The increasingly intolerant religious policies of Louis XIV (culminating in the 1685 revocation of the Edict of Nantes) triggered a barrage of oppositional literature, both abroad and domestically. The Glorious Revolution in England similarly released a cascade of political treatises in its wake, most famously Locke's *Two Treatises of Government* (1690), which was translated into French the year after its publication (see below).

In our rush to retrace our own "modern" political ideas back to the eighteenth century, however, we often overlook the fact that the new is not always the most subversive or challenging. The book that really got under Louis XIV's skin was not Spinoza's *Tractatus theologico-politicus* (1670), or for that matter Locke's *Second Treatise*, but Fénelon's *Les aventures de Télémaque* (1699). This epic novel about the son of Odysseus, written for the Dauphin's political instruction, was not only set in Homeric antiquity but steeped in classical moral precepts (along with certain Christian doctrines).[4] In the guise of Mentor, who was really the goddess Athena, Fénelon indirectly chastised Louis XIV for his excessive spending and lust for warfare, celebrating instead the joys of frugality and civic virtue. In a later text, Fénelon highlighted the political punch that ancient texts could pack:

> Did Homer not describe Calypso's island and Alcinoös's gardens gracefully without adding marble or gilding? Are Nausicaa's pastimes less worthy than the games and intrigue of women today? Our fathers would have been ashamed of these, and still some dare disdain Homer for not having predicted such monstrous conduct, at a time when the world could happily ignore it. . . . Nothing defines a spoiled nation more than this scornful luxury that rejects ancient

frugality. . . . It is our mad and cruel vanity, not the noble simplicity of the ancients, that should be corrected.[5]

Such criticism led to Fénelon's perpetual banishment in his archbishopric at Cambrai, where he died nine months before Louis XIV. *Télémaque*, however, went on to become the most influential political text of the eighteenth century: Montesquieu's Troglodytes, Rousseau's Montagnons, Diderot's Tahitians, and Voltaire's Gangarides all owe many of their qualities to Fénelon's Boeticans.[6] As Thomas Kaiser has shown, its impact was even felt at the highest level of the French state: beginning with the Regency, French rulers (in particular Louis XV) would depict themselves as peace-loving *pères du peuple*, as opposed to the traditional *rois de guerre*.[7] Fénelon's influence lasted well into the French Revolution: when the young Louis-Antoine Saint-Just left his hometown of Blérancourt to become a deputy in the National Convention, he carried his copy of *Télémaque* with him to Paris.[8]

Saint-Just did not need a French author to pique his interest in antiquity: any student who attended *collège* would have had an intimate familiarity with Roman (and some Greek) authors.[9] Such early encounters could leave young French subjects politically confused, as the writer Louis-Sebastien Mercier attested: "The names of Brutus, Cato, and Scipio pursued me in my sleep; Cicero's familiar epistles were piled into my memory. . . . It is nonetheless . . . an absolute king who pays professors to expound in all seriousness on the eloquent declamations against the power of kings."[10] But these readings also left a lasting mark. Catherine Volphilhac-Auger, for instance, has studied the persistent influence of Tacitus on Montesquieu and other eighteenth-century authors.[11] As Jacob Soll further noted, it was thanks to well-placed, marginal citations from Tacitus that the publisher and editor Amelot de la Houssaye could frame Machiavelli's *The Prince* as an anti-tyrannical treatise, thereby allowing readers such as Rousseau (who himself translated Tacitus) to declare this work to be "*le livre des républicains*."[12]

Even more than Tacitus, it was works by Plutarch, Cicero, Virgil, and Livy that continued to fire up the minds of young French boys, as well as some girls (including the future Madame Roland).[13] Echoes of Livy's *History*, accessible either in the original Latin or through the translation/adaptation by the abbé Vertot, fill eighteenth-century French political thought and fiction. This is not to say that French adolescents were republicans in the making, but rather that their political outlook was largely defined by ancient history: when Rousseau opened the *Social Contract* with the famous line "Man was born free, and everywhere is in fetters," his definition of freedom was essentially "Roman," in the sense outlined by Quentin Skinner.[14] The same holds true for Montesquieu's understanding of "public virtue" in *The Spirit of the Laws*: it was a classical concept that he could never fully "integrate . . . into his vision of the modern age."[15] It is a commonplace, yet nonetheless a fact, that most students in eighteenth-century France knew Roman history better than their own.

As with their classical learning, the *philosophes*' knowledge of ancient politics was often mediated by early-modern humanism. Machiavelli's aforementioned *Discourses*, for instance, readily available in French translation, was at the root of perhaps the most subversive political language in Enlightenment thought: classical republicanism.[16] This name is somewhat misleading, as it was not technically "classical" but rather an early-modern reconstruction of ancient polities; nor was it necessarily "republican," to the extent that it was compatible with monarchic rule.[17] It was nonetheless a political discourse through which classical political thought was transmitted and transformed. Generally speaking, classical republicanism encouraged a certain political wariness, directed primarily toward the dangers of moral corruption in politics: it was no coincidence that Rousseau chose Fabricius (a Roman consul famous for resisting enemy bribes) as the mouthpiece of his critique of modern luxury in the first *Discourse*. Conversely, classical republicans celebrated civic virtue and civil institutions as the only safeguards for preserving the state. After Machiavelli, the model ruler in this regard was commonly deemed to be Numa Pompilius, the second king of Rome, who had "civilized" the Roman *populus* through religious rituals and beliefs.[18]

Historians of eighteenth-century political thought have long recognized that many Enlightenment writers were besotted with antiquity, most famously Rousseau, who was fascinated by Sparta and ancient Rome.[19] Accordingly, we are encouraged to turn to the authors who rejected ancient models to find the roots of modern political thought. Montesquieu is thus praised for having outgrown his youthful neoclassicism (on display both in his *Persian Letters* and in his 1734 *Considérations sur les causes de la grandeur des Romains et de leur décadence*) in order to achieve "Modern" maturity in his 1748 masterpiece: "*The Spirit of the Laws* as a whole . . . is the greatest modern attack on political moralism," writes one commentator.[20] Opposing Ancients and Moderns (and their defenders) was the value accorded to commerce: decried for its corrupting influence by the former, it was celebrated for its pacifying virtues by the latter.[21] In his famous comparison of Ancient and Modern liberty, Benjamin Constant summarized the Modern attitude, declaring that "an age must come in which commerce replaces war. We have reached this age."[22]

As most of Montesquieu's other commentators recognize, however, there was still an Ancient lurking beneath the Modern.[23] Though he may not have believed that a return to the moral economy of antiquity was possible, he nonetheless regretted its passing. In fact, Paul Rahe recently argued that Rousseau's own indictment of modern society was largely cribbed from *The Spirit of the Laws!*[24] One should hasten to add that much of it also came from Fénelon. This combination of ancient and modern themes would last until the early nineteenth century: as Andrew Jainchill points out, Benjamin Constant, after blaming the Terror on Rousseau and the "liberty of the ancients," went on to extol "political liberty" as the "guarantee" of modern, individual liberty.[25]

Even the so-called Moderns, then, accepted and assimilated some of the central political precepts of antiquity; in this regard, they bore a closer resemblance to such Ancients as Dubos, who similarly sought to have the best of both worlds. Rousseau's theory of the general will was a "modern" way of resolving conceptual problems in the "ancient" notion of civic virtue.[26] Similarly, Montesquieu's doctrine of the separation of powers was primarily a reformulation of the classical ideal of a mixed government.[27] Nowhere was the imperative to "consult antiquity," in Voltaire's words, clearer than in John Adams's 1787 *Defence of the Constitutions*, half of which is devoted to the study of ancient republics.[28]

When historians search for a truly modern feature of Enlightenment political thought, they often settle on natural right theory, whose place in our own narratives of liberal modernity is so central.[29] The constant appeals by *philosophes* to the laws of nature would seem to validate this assertion and complicate our genealogy of the Enlightenment. To begin with, natural right was not an especially "French" discourse, even if its reputed modern founder, Hugo Grotius, published his *De jure belli ac pacis* (1625) in Paris, where he was living. Since natural right never made it onto the curricula of law faculties in Old Regime France, however, it did not flourish there in the same way that it did in England, the German states, the Dutch provinces, and the Swiss cantons. The dominant version of natural right theory employed by the *philosophes*, moreover, was the very "modern" interpretation offered by Locke in his *Two Treatises of Government*. Translated into French by David Mazel in 1691 (and reedited numerous times throughout the eighteenth century), this understanding of natural right theory was also expressed in Jean Barbeyrac's commentaries to his French translations of Grotius and Samuel von Pufendorf, as well as in Jean-Jacques Burlamaqui's textbooks for his students at the Geneva Academy.[30] Despite his misgivings about natural right theory, Rousseau drew strongly on this tradition in his denunciation of social inequality and political injustice, put forth in his 1755 *Discourse on Inequality*.

The role played by natural right in the French Enlightenment, however, is not quite that simple. First of all, "progressive," liberal voices were not the only ones to lay claim to it. Just as Grotius, Hobbes, and Pufendorf, in the seventeenth century, had used natural right arguments to defend absolutist government, such arguments could also be put to nondemocratic ends during the Enlightenment. One example from neighboring Geneva can serve as a cautionary tale: one of the reasons Rousseau was so critical of natural right in the second *Discourse*, as Helena Rosenblatt has shown, was because the natural-law professor Burlamaqui had thrown his support behind the patricians in their political struggle against the Genevan citizenry.[31] Later in the century, the Physiocrats also demonstrated how natural right theory was fully compatible with monarchic government, or what they called "legal despotism."[32] Their idea of executive power in fact turned the monarch into a paper king, but it also ran counter to theories of popular sovereignty.

Second, despite their adoption of Locke, the *philosophes* did not always have a "Modern" interpretation of natural right. I do not mean to suggest that they were Straussians *avant la lettre*, but rather that they often perceived natural right theory through the lens of classical representations. For instance, as I argue elsewhere, the *philosophes'* attraction to the laws of nature was often mediated by the myth of the golden age.[33] Not only did this myth of peace, perpetual spring, and free love embellish the concept of a pre-civilized time, but it greatly modified the place of natural right in society. Where Locke (in agreement with his predecessors) depicted the laws of nature as a foundation for civil legislation, he insisted that an added layer of "positive" law was necessary. In the rosy context of a golden age, however, natural right became a sufficient and complete legal body. "How brief would the codes of nations be, if only they conformed rigorously to that of Nature!" Diderot exclaimed in his discussion of Tahiti.[34] But this opinion, echoed by Rousseau, Voltaire, and a host of lesser-known eighteenth-century authors—including, to tragic ends, the leading Jacobin members of the National

Convention—also contained an exclusionary principle: whoever disobeyed the laws of nature lost their natural rights. Their version of natural right theory was thus far less liberal and rights-based than modern accounts.

To be sure, the Age of Enlightenment witnessed a range of genuinely modern developments in political thought. It was in the eighteenth century, after all, that the modern notion of political representation was fully developed. At the end of that century, at least two countries (the United States and France) had implemented representational structures of government—although in the case of France, such structures would soon be swept under the rug. Even here, however, we may question the extent to which this political achievement can be laid at the feet of the Enlightenment (at least in France). As Paul Friedland's fascinating study of representation reveals, the *philosophes* played only a minor role in the story of its evolution.[35] If Diderot's reflections on theatrical representation contributed to a radical transformation in the concept of representation (from an embodied toward a signified type), the *philosophes* did not make much of political representation in our current, democratic sense of the term.[36] This had to do in part with their lack of enthusiasm for democracy in general, although the most "democratic" among them, Rousseau, was also the one who had the harshest words for representative regimes. In France, it was the *parlementaires*, or judges versed in constitutional and Roman law, who advanced the most "modern" theory of representation; members of the *noblesse de robe*, their views were arguably more informed by older feudal notions than by works of the *philosophes*, with whom they often clashed. If an Enlightenment figure and government official such as Anne-Robert-Jacques Turgot did propose the creation of an elected, representational assembly, this institution was not to be endowed with any legislative function.[37] Only in the aftermath of the American Revolution did French political theorists begin to conceive of political representation as a viable form of government.[38] With the possible exception of Montesquieu, who spoke favorably of federative republics, of Claude

Adrien Helvétius, and of Baron d'Holbach, few *philosophes* were willing to consider political representation as a viable solution for large republics, which they tended to view as a contradiction in terms.[39]

None of this is to say that Enlightenment authors did not formulate or embrace new political ideas. On such issues as property, human rights, and criminal punishment, they championed numerous views that may rightly be considered modern.[40] The modern concept that they wielded most effectively was arguably that of public opinion. In the wake of Jürgen Habermas's influential study of the "public sphere," scholars have chronicled the ways in which public opinion materialized in the context of aesthetic judgment: Dubos himself defined "the public" as "those people who have become enlightened [*qui ont acquis des lumières*], either by reading or by engaging with the world [*par le commerce du monde*]."[41] As Joan DeJean has noted, this definition explicitly underscores how, along with the theater, it was on works of literature ("by reading") that public opinion first exercised its judgment in a self-conscious manner.[42] But this "enlightened" public did not limit its judgment to literary matters and progressively earned a constitutive role in political affairs as well: onward from the mid-eighteenth century, official state discourse sought to accommodate the demands (perceived or real) of public opinion.[43] The central importance of public opinion in the writings and practices of the Enlightenment reminds us how the chief contribution of the Moderns to the Enlightenment narrative—the spread of scientific principles throughout society—remained at the heart of its political and philosophical concerns.

8

An Ancient God: Pagans and Philosophers

If we are to fully understand the Enlightenment's abiding passion for the distant past, it may help to step back into the Quarrel to consider the arguments and beliefs defended by the Moderns. To do so is an exercise in relativity, as it soon becomes apparent that one age's moderns are another age's reactionaries. In other words, not all the causes that the Moderns defended were ones that we would today consider "modern" (in the loose sense of "progressive"). Nevertheless, on some topics, their views do sound modern: they perceived science as a means of social and philosophical transformation (a point that the Ancients did not dispute), and they celebrated female participation in the worlds of letters and knowledge.[1] The Ancients certainly held far more traditional views on the latter point, even if the only woman to actively participate in the Quarrel, Anne Dacier, intervened on behalf of the Ancients, as a translator of Homer and Plutarch.

On an array of other counts, however, the Moderns upheld positions that few would consider appealing today. Leaving aside his staunch political absolutism, Perrault closed his *Siècle de Louis le Grand* by celebrating the recent revocation of the Edict of Nantes: "Smothered Heresy, by his [Louis XIV's] pious efforts, / Offers an immortal trophy to his virtue."[2] His defense of religious orthodoxy was not unusual: the previous leader of the Moderns, Jean Desmarets, had been an equally vocal supporter of intolerance.[3] In the aftermath of the Wars of Religion, it was ultimately more "progressive" to insist on confessional unity. Our own modernity may owe more to another's Antiquity: when Voltaire sought models of religious tolerance, he looked to the English Deists, but he also turned to Julian the Apostate (along with the Ottoman sultans and the Chinese emperors).[4] In his final work, Pierre Bayle similarly chose the philosopher Themistius as the mouthpiece for arguments in favor of toleration: as Michael Hickson has argued, this choice was warranted by Themistius's actual orations, delivered in the fourth century of the Common Era.[5] It is a modernist fallacy to assume that all the values that we regard as positive today are the product of recent developments and had never been defended in the past.

The intolerance of the Moderns was directed not only toward present-day "heretics" (i.e., Protestants) but also toward the more distant religious threat of paganism. Much of the Quarrel indeed revolved around the embarrassing depictions of divine dalliances in Homer. For the Moderns, this was the "scandal" that proved beyond reasonable doubt the inferiority of the Ancients.[6] What kind of uncouth people dared represent heavenly beings in such demeaning positions (quite literally, in the case of the *Odyssey*)? Underpinning this distaste for divine transgressions was a more general problem with cultural and moral difference per se: "*comment peut-on être grec ancien?*" was the leitmotiv of the Modern criticism of Homer's age. There were, to be sure, Moderns who had less difficulty accepting variations in human society across time and space: in his *Digression sur les Anciens et les Modernes*, for instance, Fontenelle pointed to the influence of climate in shaping and transforming cultures.[7] By and large, however, it befell the Ancients to defend the principle of cultural relativism. Homeric heroes were not fit to appear in a Parisian salon? No doubt true, but let us not forget that they belonged to a different, foreign age. Rather than perceive themselves as part of an unbroken continuum linking antiquity to the present, the Ancients insisted on the vast distance separating them from the classical past, a distance that allowed them to appreciate its aesthetic dimensions without fretting about its religious attitudes. Larry Norman, who has insightfully described this attitude, points to a statement by Anne Dacier as paradigmatic of the Ancients' rapport with antiquity: "I find these ancient times all the more beautiful in that they resemble so little our own."[8]

Defenders of religious toleration and cultural relativism, the *philosophes* would have had nothing but disdain for Perrault and Desmarets's Catholic orthodoxy. But did they inherit their religious views from the Moderns' opponents? One traditional argument, underpinning the Anglo-Dutch genealogy of the Enlightenment, held that the *philosophes* were mostly Deists of an English variety, inspired by the works of John Toland, Anthony Collins, and the Earl of Shaftesbury.[9] No doubt these works played a role in shaping their attitudes toward the Catholic Church, although seventeenth-century Europe (and particularly France) was awash in a tide of skeptical and freethinking literature.[10] As Alain Niderst's intellectual biography of Fontenelle underscores, it is terribly difficult to isolate any single current of religious criticism as determinant: most *gens de lettres* read widely and gave few clear indications of which texts influenced them the most.[11]

Here as well, however, it is worth emphasizing that it did not necessarily take the emergence of "new" subversive movements to challenge ecclesiastical authority. After all, from the Renaissance and Reformation onward, scholars and elites throughout Europe had challenged, doubted, and even ridiculed Christian doctrine, often in the name of "pagan" philosophy.[12] The philological dedication to the exact reconstruction of classical texts led many humanists to embrace old ideas about nature and metaphysics, ideas that could clash head on with church doctrines, as in the case of Pietro Pomponazzi (1462–1525), professor at the University of Padua.[13] Such ideas could also result in openly neo-pagan declarations, as with Giordano Bruno, or simply lead to outright disbelief, as, for instance, among sixteenth-century Italian freethinkers such as Giulio Vanini, Alvise Capuano, Cesare Cremonini, Gaspar Varella, Paolo Sarpi, and the *libertins* of the early seventeenth century.[14] Machiavelli's last words—which, if *non vero*, are certainly *ben trovato*—expressed the erudite tendency of the age: it would be far preferable to spend eternity in Hell with the ancient philosophers than in Heaven with the angels. The *philosophes*, who did not care much for Hell anyway, would no doubt have concurred.

By emphasizing the subversive quality of classical texts, it is my intention not to argue against the importance of modern ones, but simply to counter our ingrained tendency to think of intellectual and cultural history only in terms of revolutions, discoveries, and inventions. Of course, some texts truly were revolutionary: among these, one could place Spinoza's *Tractatus Theologico-Politicus*, which Jonathan Israel locates at the center of his interpretation of the "Radical Enlightenment." Unlike the earlier freethinkers or *libertins érudits* such as Théophile de Viau, Gabriel Naudé, François de La Mothe Le Vayer, or Charles de Saint-Evremond, Spinoza alone, Israel argues, can be credited with "producing . . . a systematic philosophy explicitly at odds with the prevailing orthodoxies."[15] Although Spinoza's central role in the history of atheism is not in dispute, "producing a systematic philosophy" is a surprising criterion, however, for rewriting the history of the Enlightenment, given that an *opposition* to systematic philosophy was one of the few features that almost all *philosophes* agreed upon. As we saw, one of the earliest and most successful glosses of the *esprit philosophique* explicitly contrasted the new spirit with the *esprit de système*, which had gripped metaphysical inquiry from Aristotle to Descartes.[16] This antipathy to systematic thought may have been rooted in a Jesuitical preference for empirical demonstrations and was enshrined in the statutes of the Académie des sciences, as per its 1699 reform.[17]

It is also highly questionable whether Spinoza's entire oeuvre constitutes—or, more importantly, was perceived as constituting—a coherent entity, as Antoine Lilti points out in a review of Israel's work.[18] Israel's repeated insistence that the "Radical Enlightenment" was a tightly knit system in which atheism, democracy, and religious toleration were inextricably linked is not convincingly demonstrated. If Diderot was an atheist, he was not a republican; if Rousseau was a republican, he was not an atheist. More importantly, by bringing his own *esprit de système* to the study of Spinozism, Israel downplays the metaphysical uncertainties that nagged almost all the *philosophes* throughout their lives. Diderot described this uncertainty best in *Jacques le fataliste*: sometimes it seems as though everything is determined, but then we find ourselves believing firmly in free will. Voltaire never could quite figure out whether there was a providential God or where evil came from. And according to Jean-François Marmontel, when the topic of atheism surfaced in Baron d'Holbach's salon, it was more as a conversation piece than a belief system.[19] If atheism, unbelief, and religious skepticism in the Enlightenment were not connected parts of a systematic whole but rather separate currents that could surface in different fashions among different individuals, then it makes little sense to identify Spinoza as the source of all such critical thinking.

Ultimately, we must also come to terms with the counter-intuitive (if highly ironic) fact that many of the most critical and "dangerous" religious ideas in the seventeenth and eighteenth centuries were elaborated within the context of theological debate. Roy Porter has shown this to be the case with English Deism, and Alan Kors has studied how the concept of atheism was most fully theorized by theologians.[20] One of the key pieces in this religious puzzle was provided by the Jesuits. Not only did the Company of Jesus play an important role in sustaining a humanistic curriculum, but as Roger Pearson recently noted, they also transmitted to their students an idea of divinity that was remarkably similar to the one later formed by most *philosophes*; Voltaire's Jesuit *collège* in Paris has even been called "a nursery for *philosophes*."[21] In a bold revisionist work published a few generations ago, Robert Palmer argued that the *philosophes'* most fundamental assumptions about God and nature derived from this unlikely source as well.[22] Palmer points in particular to Luis de Molina's 1588 *Concordia Liberi Arbitrii cum Gratiae Donis*, which developed the Thomistic notion of a "state of pure nature" (*status naturae purae*), as distinct from both the state of innocence enjoyed by man in Eden and the state of sin in which he found himself after the Fall.[23] This natural state was conceived of not as a historical reality—it never actually existed—but rather as a theoretical abstraction through which man's natural faculties could be distinguished from those faculties that derive only from grace.[24] Among these faculties, according to both Aquinas and Molina, was reason; and thanks to reason, humans had access to natural law (as the ancient Roman jurists had already argued). Molina went even further, however, to argue that our human desires were not a product of the Fall but an intrinsic part of our human nature. In other words, although humankind had lapsed, we were not all that bad: because we still had reason, we could curb those desires that were unnatural and aspire to a certain degree of human justice and even happiness on earth. These notions would of course be further developed by seventeenth-century theologians and natural right theorists; in essence, however, they would inform Enlightenment ideas about nature, humanity, and divine intervention.

As we saw with the emergence of the modern concept of society, large-scale cultural shifts in religious attitudes certainly played a crucial role in making the Enlightenment narrative possible. But these large-scale shifts occurred throughout Europe and affected a whole array of new trends, such as nationalism.[25] The Enlightenment was just one of many responses to this change in *mentalités*. The question thus becomes one of determining whether specific, identifiable religious and/or philosophical developments were directly instrumental in shaping this particular response. As we have already seen, however, it makes little sense to try and pinpoint one, big, watershed moment in intellectual history capable of triggering an epistemological seismic wave. Authors who did seek to shake the foundations of European Christendom—Spinoza, for instance—were soon cubbyholed and held at a distance. The term "*Spinosiste*," in the eighteenth century, was used mostly as a slur; Spinoza's thought was ultimately less influential than his sulfurous reputation.[26] Jean-Baptiste de Boyer, marquis d'Argens (friend of Voltaire, Frederick the Great, d'Alembert, and other *philosophes*), set the tone in his influential *Lettres juives* (1738) when he spoke of "the system of Spinoza, and some other atheists, the error and horror of which I have already shown you."[27]

Simply put, religion and politics were *too* important not to have *always* been the topic of lengthy, probing, and controversial reflections. Sudden transformations in religious or political thought cannot be credited with having produced an "enlightened" opinion about God or the state, because there had already been so many sudden transformations in religious and political thought. This is, of course, not to say that religion and politics were not critical areas of inquiry for Enlightenment thinkers—the contrary is obviously true. But it was precisely because throne and altar were such important issues that the specificity of Enlightenment thought cannot have originated there.

The ways in which the *philosophes* and their allies treated religion, however, can still tell us a great deal about the Enlightenment. Indeed, just as their political arguments adopted recognizable patterns, in which ancient motifs were prominently featured, so too their thoughts about religion loosely adhered to the enlightened narrative set forth during the Quarrel. One striking example of this persistent turn to antiquity can be found in Deism. Most commentators emphasize the rationalizing drive behind Deist beliefs, often described as "rational monotheism."[28] Deist writers, or so the argument goes, sought to rid Christianity of its superstitious excesses, an exercise that could result in the abandonment of Christianity altogether.[29] There is no denying the central place of rational inquiry in the Deist reworking of monotheism. But by focusing so intently on its intellectual definition, scholars have tended to overlook the fact that Deism was also a historical narrative, with roots extending deep into antiquity. Indeed, one of the strongest and most commonly employed "demonstrations" of Deist belief was precisely its chronological primacy: in John Toland's memorable phrase, "Natural Religion was easy *first* and plain," before it was corrupted by evil priests, who in turn facilitated despotic governments, and so forth and so forth.[30] Deism was a valid and valuable faith not just because it was reasonable but because it was the first form of religious belief practiced by humanity. Voltaire repeatedly insisted on the originality: the article "Théiste" in his *Dictionnaire philosophique* (1752) claimed that "the simple adoration of a God *preceded* all the [religious] systems in the world."[31] To prove his point, he would call upon the testimony of ancient philosophers: Zoroaster, Minos, Solon, Socrates, and Cicero were invoked as evidence that monotheism was older than Christianity—or any other religion for that matter.[32] On religious matters, philosophical "progress" was not simply about leaving superstitious beliefs behind but about recovering the religious practices of the Ancients.

9

Post Tenebras Lux: *Begriffsgeschichte* or *Régime d'Historicité?*

In the previous chapters I have been primarily concerned with establishing a credible genealogy connecting the Enlightenment with the Quarrel of the Ancients and the Moderns. We have seen how the *philosophes* celebrated equally the achievements of their immediate philosophical and scientific predecessors and those of their ancient precursors. And they continued to tell a narrative in which Enlightenment derived, on the one hand, from recent discoveries and the dissemination of their knowledge and, on the other, from the rediscovery of ancient science. What this genealogy does not tell us, however, is how this narrative was received once the Quarrel had subsided. Did it retain its original signification? Or did each retelling—and this story would be retold countless times over the next seventy years—produce a new meaning? Were the latter case to prove true, moreover, we could not be sure whether the *philosophes* genuinely inherited their understanding of their own activities from Dubos and his co-participants in the Quarrel or whether they were simply borrowing freely and selectively from a larger cultural storehouse.

The daunting methodological and historical difficulties inherent in these questions become evident when we consider the fate of that Enlightenment buzzword *l'esprit philosophique*. This expression, which lay at the heart of Dubos's theory and narrative of the Enlightenment, continued to act as the calling card of the *philosophes*. Diderot proudly stated in 1749 that "we [are] in a century when the philosophical spirit has rid us of a great number of prejudices," an opinion with which the other members of the flock concurred. Voltaire observed three years later that "today . . . the philosophical spirit has progressed so far," for once in agreement with Rousseau, who also recognized "the philosophical spirit of this century."[1] Even those who disagreed with its breadth acknowledged its importance and presence: "The philosophical spirit, which seems so disseminated today, is in fact much rarer than is thought," the Swiss physiologist Charles Bonnet warned.[2] And when intellectual histories of the eighteenth century began to appear in the 1770s, it was the emergence of an *esprit philosophique* that was perceived as announcing the Age of Enlightenment: Antoine-Léonard Thomas's *Essai sur les éloges*, for instance, claims that Fontenelle and François La Mothe Le Vayer "developed in the [French] nation a philosophical spirit, which slowly became the general spirit."[3]

Crediting Fontenelle with the introduction of an *esprit philosophique*, however, highlights a first problem in trying to tease any specific intellectual content out of this expression: for Fontenelle and his fellow academicians, the *esprit philosophique* was precisely *not* new but was rather becoming more widespread in their time. On closer examination, another more serious problem crops up as well, namely that almost everyone who used this expression interpreted it differently. For Dubos, the *esprit* denoted less of an empirical than a rational attitude, what he called a "superiority of reason."[4] César Dumarsais argued, on the contrary, that it was an empirical principle, which decomposed all secondary ideas into simple, single ones, following Locke's precepts.[5] Both of these definitions at least seem to fall in the category of what Blaise Pascal called the *esprit de géomètre*, yet for Nicolas Fréret it was precisely the fact that this new spirit constituted a kind of *esprit de finesse*, more suited to humanistic genres, that made it novel and important: "The correctness of an argument [*raisonnement*] must be sought in all fields, not only those concerning natural phenomena; this critical sense [*cette critique*] provides philosophy with a large part of the moral and physical facts that it deploys."[6] Voltaire, for his part, opposed *esprit philosophique* to "*critique*," in its humanistic understanding.[7] In the *Encyclopédie* alone, there are, in fact, at least five different, including some contradictory, uses of this expression.[8]

While certain commonalities may be extracted from these varying definitions, it is clear that the *esprit philosophique* was an extremely elastic concept, to say the least. There are no *Begriffsgeschichte* studies of this term, to my knowledge, but one might also question how successful such an approach would be in this case.[9] The same may be said for many of the keywords of the Enlightenment, as Colin Jones noted;[10] and we know from Robert Darnton's research on the Société typographique de Neuchâtel that someone ordering a *livre philosophique* was just as liable to receive a pornographic pamphlet as a materialist tract.[11] Contemporaries also picked up on this ambiguity, as Charles Duclos's criticism of the Parisian elite indicates: "Alternatively given over to dissipation, ambition, or what they call philosophy . . . their ideas are never orderly, often contradict each other, and appear to them on an equal standing."[12] L'*esprit philosophique* ultimately functioned much as what the Structuralists called a "floating signifier"; capable of being affixed to a wide variety of different works, initiatives, and practices, it provided the *je ne sais quoi* that made some books and ideas philosophical and others not.[13]

The fact that "what they call philosophy" could designate such a grab bag of genres, ideas, and practices may help us unravel some of the more jarring contradictions in Enlightenment discourse. To consider but one example, this conceptual elasticity of keywords is central to the phenomenon that I have called "the Super-Enlightenment," in reference to those works and practices whose mystical and mythical dimensions strike us today as clearly contrary to Enlightenment principles but that nonetheless loudly professed their adherence to an *esprit philosophique*.[14]

At the same time, this elasticity could not be indefinitely stretched: for the "enemies of the Enlightenment," as Darrin McMahon has demonstrated, it was precisely this nominal attachment to "philosophy" that augured poorly for the fate of civilization, and particularly religion.[15] The *philosophes'* adversaries were no clearer in their usage of this term. In a mordant satire, Charles Palissot has the woman-philosopher (a double sin!) Cydalise describe her recent book of "philosophy":

> J'y traite en abrégé de l'Esprit, du bon sens,
> Des passions, des Loix, & des Gouvernemens;
> De la vertu, des mœurs, du climat, des usages,
> Des peuples policés & des peuples sauvages;
> Du désordre apparent, de l'ordre universel,
> Du bonheur idéal & du bonheur réel.
> J'examine avec soin les principes des choses,
> L'enchaînement secret des effets & des causes.[16]

A hodgepodge of various Enlightenment works, this philosophical treatise presents no recognizable thesis or system: it is simply the product of a "mind purified by philosophy."[17] But even such a semantically empty usage of this term is indicative: whatever they designated, "philosophy" and "*esprit philosophique*" were fighting words, identifying their users in a struggle that would turn violent during the French Revolution and persist well into the nineteenth century.[18]

Simply because it seems nearly impossible to pinpoint the exact philosophical content of the Enlightenment, however, does not imply that we cannot say anything about its intellectual shape or form. *Begriffsgeschichte*, or more traditional intellectual history, may simply constitute the wrong angle of approach. More promising is Daniel Brewer's suggestion that we consider the Enlightenment in terms of a "*régime d'historicité*," that is, a certain configuration of past, present, and future states.[19] Indeed, whatever the *esprit philosophique* may have been, it was always something that defined the present moment: Dubos wrote about the effect of the philosophical spirit on "our century"; for Fontenelle, the breadth of this spirit was "almost completely new." Subsequent *philosophes* maintained this emphasis on the philosophical present: in his *Poème sur la loi naturelle* (1751), Voltaire declared: "Finally, in our day, thanks to philosophy / Which enlightens [*éclaire*] at least part of Europe . . ."; and d'Alembert held that "one cannot dispute the progress of Philosophy among us," as it affected (in the present tense) all "the events which concern us, or at least affect us, our customs [*mœurs*], our works, and even our conversation."[20] A plethora of *Encyclopédie* entries similarly extolled "the philosophical spirit of the century," as Turgot called it in his *Encyclopédie* entry "Fondation." Diderot argued that "the *Encyclopedia* could only be attempted in a century of philosophy" ("Encyclopédie"); the entry "Inoculation" gushed about "this century that is so polite, so enlightened [*plein de lumières*] that we call it the *century of Philosophy*"; while the article "Observation" praised somewhat redundantly "the clarity [*les lumières*] of our enlightened [*éclairé*] century." Even more critical observers such as Duclos recognized his century's infatuation with all things philosophical: "I do not know whether my opinion of our century is too great; but it seems that a certain fermentation of universal reason is taking place."[21] This impression would last until the eve of the French Revolution, when, for instance, the abbé Sieyès wrote that "the empire of reason spreads farther every day."[22]

This constant insistence on the privileged "philosophical" condition of the present confirms Brewer's hypothesis that the "self-projection and rescripting of the present may well be one of the constitutive features of the historical-critical project of Enlightenment."[23] As Margaret Jacob has shown in a different context, the sense of belonging to a "new time" was central to the Masonic experience of "living the Enlightenment."[24] More than anything, the Enlightenment seems to have been the period when people thought they were living in an age of Enlightenment. It did not matter so much what and how these individuals were thinking or acting; what mattered was that they perceived themselves to be thinking or acting in "reasonable," "philosophi-cal," and "enlightened" ways in the present.

If the present moment was exceptional for its philosophical qualities, however, it would eventually pale in comparison to the glorious future, most memorably enshrined by Condorcet: the utopian "tenth epoch" of his *Tableau historique des progrès de l'esprit humain* promises "the destruction of inequality between nations; the progress of equality within a single people; and the true perfection of man."[25] This rosy future is also central to Kant's definition of the Enlightenment, viewed as a precursor to "an enlightened age" to come.[26] Even less optimistic *philosophes* were committed to the theoretical improvement of society, given that "progress" was a fundamental premise of the Enlighten-ment.[27] Inherited from the Moderns, this belief rested on the assumption that "men always having before them the advances or work of their predecessors, each century, through natural imi-tation, [would be] jealous to add something to what the previous centuries had left," as d'Alembert asserted in his *Essai sur les élé-ments de philosophie*, concluding that "each science would be like astronomy, which enriches and perfects itself each day through new observations added to those of the Ancients."[28] He was in fact merely reformulating what Fontenelle, Dubos, and Fréret (as well as Perrault before them) had already stated, namely that "the Moderns naturally built upon the Ancients."[29] It is this con-text that helps explain why Rousseau's argument against "per-fectibility" (the constant improvement of humanity over time) in the first *Discourse* was deemed outrageous by many, although even his criticism accepts—indeed, rests upon—the premise that the arts and science have been exceptionally developed in the present. Ultimately, it was not all that difficult to reconcile this criticism with a more optimistic vision of the future, once the ultimate goal of humanity was redefined in terms of restoring an uncorrupted, natural state of human relations, as it would be, for instance, during the French Revolution.[30]

10

Ancients and the Orient:
Translatio Imperii

In contrast to these glorious portraits of future ages, the Middle Ages often came in for bruising criticism. Countless Enlightenment works tell the same story: the enlightened present stood in sharp contrast to the "thousand years of barbarism," when society had sunk into "the deepest obscurity."[1] But despite such harsh pronouncements, this historical narrative was not a simple tale of gradual progress. First of all, how did these thousand years of barbarism end? They ended with the rediscovery of the Ancients, as Longepierre noted, rehearsing a common theme: "After the fall of Constantinople, many illustrious Greeks having sought refuge in Italy, . . . wit [*le bel esprit*] and good taste were reborn at the same time. In the midst of the ruins of ancient Greece and ancient Rome a thousand beautiful works sprung up, which, based on these divine models, captured something of their beauty and came near to their perfection."[2] This account of European cultural history bears a thematic and formal resemblance to the Modern story of a scientific revolution: in both instances, an intellectual wasteland ("gothic" desolation, on the one hand; Scholasticism, on the other) was revived thanks to a revolution in knowledge (the rediscovery of the Ancients *versus* the new philosophy of Bacon and/or Descartes), producing a "new age" of learning.³ No wonder the Ancients could so easily incorporate the Modern *régime d'historicité*: it was already there, in slightly different form. This similarity, however, should not mask the fact that the Enlightenment narrative synthesized the competing Ancient and Modern histories of the proximate past: Voltaire, d'Alembert, and Condorcet, among others, all recognized the importance of *both* the revival of ancient learning after the fall of Constantinople *and* the transformation of scientific knowledge with the advent of Bacon and Descartes.⁴

Second, just as defenders of the Ancients recognized the scientific advances of the present, the champions of the new were forced to single out moments of exceptional enlightenment in the past.⁵ If there was a Quarrel between these two groups, it was precisely because the Moderns also admitted the existence of "knowledgeable Antiquity" but simply argued that it "was never *as* enlightened [*éclairée*] as we are today."⁶ There was an unevenness to the "successive advances of the human mind," to borrow a phrase from Turgot's title: as Perrault put it, "Centuries, to be sure, vary among themselves, / Some are enlightened [*éclairés*], and others ignorant."⁷ Following Dubos, Voltaire recognized more specifically three other "happy ages . . . when the arts were perfected" in his *Siècle de Louis XIV*: the century of Pericles, the age of Augustus, and the Italian Renaissance. If the reign of Louis XIV alone "reache[d] nearest to perfection," the others were not half bad.⁸

Here again it becomes apparent that the *philosophes* owed more to the party of the Ancients than to Perrault's team of Moderns. D'Alembert, for instance, went so far as to suggest not only that antiquity could serve as a model for the arts but also that "reading the Ancients can shed much light on the study of science."⁹ Nor was it mere inspiration that his modern experimenters could find in the Ancients, since d'Alembert pointed out how "modern philosophy, in many domains, has drawn close to what was believed during the first age of philosophy." His conclusion underscored the extent to which the Enlightenment narrative was not simply a story of continuous progress but also one of rediscovering the past: "The first impressions of nature leave us with correct ideas, which we soon abandon due to uncertainty or a love for novelty, until we are forced to return to them." To be sure, d'Alembert was not suggesting that the study of classical philosophy could *replace* the contemplation of nature, but the very fact that he *also* recommended "reading the Ancients" underscores the Enlightenment's massive about-turn from the universal rejection by experimental scholars, only one century prior, of ancient learning.[10]

Such irregularity in cultural achievement presents a challenge to the "dwarves standing on giants" variety of argument, which bases the doctrine of inevitable progress on the continuous and gradual accumulation of knowledge. Rather than a progressive or stadial philosophy of history, it was the medieval *translatio imperii et studii* trope that dominated enlightened accounts of universal history.[11] The arts and sciences had peaked in given nations at given times (for instance, Periclean Greece, Augustan Rome, and Medici Florence), before passing on elsewhere (Louisquatorzian France). The astronomer and leading scientist Jean-Sylvain Bailly summed up this account in his 1775 *Histoire de l'astronomie ancienne*: "The scepter of sciences must have passed from one people to the next."[12]

By the time Bailly was writing, however, earlier nations had been added to Voltaire's list of "happy ages"; as they all lay to the east, Bailly could employ a metaphor that would soon pass into posterity with Hegel's *Philosophy of History*: the light of knowledge, "born in the Orient, as is the Sun, proceeds like this star toward the Occident, and in a slow revolution must, like the sun, pass around the world."[13] In large part thanks to Voltaire, whose correspondence with Bailly was published in the sequel to the *Histoire de l'astronomie ancienne*, China and India had joined the ranks of Athens, Rome, Florence, and Paris in the procession of glorious civilizations. These Oriental Ancients differed from their Occidental siblings in that they not only elevated the arts and sciences to a near pinnacle of refinement but most likely invented them in the first place as well: in his 1756 *Essai sur les mœurs*, Voltaire instructed his readers to "cast your gaze first of all on the Orient, cradle of the arts, which gave the Occident everything."[14]

This diffusionist model of culture was not in itself novel: only the names had changed. It had been traditional before Voltaire to ascribe a similar role to Egypt, a genealogy that continued to be accepted in certain enlightened (particularly Masonic) circles.[15] But substituting India for Egypt as the "cradle of pagan superstition, the Sciences, and the Arts"[16] opened up a dizzying new historical possibility: what if these Indian Ancients had in fact been more modern than we are today? This was the conclusion reached by Bailly, according to whom contemporary Europeans were only beginning to rediscover the full extent of scientific knowledge once available to mankind: "Our century is so enlightened, Europe today is witnessing the apogee of its scientific glory: what does it matter that our epoch was preceded by another? . . . What we have done could have been achieved before us."[17] A similar conclusion had already been proposed by Antoine Court de Gébelin in his widely read *Monde primitif:* there was an "ordre ancien et éternel" that could serve as a basis for future society.[18] Not all Enlightenment figures bought into the idea of a "wisdom of the Ancients" (in Bacon's words) that could be rediscovered only in their texts; for many, valuing the Ancients was more a matter of merely appreciating their accomplishments. At the same time, it was often convenient for the *philosophes* to exaggerate the glories of antiquity, if only to indirectly criticize the present, exceptional as it was.

Enlightened Institutions (I): The Royal Academies versus the Republic of Letters

One of the arguments for locating the origins of the Enlightenment outside France is that countries such as England or the Netherlands had already put into practice the philosophical and cultural ideals that the French *académiciens* were merely talking about. Indeed, at the time Dubos was writing, both England and Holland had a tradition of public lectures on natural philosophy;[1] and rulers in these countries had embraced many of the political and religious values (e.g., toleration or relative freedom of expression) that would later be held dear by the *philosophes*. Does it really matter, then, if the French put into words what others were already doing? Ultimately, the Enlightenment was about social transformation; if societies were already being transformed in England and the Dutch provinces, then surely they can claim precedence over the French.

The interest in national Enlightenments, as I noted previously, runs the risk of nationalizing the debate over the Enlightenment, and I do not wish to suggest that everything that mattered in the eighteenth century began in Paris. I do believe, however, that pre-1720 societal and discursive (as opposed to, say, scientific) changes in England and Holland had little immediate impact on French society or thought, whereas the French narrative of the Enlightenment *did* have a significant impact on its various European versions (which is not to say they were not equally influenced by local traditions).

There is no opposition, moreover, between theory and practice in this French genealogy of the Enlightenment: the Parisian *académiciens*, after all, were themselves reacting to the considerable progress of new philosophical and scientific ideas in French society. As Fontenelle and others remarked, it was not so much the *lumières* that were new, but the fact that they were increasingly disseminated (*répandues*).[2] This observation may even be favorably compared with Joseph Addison's statement in the *Spectator* that he hoped to bring "Philosophy *out* of the closets and libraries, schools and colleges, to dwell in clubs and assemblies, at tea-tables and in coffee-houses"—a wish that, when he formulated it in 1711, was still prospective.[3]

In France, by contrast, the new philosophy had already become so fashionable that it was an object of satire: "People here are very keen on the sciences, but I am not sure whether they are truly learned," Montesquieu has the younger of his two Persian travelers, Rica, comment.[4] According to Dubos, this trend had already been apparent in Paris much earlier—by 1675—when "even women were then studying the new systems which many people taught in Paris in vernacular language," adding how "there is fashion among us for sciences as for clothes."[5] His observation is in fact supported by contemporary sources such as Molière's 1672 mocking play *Les femmes savantes* (who constitute their own academy), as well as by more recent historical accounts: Erica Harth, for instance, has described how "from the 1640s to the 1660s the salons were beset by a craze for Cartesian philosophy."[6] This was no passing fad and would be celebrated as a sign of cultural progress by Fontenelle, whose *Entretiens sur la pluralité des mondes* (1686) heralded the conversion of the fictional marquise de G. to "the party of philosophy."[7] The Jesuit priest Gabriel

Daniel was still mocking the modish interest in the new science in 1690: "It was these same individuals [the Jansenists] who made philosophy fashionable for women."[8] In fact, François Azouvi has chronicled how it was largely thanks to the worldly successes of Cartesianism that it eventually managed to replace Scholasticism in the French universities and *collèges*.[9] Public experiments were performed at the Sorbonne from the 1690s onward, and this "general enthusiasm for science and experimentation, particularly among women," would continue unabated throughout the eighteenth century, reaching a climax with the Mesmerist craze of the 1780s.[10] At the midcentury, the world-weary marquis de Vauvenargues quipped that "philosophy has its fashions just as do clothes, music, architecture, etc."[11] That said, the association between philosophy and fashion was not always viewed so negatively: after all, the editors of the *Encyclopédie* placed their work under the sign of "this philosophical spirit, so fashionable today [*si à la mode aujourd'hui*]."[12]

In addition to its success among the worldly elite, the new science had made its impact on a number of critical institutions. While we have grown accustomed, since Habermas, to look primarily toward the salons, coffeehouses, Masonic lodges, and other public spaces for social evidence of a nascent Enlightenment, Dubos identified two other institutions. The first pillar of the new science, according to Dubos (in agreement here with many others), was the Académie des sciences, along with the other French academies, and their foreign equivalents, such as the Royal Society.[13] The symbolic importance of the academies' contributions to the Scientific Revolution may not hold up to historical scrutiny, but in the establishment of an Enlightenment narrative, they occupied a central place (not the least, one can only imagine, because so many key writers of this period were themselves *académiciens*).[14] It was, after all, within and between the academies that the Quarrel of the Ancients and the Moderns primarily took place; and by the 1770s these institutions had become the de facto headquarters of the *philosophes*.[15]

It would, of course, be an exaggeration to suggest that Louis

XIV, founder of the academies (expect for the Académie française), ought accordingly to be viewed as the father of the Enlightenment; the primary purpose of the academies, after all, was not to disseminate knowledge—deliberations in the Académie des sciences remained secret until the 1690s—but rather to augment the glory of the French nation.[16] But there was a basic convergence of interests between the French Crown and the *philosophes*: both sought, in the words of the person who came closest to uniting them, to "overturn the sterile monuments" of feudalism and tradition.[17] By the time (1757) Turgot published this statement—as a civil servant (and future *intendant*) writing in the *Encyclopédie*—the *philosophes* were becoming increasingly aware that the state could be a fickle ally: hence, Diderot's assertions that the *Encyclopédie* could not be overseen by the government.[18] But this relative demand for independence must be recognized as a departure—and a brief one at that—from an earlier configuration in which the state was perceived as the necessary sponsor of the Enlightenment, with the academies as its chief institutions.

This faith in the benevolent power of the state and in state-sponsored academies is what ultimately distinguishes the French narrative of Enlightenment from similar, more cosmopolitan notions about a philosophical age that were circulating in the Anglo-Dutch Republic of Letters around the same time as the Quarrel of the Ancients and the Moderns was taking place.[19] These scholars—mostly Protestants, many exiled by the revocation of the Edict of Nantes in 1685—defended beliefs that would later inform the Enlightenment project as it was understood across Europe, most notably religious toleration, freedom of expression, skepticism toward the miraculous, and an insistence on rule-based government. They have accordingly been presented as the true precursors of the *philosophes*. Yet there is a fundamental and decisive difference between them. The Protestants perceived themselves as part of a diffuse and scattered network, of a Republic of Letters that existed more in their minds than in reality; their core virtue, as John Marshall has written, was *amicitia*, the Ciceronian "bonding of individuals in intellectual friendship."[20] For the French, by contrast, the Enlightenment was immediately and intrinsically connected with the social transformation of the most powerful monarchy on the Continent, and with a specific capital, Paris.[21] The *philosophes* valued intellectual friendships, to be sure, but placed far greater emphasis on engaging with society at large: if the ideal portrait of the scholar displayed him in his library, writing for his intellectual peers, the *philosophe* presented himself as a man of the world, corresponding with monarchs; defending humanity, truth, and freedom; or holding court like a Roman senator.[22] Though Enlightenment authors also developed extended correspondence networks, they concentrated their intellectual efforts on the great capitals of Europe, writing less for each other than for the rulers, ministers, and elites of society.

The Protestant scholars active in the Anglo-Dutch Republic of Letters were very much involved in the political activities of the day, from the absolutist maneuvers of Louis XIV to the English Glorious Revolution. In many respects, however, such direct engagement in political affairs was unusual for the wider European Republic of Letters. Humanist scholars could be loyal servants to a monarch, but they also recognized, in Peter Miller's words, "the conflict between service and scholarship."[23] Even when partaking in the *vita activa*, they remained nostalgic for the *vita contemplativa*. As Jacob Soll has shown, those who did put their scholarly efforts to work for the state could become victims of the conflicting objectives of politics and scholarship, as they sometimes found themselves forbidden to publish their studies.[24]

Complicating matters is the fact that the *philosophes* continued to refer to their literary world as a *république des lettres*. The continued use of this label has led John Pocock to argue that they "annex[ed] the term . . . from the Netherlands-based operators who had formerly conducted it" and to whom "the name and vocabulary of Enlightenment may justly be applied."[25] But this expression was in fact already commonplace in early seventeenth-century France; Jean-Louis Guez de Balzac was employing it routinely by 1648, thirty-six years before Bayle.[26] By the eighteenth century, it had simply become a label designating the world of scholarship and writing.

What sort of relationship did exist, then, between the Enlightenment and the Republic of Letters? Dena Goodman describes the former as "a moment in the history" of the latter and largely uses the terms interchangeably.[27] This usage may correspond to the discursive practice of the *philosophes* themselves but leaves genealogical questions unanswered. Anne Goldgar has gone in the opposite direction, suggesting that the relation between the Republic of Letters and the Enlightenment was one of considerable disruption: on the one hand, "the old Republic ... was essentially directed inward. Its concerns were the concerns of scholarship, and its audience conceived largely as itself," whereas the new members of the Enlightenment "claimed a role in a mission to change society." Accordingly, "Enlightenment writers behaved toward the conservative members of the Republic of Letters . . . much as the seventeenth-century aristocrats had behaved toward their *nouveaux riches* neighbors."[28]

This attitude was certainly on display in some of the earliest texts of the Enlightenment: Montesquieu's *Persian Letters*, for instance, offers a series of satirical portraits of scholars, including an obnoxious astronomer who boasts about corresponding with "a man in Stockholm, another in Leipzig, and another in London, whom I have never seen, and no doubt shall never see."[29] By the time of the *Encyclopédie*, however, the *philosophes* appeared almost to have forgotten about the early-modern *respublica litteraria*, to the point that Diderot could propose reinventing it: "It would not be wasteful to establish correspondences between the principal centers of the educated world. . . . We would exchange information about our practices, customs, publications, works, machines, etc."[30] No fundamental disaccord seems to have existed, in other words, between *philosophes* and *savants*: as

Lawrence Brockliss has argued, their social networks overlapped considerably, even when their scholarly interests did not collide.[31] Precisely because the old Republic of Letters persisted in good stead throughout the eighteenth century, however, it is hard to imagine how an intellectual movement as substantively different as the Enlightenment could have emerged from it.

Enlightened Institutions (II): Universities, Censorship, and Public Instruction

Another institution that, according to Dubos, fueled the *esprit philosophique* was the university. As evidence for this assertion, Dubos points to how "forty years ago [updated to "sixty" in the 1733 edition] no professor at the University of Paris would have dared teach [Copernicus's] system. Nearly all teach it today [i.e., in 1719]."[1] The professors at the Ecole de medecine de l'Université de Paris had similarly come to accept Harvey's circulation theory, which had also encountered stiff resistance when it was first proposed. Dubos's assertions fit with recent studies on the evolution of university curricula: according to Brockliss, Cartesian philosophy became accepted in French universities in the 1690s; and the turn of the century, more generally, marked a turning point in the instruction of the sciences.[2]

While the universities clearly did not belong to the avant-garde of the "new philosophy," Dubos's remarks nonetheless call to mind Alan Kors's suggestion, made in his masterful study *D'Holbach's Coterie*, that the university played a much larger role in the education of the *philosophes* than is usually acknowledged.[3]

As he notes, with the exception of Voltaire and Rousseau, most other Enlightenment figures spent time at a university (this was particularly true in Scotland, Hanover, and Prussia). In fact, the role of both universities and *collèges* (i.e., the equivalent today of high school) may have been even more critical with respect to the many students who did not go on to become *philosophes*. As Brockliss observed, "In disseminating the new science, [the *collèges*] ensured the French *philosophes* an audience that could comprehend what they were trying to do, irrespective of whether or not it sympathized with their conclusions."[4] This sort of assistance to the Enlightenment project was indeed an unintended consequence: most French *collège* and university professors frowned upon the writings of the *philosophes*. Yet simply by promoting Cartesian physics and philosophy, professors validated the *philosophes'* claim that they lived in a *siècle de lumière*, in which intellectual matters were examined with a new *esprit philosophique*.

Kors's insight has mostly fallen on deaf ears. While the material and intellectual support that universities provided for the Scientific Revolution is increasingly recognized, their contributions to the Enlightenment remain categorically denied, as this assertion suggests: "In France in the eighteenth century, the university ceased to have any marked influence on the intellectual life of French society and the course of enlightened discussion there."[5] To back up his claim, this author points to d'Alembert's 1754 article "Collège" in the *Encyclopédie*, which is characterized as "unqualifiedly condemnatory and at the same time demand[ing] fundamental reforms."[6] But this description ignores d'Alembert's praise of the university in this very entry: "Despite the steady dissemination of true philosophy in France, it remains much more difficult for it to infiltrate institutions [*les corps*] than individuals. . . . The University of Paris, composed of individuals who are not constituted into any regular or ecclesiastical body, will have less trouble in shaking the yoke of prejudice that still determines the colleges [*écoles*]."[7]

Compared with the tightly run *collèges*, the university was thus clearly deemed to be far more open to philosophical innovation, a fact that d'Alembert credits in no small part to Charles Rollin, rector of the University of Paris between 1694 and 1696 and "one of the men who has worked most effectively for the education of the young."[8] D'Alembert would have been well aware of the university's liberal attitude, as it had been indirectly responsible for the first major crisis of the *Encyclopédie*: the revelation that one of its contributors, the abbé de Prades, had received a doctorate in theology from the University of Paris for a dissertation that challenged Catholic orthodoxy.[9] Finally, d'Alembert's comments also highlight his adherence to the belief that the Enlightenment was a matter less of inventing a *new* philosophy than of ensuring that "*true* philosophy" be diffused throughout society. Indeed, the very goal of the encyclopedic venture, as Diderot famously wrote in a subsequent article, was not to champion a new way but to "change the *common* way of thinking."[10]

"Common" is certainly not to be confused with "popular": only a fraction of French subjects attended *collège* or university, and only a fraction would read the *Encyclopédie*.[11] But the *philosophes* did not cast their nets very widely: they sought mostly to enlighten those who were already "a bit enlightened [*un peu éclairés*]," as Fontenelle put it; as for the "people," he continued, "they are destined to be perpetually fooled [*à être la dupe de tout*]."[12] The diffusion of a philosophical spirit thus featured in the Enlightenment project in two distinct respects: on the one hand, the stated goal of Enlightenment philosophy was to influence and change *elite* beliefs and practices (often with the general welfare in mind, but only indirectly: one might call this trickle-down humanitarianism); on the other, one of the conditions of possibility for the Enlightenment to occur was the *prior* transformation of elite beliefs and practices. In other words, and to put it somewhat paradoxically, for there to be an Enlightenment, certain people already had to be enlightened. The chicken came before the egg. This apparent paradox vanishes, however, if one accepts the thesis presented above, namely that the foundational act of the Enlightenment was narratological and not epistemological.

In the wake of Dubos's *Réflexions critiques*, a third institution emerged as a paradoxical bastion serving the cause of the *philosophes*: state censorship. In a remarkable new study of censorship in eighteenth-century France, Raymond Birn forces us to acknowledge that regarding most matters of censure the *philosophes* and the state were on the same side.[13] Religious works that could be judged "fanatical" and harsh criticisms of Enlightenment figures and ideas were often refused the royal printing *privilège*, whereas the system of tacit permissions (and relative ease with which forbidden texts could enter France from abroad) ensured that most Enlightenment works were readily available. The well-known instances of "spectacular" censorship—such as of Helvétius's *De l'esprit* in 1758–59 and Rousseau's *Emile* in 1762—were mostly cases of rivalry between competing censuring powers (the Council of the King, the Parlement of Paris, the archbishop of Paris, and the University of Paris). The well-known anecdotes about Malesherbes, *directeur de la librairie* (responsible for book censorship), hiding Diderot's papers in his own home after the printing privilege for the *Encyclopédie* was revoked in 1759, or of Sorbonne censors having banned books sent from foreign publishers directly to Sartine, the police lieutenant general of Paris, the better to avoid border checks, appear less as anomalies than as symptomatic of a larger pattern. Given the *philosophes'* powerful allies at court—which included, for a while, Louis XV's own mistress, Madame de Pompadour, who had herself painted with the *Encyclopédie*, Montesquieu's *De l'esprit des lois*, and Voltaire's *Henriade* in the background—this loose alliance between state and Enlightenment is not all that surprising.[14] Perhaps the most symbolic event of the Enlightenment was not the publication of pornography libeling the French queen but rather the fact that Marie-Antoinette was among the cheering theater audience that greeted Voltaire on his last appearance in Paris.[15]

It is difficult to abandon our impression of the subversive *philosophes* challenging the inequities of Old Regime justice and crushing *l'infâme*. And in some respects, there is no reason we should: Enlightenment writers did seek to redress social and cultural wrongs, waging battles that often pitted them against the state. But we must remember that "the state" in the eighteenth century was an incredibly fragmented body, constituted of interdependent parts that often thought and acted independently.[16] When Voltaire took on the Parlement of Toulouse, in the Calas affair, he knew he could count on the support of his good friend the duc de Choiseul, Louis XV's minister of foreign affairs. In fact, an impressive series of "philosophical" ministers and administrators served France throughout the eighteenth century: the chancelier d'Aguesseau, the marquis d'Argenson (minister), Charles-Augustin de Ferriol d'Argental (intendant), Malesherbes (minister), Sartine (lieutenant general of police for Paris and later minister), Turgot (minister), Necker (minister), Loménie de Brienne (minister), and many others sympathized with and supported the *philosophes*. One would also have to add to this list the names of some of the most illustrious families in France, such as the duc de Nivernais (who protected Montesquieu after the publication of *De l'esprit des lois*), the duc de Richelieu (Voltaire's close friend), and the duc de Luxembourg (an admirer of Rousseau).

The close alliance between academicians, scholars, professors, and philosophers, on the one hand, and members of the high aristocracy and government, on the other, can be seen as an essential precondition for the Enlightenment's success. This alliance is also evident in the fact that most *philosophes* occupied official posts. Voltaire was a royal historiographer and member of the Académie française, of which d'Alembert rose to become the perpetual secretary, and to which a great many other *philosophes* belonged. Many of the censors employed by the Crown to suppress seditious works were friends of the *philosophes* or *philosophes* themselves.[17] Before embarking on an academic career, Dubos had been a secret diplomatic emissary for the Ministry of Foreign Affairs. So matter-of-fact was this arrangement that Rousseau's friends could simply not understand why he refused state patronage, and thought him mad.[18]

Of course, an equal, possibly larger, number of ministers and *grands* were overtly hostile to the Enlightenment and did their utmost to muzzle its most vocal representatives. During certain times of crisis, such as the 1750s and 1770s, the *dévôt* party at court—led by the Dauphin himself until his death in 1765, and later by the count de Vergennes—or the Jansenists in parlement managed to get the upper hand and convince Louis XV to crack down on Enlightenment works and reject enlightened reform projects.[19] The state, to put it bluntly, was never completely in cahoots with the *philosophes*. As their enemies coalesced into a Counter-Enlightenment movement, from the 1750s onward, this opposition adopted an even more intransigent and combative attitude, further polarizing the pro- and anti-*philosophe* factions both at court and in the public.[20] These later developments, however, do not modify the fundamental point that there was always a pro-Enlightenment party within the fragmented state as well; it did not win every policy battle, but without it, the Enlightenment as we know it could not have existed.

13

Worldliness, Politeness, and the Importance of Not Being Too Radical

More than any institution, it was another social transformation that, in the eyes of many contemporary observers, distinguished the present age from centuries past. This transformation had begun around the same time as the new science but occurred in a very different area, *les mœurs*. According to the champion of the Modern cause Charles Perrault, the French in the time of Richelieu had become "polite," or, to use his preferred term, "gallant."[1] The overly "Modern" connotations of gallantry would ultimately bring this aristocratic concept into disfavor: Dubos, for instance, follows Boileau in deriding it as "the affectation of expressing feelings to women out of politeness when one has none."[2] While disparaging fops whose worldly success was due only to their "scintillating imagination, agreeable conversation, and light reading," the *philosophes* nonetheless generally adhered to the norms of polite society that dictated etiquette in the salons and correspondence.[3]

The alliance between *gens de lettres* and *le monde* went well beyond a shared culture of civility to inform the genesis and intellectual conditions of the Enlightenment.[4] As historians studying the social conditions of literary life in the Old Regime have shown, these two groups developed an almost symbiotic relationship. Beginning in the seventeenth century, authors stopped depending directly on wealthy patrons, yet became increasingly indebted to a new patron: the state.[5] In the eighteenth century, authors also became more dependent on the positive recognition by society—*le monde*—of their literary value.[6]

One of the key sites where this recognition was debated and awarded was the salon. Our earlier understanding of the salons as places of lively philosophical debate has been challenged by Antoine Lilti's magisterial thesis, in which the salons figure more as sites of aristocratic patronage: *gens de lettres* and aristocrats might frequent the same salons but often on different days or at separate meals.[7] Even the *philosophes* who were fortunate (and fortuned) enough not to depend on aristocratic largesse for survival were still dependent on the social elite for their cultural and political support. But this does not mean that the salons played no intellectual role in the Enlightenment. Indeed, for the Enlightenment to exist at all, there had to be an audience prepared to approve of, and on many occasions defend, works by Enlightenment authors. To the extent that it was fashionable to present oneself as "enlightened," authors seeking to curry favor with the worldly elite had to appeal to this client base. Part of this appeal was no doubt the novelty, even the "edginess" (to lapse again into marketing talk), associated with the *esprit philosophique*, yet already by the 1680s, this fashion was also fairly tame: one no longer risked the stake, for instance, by arguing that the Copernican system was correct.

Some historians have suggested that this *esprit philosophique* was in fact too tame, and that the alliance between *gens de lettres* and *le monde* was little more than a sellout. The *philosophes* may have largely escaped state censure, but as Robert Darnton reminded us, this may have been because they were too cozy with the authorities: Beaumarchais's incendiary *Marriage of Figaro* was censored by none other than Jean-Baptiste-Antoine Suard, a member of the *coterie holbachique* and d'Alembert's protégé in the Académie française.[8] There are, of course, plenty of examples of an entirely opposite attitude: one of Diderot's last texts was a direct address to Louis XVI, whom he berated (using the informal *tu*) for abetting luxury at court while the nation was plunged into poverty.[9] This dichotomy between apparent conformism, on the one hand, and pointed criticism, on the other, was codified by Jonathan Israel into a two-speed theory of the Enlightenment: in his account, *philosophes* of Voltaire's and Montesquieu's streak formed part of a "mainstream Enlightenment," to which he opposes a "Radical Enlightenment," which championed Spinozist beliefs in atheism, democratic government, and religious toleration.[10]

There is no doubt that radical thinkers thrived on the fringes of the more established intellectual milieu in the eighteenth century (as they had, indeed, in preceding centuries). Both Israel and Margaret Jacob before him have cast light on the clandestine networks of freethinkers, stretching across England, Holland, and France, who produced and disseminated a series of philosophically, religiously, and politically "scandalous" works. Nor is there any doubt that these works were passed around and read in Enlightenment circles, since they are cited (often critically) by the *philosophes*. But what impact did they really have on the intellectual and social history of the Enlightenment? As we have seen, what makes the Enlightenment distinctive in the social history of ideas (and, *a fortiori*, what defines the Enlightenment) is precisely the fact that its main proponents—especially in France, but there are plentiful examples elsewhere—struck a balance between intellectual daring and worldly conventions in order to forge an alliance with the educated elites and rulers. Had they been too radical, their philosophy would have been anathema to this public and to some of their own colleagues. In this regard, as Margaret Jacob suggests in her new work with Lynn Hunt and Wijnand Mijnhardt, it was in fact writers such as Bernard Picart who were truly "radical": author of an encyclopedic study of religions, Picart made the concept of religious toleration palatable to a large number of readers through his subtle comparisons.[11] If this work had exhibited a materialist, atheistic attitude, it would never have been read by as many people. The same can be said about the *Encyclopédie*: Israel claims that it did *not* "reflect the views and perspectives of the leading figures of the French moderate mainstream—Voltaire, Montesquieu, Maupertuis, and Turgot."[12] But thanks to new research tools developed by the ARTFL Project at the University of Chicago, which can identify uncited and unattributed passages from other works, we know that the opposite is true: Montesquieu's *De l'esprit des lois*, for instance, is excerpted over five hundred times, in more than one hundred fifty entries, mostly without acknowledgment, and even constitutes the bulk of such important articles as "Aristocratie," "Démocratie," "Esclavage," "Fief," "Impôt," "Loi," "Monarchie," "République," and "Succession à la couronne."[13] Voltaire's *Essai sur les mœurs* is cited almost as often.

Because the political objectives pursued by radical authors bear a greater resemblance to modern democratic values, it is tempting to depict those authors as our direct forebears. Succumbing to this sort of heroic narrative, however, can make for bad intellectual history. In Israel's account, the diffusion and battle of ideas hardly matter at all: the radicals were fated to win from the start. Beliefs in secularization, toleration, and equality, he suggests, "*were bound to* precipitate a European and American revolutionary process, of a type never before witnessed," adding, "the advent of republican and democratic political ideologies . . . *followed directly*" from these "revolutionary philosophical, scientific, and political thought systems." Viewed from this perspective, the "moderate mainstream Enlightenment . . . proved to be much the less important."[14] In his Whiggish history, the *philosophes* are but men in wigs. Leaving aside the gross historiographical problems with this narrative, it occludes the significant impact that the so-called mainstream Enlightenment had on individuals across Europe and the world. While they were far from omnipotent, the *philosophes* undeniably had a part in encouraging sovereigns to revise penal justice systems, institute greater religious toleration, reform religious orders, and even in some instances (such as Tuscany and Russia) take steps toward major constitutional reform.[15] In France, under the influence of the *philosophe*-minister Turgot, Louis XVI proclaimed at the beginning of his reign that he wished "to reign only by justice and laws," a far cry from the *tel est nostre plaisir* of earlier monarchs (and from his own claim, as his rule was collapsing, "It is legal because I wish it to be" [*C'est légal parce que je le veux*]).[16] He later chose as chief finance minister a Genevan Protestant whose salon was home to many *philosophes* and whose wife raised funds for a sculpture of Voltaire.[17] Vivian Gruder has recently shown how it was in large part thanks to the "enlightened" views of the aristocratic Notables assembled in 1787–88 that the king came to summon the Estates General, thereby precipitating the French Revolution.[18]

The Revolution in fact *set back* reforms across Europe for many decades, as sovereigns balked at the political turmoil in Paris. This is not to suggest that the reform movements encouraged by the *philosophes* would ultimately have been better for more people than the revolutionary programs launched by the French in 1789, but simply to emphasize that the Enlightenment had a very significant impact on countless lives in eighteenth-century Europe.[19] Conversely, Israel's radicals may have promoted some of the values that modern Western societies would ultimately embrace, but they had very little influence in bringing about their adoption. It was arguably much more "radical" to advocate and fight for slighter social changes, many of which actually succeeded.

Rather than divide the Enlightenment into querulous groups—a division, moreover, that does not correspond to historical experience—it makes more sense, I would suggest, to recognize that the alliance between *gens de lettres* and *le monde* was constantly in the process of being renegotiated. Both sides had their limits, as they discovered repeatedly throughout the numerous *affaires* of the eighteenth century. Many *philosophes* tested these limits, seeing what they could get away with, and developing complex publication strategies to trick the authorities into publishing more audacious works (when they did not choose, as Diderot, essentially to refrain from publishing them altogether).[20] A certain radicalization may also have occurred over time, from Fontenelle to d'Holbach, as the *philosophes* discovered that their public was developing an appetite for more adventurous thought. Yet as Alan Kors emphasized, even the most hardened atheists of the Enlightenment married in churches and fretted about receiving a proper Christian burial.[21] This is not to say that they were insincere in their unbelief but rather that they kept it mostly under wraps. Those members of the *coterie d'holbachique* who did espouse atheism believed that it would be dangerous to share their sentiments with the *bas peuple*, in accordance with widespread Enlightenment notions about the need for a "double doctrine."[22]

The worldliness of the *philosophes* also explains why their major contributions did not come in the form of scientific experimentation, or even (with a few obvious exceptions) philosophical treatises, but rather were expressed in novels, plays, essays, dialogues, and histories, that is, *belles-lettres*. The *philosophes* were *gens de* lettres in a literal sense, Peter Gay reminded us.[23] Voltaire may have devised experiments with Emilie du Châtelet, but it is for his literary output that he was known and is remembered; the works by Rousseau, Montesquieu, Adam Smith, and Kant that have entered into the political, economic, and philosophical canons are ultimately less representative of the Enlightenment's scholarly output (if clearly more important to us today) than are the flurry of texts by famous or unknown authors seeking to disseminate the *esprit philosophique*. Kant was the far greater philosopher, but the emblematic work of Enlightenment philosophy is the *Encyclopédie*, not the three *Critiques*. To phrase it differently, the primary and initial goal of *philosophes* across Europe was to demolish Scholastic prejudices and *idées reçues* and not necessarily to produce original thought. This kind of philosophy ran the risk of appearing overly skeptical, as one of its earliest observers remarked: "Our century's characteristic seems to be to subject everything to absolute doubt," Fréret cautioned in 1724, not sounding a particularly radical note; "we take pride in this dangerous philosophy, whose only goal is to destroy everything, without ever building anything."[24] But this characteristic also explains why a cultural movement rooted in astronomical and medical observations would turn to more popular genres, such as *contes* and poetry, to advance its cause.

14

From Enlightenment to Revolution: A Shared History?

By 1789, the program of Enlightenment announced seventy years earlier seemed well on its way to being fulfilled. Monarchs across Europe found it advantageous to let it be known that they were advised by *philosophes*; academies flourished not only in major capitals but also in provincial towns; and more than ever before, the philosophical ideals associated with the new science were embraced by wide swathes of society. These transformations do not validate the old celebration of the Enlightenment as an age of progress and reason: as the Mesmer affair demonstrated, the growing interest in science could translate into knowledge about the natural world just as well as it could inspire supernatural fantasies.[1] Even in this instance, however, the state's response revealed the power and prestige now accorded to knowledge specialists, to wit, members of the academies of science and medicine. A royal directive charged a committee from these academies to evaluate Mesmer's claims and to issue a report, which the king subsequently enforced.[2]

In many other respects, the philosophical and social demands of the Enlightenment were in the process of being met. To take another example, Louis XVI asked Jean-Sylvain Bailly, a leading member of the Académie des sciences, to head a team to evaluate the Hôtel-Dieu, a hospice for the poor.[3] Not only was Bailly's highly critical report—demanding better hygiene, more beds, and more funds for the hospital—an immediate publishing success, but it was also very well received by the king, who signaled his willingness to follow the astronomer's recommendations. As it turned out, he never got the chance: the last report (of three) was issued in 1788, a year before the French Revolution.

Even a cursory overview of the debates about the relations between the Enlightenment and the French Revolution, a perennial topic of discussion, is beyond the scope of this study.[4] It is nonetheless worth pausing to consider what the Revolution may reveal in retrospect about the Enlightenment narrative. To begin with, it seems fair to say that the events of 1789 caught most *philosophes* who lived to witness the Revolution—and many, including Helvétius, Voltaire, Rousseau, Diderot, and d'Holbach, did not—off guard. Condorcet may have embraced republicanism and joined forces with Tom Paine in 1791, but in 1789 he came out against the calling of the Estates General.[5] Guillaume-Thomas Raynal himself—who had spent seven years in exile for publishing the third edition of his *Histoire philosophique* under his own name and had enthusiastically welcomed the American Revolution—skewered the entire French revolutionary process in a letter to the National Assembly in 1791.[6] All the other members of the *coterie holbachique*, barring Jacques-André Naigeon, were similarly alarmed, when not horrified, by the upheavals that turned their familiar world upside down.[7] If some cautiously embraced the Revolution at its beginning, almost all had moved firmly to the royalist camp even before the first signs of the Terror. The revolutionaries returned the favor, criticizing, prosecuting, and even executing members of what Robespierre called the "sect of *Encyclopédistes*."[8]

The few individuals who did bridge the Enlightenment and the Revolution reveal the chasm separating the two. Bailly again offers an illuminating example. At the height of his popularity for his role in the Hôtel-Dieu commission, he was literally thrust into revolutionary politics without really having sought to be involved. He was nominated to the electoral assembly of Paris, where he became the first Parisian elector (out of 407) to be selected as a deputy of the Third Estate. He in fact sought to resign this honor, tellingly informing his colleagues, "I owe the better part of my fortune to favors and pensions from the government."[9] They sent him to Versailles all the same, where he became the first president of the newly constituted National Assembly on June 17. It was in this role that he was immortalized by Jacques-Louis David in his famous sketch *Le serment du jeu de paume* (1791): Bailly is the central figure, administering the oath to the other deputies.

If this story so far suggests a certain compatibility between Enlightenment social advocacy and revolutionary politics, the second half of the story puts this impression to rest. Bailly's next—and last—official position was as mayor of Paris. Here his popularity quickly dwindled: unable to cope with the rising cost of bread or the polarizing effect of the Civil Constitution, Bailly quickly fell out of touch with an increasingly radicalized population.[10] The coup de grâce came after the king's aborted escape attempt, the so-called flight to Varennes.[11] In reaction to this slight, a crowd gathered on the Champ-de-Mars to sign a republican petition. The assembly became somewhat disorderly, and Bailly and Lafayette (the head of the National Guard) declared martial law; when the crowd did not disperse, the soldiers opened fire, killing a dozen or so participants. Shortly thereafter, Bailly resigned as mayor of Paris and tried to retire from public life, but to no avail: he would be tried by the revolutionary tribunal and executed two years later, in November 1793.

Bailly's unfortunate story highlights the wide gap that separated the Enlightenment emphasis on social instruction and the revolutionary demand for popular participation. In response to the question of how individuals prone to daring and "revolutionary" pronouncements could end up shying away from the defining revolutionary event of their time, Alan Kors reminded us that "the philosophes loved to write with fire—to shock, to warn, to predict, to exercise their rhetoric."[12] It might be argued that the revolutionaries took this rhetoric literally and were faithful to the letter, if not the spirit, of the Enlightenment. Revolutionary debates were certainly framed in terms that would have been very familiar to the *philosophes*, but despite constant references to Rousseau, Montesquieu, and Locke, their particular theories and definitions were usually reinterpreted in novel ways.[13] More than anything, the revolutionaries used the Enlightenment as a form of legitimation: through the "pantheonization" of Voltaire and Rousseau, through a variety of festivals and rituals, the revolutionaries created the illusion of an intellectual lineage that tended not to exist.[14]

Even in the absence of genuine filiation, the Enlightenment did arguably transmit a certain number of features to the Revolution. I will limit myself to discussing two, beginning with the similarity of their respective *régimes d'historicité*. Indeed, like the Enlightenment, the Revolution was predominantly defined in terms of a new present. Already before the calendar reform of Year II (1793), the momentous events of 1789 were perceived as ushering in a new age, a "Year I of Liberty."[15] Revolutionary festivals may have celebrated a number of varied events, but each also served to highlight the "mythic present" of the Revolution.[16] Even this exceptional present, however, was not complete: as Robespierre informed the Convention in February 1794, the French people may have advanced two thousand years ahead of their European brethren since 1789, but they had still only reached the halfway point.[17] The resemblance between this narrative and its Enlightenment precursor becomes evident when one considers that at precisely the same moment Condorcet, on the run as a Girondin outlaw, was sketching his own vision of a perfected "tenth epoch" in human history.[18]

The historical narrative of the Revolution also dealt similarly with the past. On the one hand, if the present was so remarkable it was because it had broken so spectacularly with the immediate past, quickly stylized as an ancien *régime*. This sense of a clean break was also conveyed by the very term "revolution," which in eighteenth-century French no longer designated an astronomical return but rather described an epochal transformation.[19] On the other hand, the farther back one delved into the past, the more positive models one could find for the future. Antiquity was, of course, a favorite "realm of memory" for the revolutionaries: as Marx famously quipped, the French Revolution was conducted "in Roman costumes and with Roman phrases."[20] He was only partially exaggerating: Livy, Cicero, and Plutarch no doubt influenced the revolutionaries nearly as much as Montesquieu, Voltaire, and Rousseau did.[21] And like the Ancients a century before them, the revolutionaries valued antiquity in large part for its greater proximity to nature: the Jacobins turned to Egyptian symbols and gods in an effort to invest their political agenda with natural authority.[22] Even the revolutionary calendar, beginning as it did on the fall equinox, when the day was equal to the night, registered this natural rhythm.

The Enlightenment also seems to have bequeathed to the Revolution its sense of a universal mission. It has often been noted that the (successful) American Revolution never launched a revolutionary tradition in the way that the (unsuccessful, in the short term) French Revolution did.[23] This difference can mostly be explained by the fact that the American colonists argued their cause primarily in the language of British constitutionalism.[24] While writers such as Thomas Paine had already portrayed the American struggle in universal terms, the idea of a worldwide revolutionary movement truly took hold only after the fall of the Bastille.[25] To be sure, this idea was supported by actual revolutionary stirrings in other European countries. But it was also an idea heavily promoted by the French revolutionaries themselves. Arguing in favor of additional repressions, Louis-Antoine Saint-Just proclaimed, "The measures that will be presented to you . . . will rid the Republic and the Earth of all accomplices. . . . No rest until the enemies of the Revolution and the French people have been exterminated!"[26] As with the Enlightenment, this universal process was perceived as beginning in France, more specifically in Paris, from whence it could be disseminated throughout the world. In both cases, universalism did not preclude nationalism but rather depended on it.

France and the European Enlightenment

If the ideals of the French Revolution could be so quickly exported (before they were imposed by force), it was also because the rest of Europe was already in the habit of following intellectual and other fashions set in Paris. Until now, I have mostly discussed the role played by French *académiciens* and other writers in synthesizing an assortment of observations about the past and present states of society, culture, and learning into a unified concept, or narrative, of the Enlightenment. But France also played another role in this story, which was one of distribution. The Enlightenment, after all, was primarily disseminated in the form of a commodity, namely, books.[1] Because French culture enjoyed an almost hegemonic status in eighteenth-century Europe, theories and definitions devised in Paris could reach audiences across the Continent (and across the Atlantic), benefiting from well-established trade networks, as well as new ones, such as Freemasonry.[2] French was, moreover, the language spoken at most foreign courts, as well as by the aristocratic (even bourgeois) elites of most European countries.[3] Indeed, such was the breadth of the French language that in 1783 the Berlin Academy could propose, as its prize competition question, "What has made French the universal language?"⁴

The universality of French cannot of course be construed as a yardstick for the diffusion of Enlightenment ideas: a fascination with Versailles and French theater had made France fashionable well before Voltaire.⁵ But these two high points in French culture were not all that distinct in people's minds. Voltaire himself had credited the *grand siècle* as a precursor for Enlightenment, arguing that "healthy philosophy only became known at this time. . . . [F]rom the last years of Cardinal Richelieu until those following the death of Louis XIV, a general revolution has taken place in our arts, our minds, and our manners, as it has in our government." This "revolution," he added, "will provide an eternal monument to the true glory of our nation [*patrie*]." His following commentary on the spread of this "revolution" is most pertinent to the argument developed here: "This fortunate influence did not even stop in France; it spread to England; it triggered a much-needed emulation from this spiritual and hearty nation; it brought taste to Germany, sciences to Russia; it even revived a languishing Italy, and Europe owes its politeness and sense of society to the court of Louis XIV."⁶

While Voltaire was not an unbiased observer, it is telling to find, in the same breath, an account of the French genealogy of the Enlightenment and of its subsequent diffusion throughout Europe. The present chapter, through a rapid *tour d'horizon* of case studies, seeks more modestly to establish that almost all of the European centers and figures of the Enlightenment were exposed to the writings of the *philosophes*. Of course, "exposed to" is not tantamount to "influenced by." But the French narrative of the Enlightenment, as we have seen, was sufficiently open-ended that it could be appropriated by almost anyone for almost any political or intellectual purpose. It is precisely this open-endedness that makes the French narrative the most likely candidate for providing a template for other national, confessional, or regional Enlightenments, even though on many counts they may have differed from the French model. By retracing the spread of French Enlightenment texts, accordingly, I wish only to show that writers in other European countries (or colonies: New England would be another obvious case) were reading works that, among many other topics, defined and illustrated the Enlightenment. Reading Voltaire does not make you a Voltairean; but it does give you a good sense of what the Enlightenment was about.

Let us begin in Scotland, which is often lumped together with England as forming a "British Enlightenment."[7] As Roger Emerson reminds us, however, we should dispense with the assumption that geographic proximity was paramount: "Many Scots were more familiar with Holland and France than with England and knew Paris better than London.... [P]olite standards of taste owed as much to the French as to Addison."[8] There was moreover a long tradition of Scottish-French entente, which resulted in "close connections" between their respective universities.[9] Such closeness is perhaps most apparent in the case of the most renowned figure of the Scottish Enlightenment, David Hume. Hume acquired his knowledge of France firsthand, visiting Paris in 1734, before settling down for three years at the Jesuit *collège* of La Flèche, Descartes's alma mater. Here Hume wrote *A Treatise of Human Nature*, taking advantage of the remarkable library at La Flèche and possibly also reading clandestine French works, such as Voltaire's *Lettres philosophiques*, published the year Hume arrived in France.[10] He returned to Paris for another three years in 1763, where he was lionized by the *philosophes* and enjoyed himself so much that he considered staying there for good.[11]

The influence of this French connection, and more specifically of the Enlightenment narrative, on Hume's thought is evident from his very early work onward. In his 1742 essay "Of the Rise and Progress of the Arts and Sciences," which has been described as "the first major Scottish presentation of a theory of historical stages,"[12] Hume emphasized the central role played by society, as opposed to individual geniuses, in the development of learning: "Though the persons who cultivate the sciences with such astonishing success as to attract the admiration of posterity, be always few in all nations and all ages, it is impossible but a share of the same spirit and genius must be antecedently diffused through the people among whom they arise."[13] This shift in focus away from "great men" to civilized moments is very reminiscent of Dubos's discussion of the *esprit philosophique*, as is Hume's insistence that "modern notions of *gallantry*" greatly contributed to the current refinement in the arts and sciences.[14] Such refinement, Hume noted in other essays, currently made French and English gentlemen "the most civilized in the most civilized nations," and France the nation that "has carried the arts and sciences as near perfection as any other."[15] His praise of Britain was somewhat more limited, mainly due to "corruption [which] may seem to increase of late years."[16]

If Hume seemed to come down on the side of the Moderns, he in fact struck the same middle ground as Dubos and the *philosophes*. "The models left us by the ancients gave birth to all the arts about two hundred years ago, and have mightily advanced their progress in every country of Europe," he openly acknowledged, before concluding, "The ancients had left us models in every kind of writing, which are highly worthy of admiration."[17] At the same time, where the leading English defender of the Ancients, Jonathan Swift, had mocked the Royal Society in his satire of the "grand Academy of Lagado," Hume placed Galileo and Newton "at the top of human kind" for their "genius and capacity."[18] Hume's narrative of human progress was thus a dialectical synthesis of ancient and modern achievements, remarkably similar to the French narrative of Enlightenment. This is not to suggest that Hume introduced no new elements: indeed, in his narrative, as in many subsequent Scottish works, commerce, political freedom, the rule of law, and changes in government occupy a far more important place than in comparable accounts by Dubos or Voltaire. Yet this is precisely what made the French narrative of Enlightenment ideally suited for export: it offered a basic model that could be modified at will.

The French influence on Scottish writers only continued to

grow as the century wore on. William Robertson's "View of the Progress of Society in Europe" identified "manners" as a key measure of social improvement, with a nod to the crucial influence of Voltaire's *Essai sur les mœurs*.[19] Montesquieu's *Spirit of the Laws* was even more influential, not only for Robertson but also for Hume (who corresponded with the author), Adam Ferguson, John Millar, and Adam Smith.[20] Smith's own relations with the *philosophes* were no less intimate than Hume's. Smith, who once considered Rousseau to be the only original French philosopher since Descartes, drew on the Genevan's concept of pity (as developed in the second *Discourse*) for his own discussion of sympathy in *The Theory of Moral Sentiments* (1759).[21] Smith subsequently traveled to the Continent, meeting Voltaire (whom he considered "the most universal genius perhaps which France has ever produced") at Ferney, and studying with Quesnay, the leader of the *économistes*, or Physiocrats. While Smith ultimately departed from the Physiocratic doctrine, he nonetheless regarded Quesnay's theory as "the nearest approximation to the truth that has yet been published upon the subject of political economy . . . with all its imperfections" and nearly dedicated *The Wealth of Nations* to him.[22]

The French narrative of the Enlightenment might be expected to have had more trouble integrating cultures where "national" philosophical traditions were more firmly established, as in the German states. Ian Hunter, for instance, suggested that the three traditions vying for prominence at the University of Halle—Thomasian civil philosophy, Pietist theology, and Wolffian metaphysics—represented "rival Enlightenments." Hunter's justification for using this term bears some resemblance to the argument presented above: he notes how certain commentators (around 1710) claimed that they "stood on the threshold of a new enlightened epoch."[23] Since this narrative concerns only the world of learning, however, and not society, it does not really differ from earlier "epochal" claims concerning the new science (à la Thomas Sprat, for instance). What makes this argument particularly unconvincing is the remarkable time lag between the moment Hunter is examining and the emergence on the German scene of a more fully self-aware concept of *Aufklärung* in the 1780s. By that time, the debate over "What is Enlightenment?" was pitched in specifically social terms. Moses Mendelssohn, for instance, defined Enlightenment according to "its dissemination through all estates," among other traits.[24] Kant similarly defined Enlightenment in terms of "mankind," not simply philosophers.

By the 1780s, moreover, the German states had been culturally saturated with French works.[25] French theater, in particular, was hugely popular in German courts, with many plays performed in French.[26] News about the Enlightenment in France was also widely diffused by the *Correspondance littéraire*, edited mostly by Grimm, which went out to over half a dozen German courts.[27] Works by the *philosophes* were readily available as well; it was in the Prussian city of Stettin that Catherine II developed her adolescent appreciation of Voltaire.[28] One of the main conduits for the French Enlightenment in Prussia was of course Frederick II, who made Montesquieu, Voltaire, Maupertuis, Boyer d'Argens, Diderot, La Mettrie, and Lagrange members of the Berlin Academy of Science and tried to lure many others (such as d'Alembert and Condorcet), in addition to offering refuge to *philosophes* on the lam, such as Helvétius.[29] Kant's hero worship of Rousseau, whose portrait hung in his study, is legendary, if not unusual, since much of educated Europe shared his enthusiasm for *Emile* (surpassed only by an obsession with *Julie*).[30] Finally, one of the clearest indications that the Enlightenment was perceived as primarily a French affair can be discovered among its detractors: before Johann Gottfried von Herder reacted against French philosophy, he had sought to mold himself into a *philosophe*.[31]

States did not need to have a Francophile ruler for French philosophy to be appreciated, but it certainly helped.[32] Another telling case in this regard is Russia, where the Enlightenment is still known as "Voltairism," or *Volterianstvo*.[33] Tellingly, as Natalie Bayer has noted, this term "denoted everything from religious freethinking to the imitation of the French fashion."[34] While the Russian attraction to all things French can be traced back to Peter the Great, it was his daughter, Elizabeth Petrovna, who made French style de rigueur in Russian court society.[35] Her daughter-in-law, Catherine II, built on this cultural foundation, importing or translating French Enlightenment works by the cartload—literally, in the case of Diderot's and Voltaire's libraries. While the educated classes read the *philosophes* in the original language, the tsarina also sponsored a massive translation effort, in which French works accounted for about three-quarters of the final output (German came in second, at around one-fifth; English works were hardly present at all).[36] The tsarina's dedication to the French Enlightenment no doubt served her own publicity purposes, yet her own works bear its unmistakable influence: for instance, her proposal for the reform of the Russian state, known as the *Nakaz*, was largely cribbed from *The Spirit of the Laws*.[37] She relished the image presented to her by Voltaire, among others, of a civilizing monarch, in the vein of Peter the Great, who broke with the prior backwardness of Russia to found a future-looking empire.[38]

This crushing fad for French philosophy may not seem particularly unusual in a country undertaking a crash course in "Westernization." The same argument might be made for Poland, where the Enlightenment was also perceived as a French phenomenon, with the French language, "as the reformer Stanisław Konarski observed, [being] for Poles what Greek had been for the Romans."[39] Yet in fact, a very similar story can be told about the European region with the longest history of shared cultural ties with France, namely, Italy.

A key figure in the Italian Enlightenment is Francesco Algarotti, who traveled to France in 1735, where he befriended Voltaire; shortly thereafter he published his most famous work, *Il Newtonianesimo per le dame* (1737), modeled on Fontenelle's *Entretiens sur la pluralité des mondes*.[40] The impact of the Enlightenment narrative on this work is striking: when asked by the marquise to explain Newtonianism, the narrator launches into a history of philosophy, from the earliest times, through India, Egypt, Greece,

Rome, the Middle Ages, before finally reaching the seventeenth century and, in particular, Galileo.[41] Though he is often critical of the Ancients, who suffered from an *esprit de système* (20), he reserves sharp barbs for some of the Moderns, too: "The Moderns [an apparent reference to Cartesians] had their partisans as well, who were no less enthralled or opinionated than those of the Ancients: every day the stubbornness of the old School was mocked, without their recognizing that they were guilty of the same mistakes" (31). Algarotti thus subscribed to the same "post-partisan" account of the Ancients and the Moderns, expressing his admiration for both ancient works of literature (5) and the rare few—two, to be exact—ancient philosophers who acknowledged the need for empirical observation (20). At the same time, he celebrated the current age for its return to this fundamental principle: "This is the practice of the best philosophers today and of the knowledgeable societies founded by generous sovereigns and upheld by the taste of all peoples" (34). While his history of philosophy focused mostly on great scientific breakthroughs, the overall purpose of his book was clearly to disseminate Newtonian thought throughout society via the support of women. After the marquise expresses her desire to become *newtonienne*, the narrator exclaims, "Here is the surest way to spread Newtonianism and to make it fashionable" (15). Algarotti's marquise later came to life in Countess Clelia Grillo Borromeo, who sought to found a new Italian Academy on the Parisian and British models.[42]

As in Scotland, however, it was arguably Montesquieu's *Spirit of the Laws* that made the greatest impact on Italian thought: this was the work that sparked Cesare Beccaria's interest in criminal justice, an influence that in turn facilitated the reception of his own *Dei delitti e delle pene* (On Crimes and Punishments) in France.[43] Montesquieu's masterpiece also inspired reformers in Naples, such as Antonio Genovesi, whose annotations were published alongside its Italian translation.[44] Naples had its own vibrant intellectual tradition, to be sure, yet the poor abbé Galiani nonetheless pined for the salons of d'Holbach and Madame d'Epinay, after being sent back to Naples for a diplomatic indiscretion.[45] His compatriot Giambattista Vico, meanwhile, suffered from intellectual neglect, having published his "massive defense of the humanities" in an age when "natural philosophy seemed the cutting edge of human thought."[46] Vico's rejection of Cartesian principles in humanistic matters has in fact been read as a distinctly anti-Enlightenment move.[47] Given the mythical status of Descartes's and Bacon's break with Scholasticism in every Enlightenment narrative, this attitude—along with Vico's idiosyncratic theory of historical cycles—helps explain his poor reception in his time.

These examples should not be misread as an old-fashioned attempt to argue that the Scottish, Prussian, Russian, Tuscan, or Neapolitan Enlightenments were pale copies of a French model. This very brief sketch of how the French Enlightenment was disseminated throughout Europe is intended only to depict how the French narrative of the Enlightenment would have been readily available to readers, rulers, and philosophers across Europe, in a way that no comparable English, Dutch, German, or other national concept would have been. In other words, someone somewhere may have independently described their age in terms similar to, say, Dubos, Fontenelle, or Voltaire, but until it can be shown that this description circulated beyond the borders of a letter or a country, it does not fundamentally challenge the argument presented here.

It is moreover rather ironic that the two candidates rivaling France for the honor (if it is one) of having formulated the first theory of the Enlightenment did not produce particularly visible or viable enlightened movements. The Netherlands witnessed an outbreak of religious and political freethinking in the wake of the revocation of the Edict of Nantes (1685).[48] Yet this movement was spurred by French Huguenot refugees who remained on the outskirts of Dutch society and culture: "They [the refugees] were hardly interested in the ideas current in their adopted fatherland," Wijnand Mijnhardt commented. Conversely, they had little influence on the intellectual traditions of their hosts: "To the majority of Dutch intellectuals [their] ideas bore little relevance."[49] Amsterdam may have served as a publishing hub for the "forbidden best-sellers" of the Enlightenment, yet as the publisher Marc-Michel Rey allegedly told Rousseau, "We may print you, but we do not read you." After its golden age of art and power in the seventeenth century, the Dutch Republic was seen by most observers as having slumped into a period of decline. Simon Schama has described how the once glorious universities of the Low Countries (including Leiden) lost their intellectual spark, and the nascent debate clubs and journals "studiously avoided anything that could be construed as politically controversial." Schama concluded that the idea of the Dutch Republic served mostly as "an idealized projection of the [French] Enlightenment's own self-image," whereas the republic was hardly the freethinking paradise its admirers made it out to be.[50] Hume had come to a similar conclusion long before: "Multitudes of people, necessity and liberty, have begotten commerce in Holland; but study and application have scarcely produced any eminent writers."[51]

As for England, Franco Venturi himself, one of the first historians to emphasize the importance of studying Enlightenment centers outside France, argued that ideas of reform and social instruction never really coalesced in England into a movement that could be said to constitute an Enlightenment.[52] In other words, there was no group of individuals who self-consciously identified themselves in this way. Venturi's opinion was also held by a contemporary source, Edmund Burke, who noted how "a cabal, calling itself philosophic, receives the glory of many of the late proceedings" in revolutionary France, whereas there was "no party in England, literary or political, at any time, known by such a description."[53]

Given that Burke blamed the "philosophic cabal" for the revolutionary affairs under way in France, his testimony may be viewed with suspicion. At the same time, one would be hardpressed to find any group of English citizens that conceived of itself or of its aims in enlightened terms before, say, the Rational Dissenters of the late eighteenth century (such as Richard Price and Joseph Priestly).[54] If this is the English Enlightenment, it is certainly a latecomer. One could argue that it did not take such a self-conscious description for the "phenomenon" of the Enlightenment to occur in England, and Roy Porter has counted the ways in which *British* writers and politicians acted in ways, and defended positions, that certainly look or sound "enlightened." Leaving aside this problematic lumping together of Scottish and English authors,[55] we return to the larger issue of distinguishing between Enlightenment ideas and practices in particular and political or religious debates more generally. When one considers the cultural context of *English* intellectual life, its differences with corresponding Continental equivalents loom large. Most significantly for the argument developed here, the English *régime d'historicité* differed drastically from the narrative developed in France and adopted around Europe. As Margaret Jacob has notably shown, the story of the Scientific Revolution, in English accounts, was inextricably tied up in a national history of the Glorious Revolution.[56] This entwinement is characteristically visible in the somewhat hyperbolic, yet nonetheless representative "allegorical poem" by John Desaguliers, *The Newtonian System of the World, the Best Model of Government*, in which the law of attraction binding the planets to the sun is favorably compared to the parliamentary monarchy secured in 1688–89.[57] While this narrative might have resonated in the Dutch provinces (home to William of Orange), it had far less impact in France and elsewhere on the Continent, where most monarchies were seeking to emulate Louis XIV's absolutist system incarnated at Versailles—a very different solar metaphor. This English narrative was also profoundly Protestant, with divine Providence and the struggle against Catholicism playing determining roles.[58]

Most importantly, this narrative was much more "conservative." The achievements of the Glorious Revolution and the Hanoverian Succession had brought Protestant British subjects a set of political, religious, and legal rights unique in Europe.[59] This was a legacy to be preserved, not a goal to be achieved. Even John Wilkes—who arguably presents the strongest case for an English

Enlightenment and was hailed as a fellow *philosophe* by the likes of Diderot, d'Holbach, and Voltaire—celebrated the revolution of 1688–89 as "this most auspicious period" when "the disputes of prerogative, of privilege, and of liberty subsided."[60] English reform movements in the eighteenth century focused on restoring the "spirit of liberty" of 1688 by preventing governmental corruption and ensuring fair elections:[61] "Our present political liberty," Wilkes continued, "owes its very existence indeed to the *Revolution*, but we may justly regard its continuance as too precarious, its security as ill established."[62] It is this dual commitment to liberty and tradition that can make someone like Burke both an "enlightened" figure, in Porter's account, and a founding father of the modern conservative movement. It is hard to imagine a similar outcome for Diderot, Hume, Beccaria, or even Kant.

Because of its unique and more liberal policies, England was no doubt a source of fascination for Continental writers. Precisely due to its unique status, however, England was often perceived as "a phenomenon to be understood and marveled at . . . rather than a model to be imitated."[63] And while English thinkers such as Newton and Locke towered over the *philosophes*, particularly in the aftermath of Voltaire's *Lettres philosophiques* (1734) and Condillac's *Essai sur l'origine des connaissances humaines* (1746), they did not feature prominently in the elaboration of the Enlightenment's conceptual framework, as the latter was historical, not epistemological. One might even say, somewhat perversely, that it was their inclusion in the French narrative that made Newton and Locke the giants of the Enlightenment.

16

Conclusion: Modern Myths

The narrative that lay at the heart of what we now know as the Enlightenment was more than just a story: it was and remains a "master narrative" of modernity, even a myth.[1] The genesis of this myth can be found in the Quarrel of the Ancients and the Moderns, which consumed French intellectual life for over thirty years. Although it would be pointless to try and date the exact moment when the Quarrel ended and the Enlightenment began, Dubos's work may serve as a convenient marker, underlining as it does the necessary combination of both Ancients and Moderns in the self-conception of the Enlightenment. His *Réflexions critiques* was certainly not the first work *of* the Enlightenment, but it can arguably lay claim to being the first work *about* it. In saying this, I do not mean to imply, in a Foucauldian vein, that it was impossible to conceive of the Enlightenment before key expressions such as *esprit philosophique* emerged to designate it. Rather, Dubos's work first combined the narrative, characters, and discourse of Enlightenment that would underpin, and be repeated in, the vast majority of subsequent texts by *philosophes*, enlightened rulers, and fellow travelers.

Calling this narrative a myth underscores its constructed and partial nature, reminding us that this story should not be mistaken for an accurate history. But it also draws attention to the particular force of this narrative. As the French political writer Georges Sorel once wrote, myths are what provide us with an overarching sense of meaning for our actions: "Men who are participating in great social movements always picture their coming action in the form of images. . . . I proposed to give the name of 'myths' to these constructions."[2] Sorel's examples were taken not from ancient Greece but from European history: ranging from the early Christians to the Risorgimento fighters, they might well have included the *philosophes*. What made myths such powerful mental constructions, Sorel argued, is that they cannot be disproved. This was indeed the case with the Enlightenment narrative: despite the many articles in the *Encyclopédie*, for instance, that highlighted medical discoveries occurring well before the Scientific Revolution, the story line remained unchanged.[3] The narrative of a "new science" progressively dismantling all remnants of superstition and Scholasticism in its way was too central to the self-perception of the *philosophes*. Their very identity depended on it; the consciousness of their place in this historical trajectory, which crested in the present, endowed their worldly interventions with greater meaning.

As with all identities, however, the Enlightenment persona had something borrowed and something new. There is a tendency among scholars today to brandish Kant's famous essay as a one-stop shop for defining the Enlightenment, yet in only very few cases was the Enlightenment "*mankind*'s exit from its self-incurred immaturity," through "the courage to use [one's own understanding] without the guidance of another."[4] For the most part, the Enlightenment was rather a matter of exchanging one type of guidance for another. The role of the *philosophe* was precisely to "instruct and civilize the nation," Voltaire wrote.[5] To become "enlightened" was to think and act in accordance with a new set of norms, but these norms were only rarely self-imposed. In other words, there was just as much fashioning as self-fashioning going on in the production of the Enlightenment— hence Rousseau's complaint about how it was often little more than a "fashionable little philosophy."[6] This complaint, which unwittingly underscores the Enlightenment's cultural capital, illuminates why *le monde* was more than happy to be associated with *gens de lettres*.[7]

In another classic essay on the Enlightenment, Michel Foucault argued that "modernity is distinct from fashion, which does no more than call into question the course of time; modernity is the attitude that makes it possible to grasp the 'heroic' aspect of the present moment."[8] But one may question the extent to which modernity can be so easily distinguished from fashion. Etymology, of course, unites them, at least in French: *mode* (fashion) shares the same Latin root (*modo*) as "modern" and "modernity." And as Foucault noted, both designate an object or idea that is temporally defined in relation to the present. More importantly, modernity is an equally shifty concept: it does not change, like fashion, with the seasons, but its slower tempo should not lead us to overlook its transformations. In the early twentieth century, it was modern to be an atheist and a communist; in the early eighteenth century, it was modern to be a religious orthodox and an absolutist. Who knows what will define modernity in the twenty-first century?

By emphasizing this parallel, I certainly do not wish to suggest that the Enlightenment was nothing more than a fashion for a set of ideas and social practices; rather, I wish to question what we gain by defining the Enlightenment in terms of modernity. Yes, some of the values defended by the *philosophes*, their patrons, and their readers are values that we still hold dear today. But their modernity was very different from ours: it was a modernity in which large democratic states seemed unfeasible, if not impossible; religion was not just the opium of the people but an important social institution; and patronage, if not monetary, then at least political, was a simple fact of life. In this unfamiliar context, beliefs that we champion or deride today could have a very different meaning. While the desire to retrace the genealogy of our own modernity is an honorable pursuit, it should not come at the expense of rewriting the genealogy of the past.

Abbreviations

ARTFL   The FRANTEXT database, run by the ARTFL
Project at the University of Chicago: http://
artfl-project.uchicago.edu/

CORPUS   *Le corpus des œuvres de philosophie en langue française*:
http://www.lib.uchicago.edu/efts/ARTFL/databases/
bibliopolis/cphil/

ECCO   Eighteenth Century Collections Online: http://find
.galegroup.com/ecco/

Encyclopédie   *Encyclopédie, ou Dictionnaire raisonné des sciences, des
arts et des métiers*, ed. Denis Diderot and Jean-le-Rond
d'Alembert. University of Chicago: ARTFL Encyclopédie Project (Winter 2008 edition), ed. Robert
Morrissey, http://encyclopedie.uchicago.edu/

GALLICA   Digital library of the Bibliothèque nationale de France:
http://gallica.bnf.fr/

VOLTAIRE   *The Voltaire électronique* database: http://efts.lib
.uchicago.edu/efts/VOLTAIRE/index.html

Notes

INTRODUCTION

1. Stéphane Van Damme, *Paris, capitale philosophique: De la Fronde à la Révolution* (Paris: Odile Jacob, 2005); I return to the question of diffusion in the final chapter.

2. Peter Gay, *The Rise of Modern Paganism* and *The Science of Freedom*, vols. 1 and 2 of *The Enlightenment: An Interpretation* (New York: Knopf, 1966–69).

3. Paula Findlen and Kenneth Gouwens, "Introduction: The Persistence of the Renaissance," *American Historical Review* 103, no. 1 (1998): 51–54.

CHAPTER ONE

1. Carl Becker, *The Heavenly City of the Eighteenth-Century Philosophers*, 2nd ed. (New Haven, CT: Yale University Press, 2003); Jürgen Habermas, *The Structural Transformation of the Public Sphere: An Inquiry into a Category of Bourgeois Society*, trans. Thomas Burger (Cambridge, MA: MIT Press, 1992); Haydn T. Mason, ed., *The Darnton Debate: Books and Revolution in the Eighteenth Century*, Studies on Voltaire and the Eighteenth Century, vol. 359 (Oxford: Voltaire Foundation, 1998); and Jonathan Israel, *Enlightenment Contested: Philosophy, Modernity, and the Emancipation of Man, 1670–1752* (Oxford: Oxford University Press, 2006).

2. Anthony Grafton, "Introduction: Notes from Underground on Cultural Transmission," in *The Transmission of Culture in Early Modern*

Europe, ed. Anthony Grafton and Ann Blair (Philadelphia: University of Pennsylvania Press, 1999), 1–7 (quotation on 2). See also Linda Kirk, "The Matter of Enlightenment," *Historical Journal* 43, no. 4 (2000): 1129–43 (quotation on 1132).

3. Jonathan Israel, *Radical Enlightenment: Philosophy and the Making of Modernity, 1650–1750* (Oxford: Oxford University Press, 2002); Israel, *Enlightenment Contested*.

4. Antoine Lilti, "Comment écrit-on l'histoire intellectuelle des Lumières? Spinozisme, radicalisme, et philosophie," *Annales HSS* 64 (2009): 171–206. My thanks to the author for sharing this penetrating study, to which the present arguments are greatly indebted, while still in manuscript.

5. Greg Urban, *Metaculture: How Culture Moves through the World* (Minneapolis: University of Minnesota Press, 2001).

6. R. R. Palmer, *Catholics and Unbelievers in Eighteenth-Century France* (1939; New York: Cooper Square Publishers, 1961); and Alan Charles Kors, *Atheism in France, 1650–1729* (Princeton, NJ: Princeton University Press, 1990).

7. Franco Venturi was one of the first to encourage historians to examine other European Enlightenments; see his *Settecento riformatore*, 5 vols. (Turin: G. Einaudi, 1969–76), the third volume of which was translated as *The End of the Old Regime in Europe, 1776–1789*, trans. R. Burr Litchfield, 2 vols. (Princeton, NJ: Princeton University Press, 1991). See also Roy Porter and Mikuláš Teich, eds., *The Enlightenment in National Context* (Cambridge: Cambridge University Press, 1981).

8. See esp. Margaret Jacob, *The Radical Enlightenment: Pantheists, Freemasons, and Republicans* (London: George Allen, 1981); John Pocock, *The Enlightenments of Edward Gibbon*, vol. 1 of *Barbarism and Religion* (Cambridge: Cambridge University Press, 1999); and John Marshall, *John Locke, Toleration, and Early Enlightenment Culture: Religious Intolerance and Arguments for Religious Toleration in Early Modern and "Early Enlightenment" Europe* (Cambridge: Cambridge University Press, 2006).

9. J. B. Shank, *The Newton Wars and the Beginning of the French Enlightenment* (Chicago: University of Chicago Press, 2008). I return to this important work in later chapters. Scholars who have emphasized the place of Newtonian thought in the formation of the Enlightenment include Margaret Jacob, in *Radical Enlightenment*; and Roy Porter, in *The Creation of the Modern World: The Untold Story of the British En-*

lightenment (New York: Norton, 2001), originally published as *Enlightenment: Britain and the Creation of the Modern World* (London: Allen Lane, 2000).

10. This literature is surveyed in Craig Calhoun, *Habermas and the Public Sphere* (Cambridge, MA: MIT Press, 1992); and James van Horn Melton, *The Rise of the Public in Enlightenment Europe* (Cambridge: Cambridge University Press, 2001).

11. See esp. Margaret Jacob, "Radicalism in the Dutch Enlightenment," in *The Dutch Republic in the Eighteenth Century: Decline, Enlightenment, and Revolution*, ed. Margaret C. Jacob and W. W. Mijnhardt (Ithaca, NY: Cornell University Press, 1992), 229–33; see also Margaret Jacob, *Living the Enlightenment: Freemasonry and Politics in Eighteenth-Century Europe* (Oxford: Oxford University Press, 1991).

12. As Jacob herself recognizes: "culture permits—it does not determine" (*Living the Enlightenment*, 180).

13. See, e.g., the conclusion to Court's *Monde primitif*, which includes a paean to Louis XVI: Antoine Court de Gébelin, *Monde primitif considéré dans son génie allégorique et dans les allégories auxquelles conduisit ce génie . . .* , 9 vols. (Paris: n.p., 1773–81), 8: lxvii–lxix. On Court's political views, see Anne-Marie Mercier-Faivre, *Un supplément à l'"Encyclopédie": Le "Monde primitif" d'Antoine Court de Gébelin* (Paris: Champion, 1999).

14. Antoine Lilti, *Le monde des salons: Sociabilité et mondanité à Paris au XVIIIᵉ siècle* (Paris: Fayard, 2005). Lilti's account notably challenges Dena Goodman's earlier study, *The Republic of Letters: A Cultural History of the French Enlightenment* (Ithaca, NY: Cornell University Press, 1994).

15. David A. Bell, *The Cult of the Nation in France: Inventing Nationalism, 1680–1800* (Cambridge, MA: Harvard University Press, 2001), 32.

16. Jonathan Sheehan proposed a "media-driven concept of the Enlightenment" in "Enlightenment, Religion, and the Enigma of Secularization: A Review Essay," *American Historical Review* 108, no. 4 (2003): 1061–80.

17. Clifford Siskin and William Warner, eds., *This Is Enlightenment* (Chicago: University of Chicago Press, 2010).

18. Robert Darnton, "The News in Paris: An Early Information Society," in *George Washington's False Teeth* (New York: Norton, 2003), 25–75.

19. Ann Blair and Peter Stallybrass, "Mediating Information, 1450–1800," in *This Is Enlightenment*, ed. Siskin and Warner, 139–63.

20. On this distinction, see Joshua Landy, "Philosophical Training Grounds: Socratic Sophistry and Platonic Perfection in *Symposium* and *Gorgias*," *Arion* 15, no. 1 (2007): 63–122; and, by the same author, *How to Do Things with Fiction* (forthcoming).

21. On Voltaire's irony, see Jean Starobinski, "Voltaire's Double-Barreled Musket: On the Philosophical Style of *Candide*," in *Blessings in Disguise; or, The Morality of Evil*, trans. Arthur Goldhammer (Cambridge, MA: Harvard University Press, 1993), 84–100.

22. Pocock, *Enlightenments of Edward Gibbon*; and more recently his "Historiography and Enlightenment: A View of Their History," *Modern Intellectual History* 5, no. 1 (2008): 83–96. See also Sankar Muthu, *Enlightenment against Empire* (Princeton, NJ: Princeton University Press, 2003). Against this increasingly accepted tendency, see John Robertson, *The Case for the Enlightenment: Scotland and Naples, 1680–1760* (Cambridge: Cambridge University Press, 2005).

23. Peter Gay, *The Rise of Modern Paganism*, vol. 1 of *The Enlightenment: An Interpretation* (New York: Knopf, 1966), 3.

24. Hermann Abert, *W. A. Mozart*, trans. Stewart Spencer, ed. Cliff Eisen (1923–24; New Haven, CT: Yale University Press, 2007), 510. As Eckhart Hellmuth confirms, "The German territories . . . were dominated by a moderate, enlightened spirit that clearly diverged from its more critical Western European counterparts"; see his "Enlightenment and Government," in *The Enlightenment World*, ed. Martin Fitzpatrick, Peter Jones, Christa Knellwolf, and Iain McCalman (New York: Routledge, 2004), 443.

25. Denis Diderot, *Réfutation suivie de l'ouvrage d'Helvétius intitulé "L'homme*," in *Œuvres complètes*, vol. 2 (Paris: Garnier, 1875) [ARTFL], probably written in 1774. Diderot takes Helvétius to task for his defense of democratic government, among other radical proposals (1.4.11; 390). In *A Revolution of the Mind: Radical Enlightenment and the Intellectual Origins of Modern Democracy* (Princeton, NJ: Princeton University Press, 2009), published after the present manuscript was completed, Israel acknowledges this criticism.

26. Lilti, "Comment écrit-on l'histoire intellectuelle des Lumières?" 186. Lilti points, for instance, to Peter Friedrich Arpe.

27. Ian Hunter, "Multiple Enlightenments: Rival *Aufklärer* at the University of Halle, 1690–1730," in *Enlightenment World*, ed. Fitzpatrick

et al., 576–95; and by the same author, *Rival Enlightenments: Civil and Metaphysical Philosophy in Early Modern Germany* (Cambridge: Cambridge University Press, 2001). I return to Hunter's work in chapter 15.

28. Although this entire book is greatly indebted to comments by Keith Baker, I owe this particular distinction entirely to him.

29. Paul Hazard, *La crise de la conscience européene* (Paris: Livre de Poche, 1935); translated as *The European Mind, 1680–1715*, trans. J. Lewis May (London: Hollis and Carter, 1953).

30. Niklas Luhmann, *Art as a Social System*, trans. Eva M. Knodt (Stanford, CA: Stanford University Press, 2000). Luhmann defines second-order observations as "observations of observations" (55). See also Hans Ulrich Gumbrecht, *The Production of Presence: What Meaning Cannot Convey* (Stanford, CA: Stanford University Press, 2004), 38–41.

31. Steven Shapin, *The Scientific Revolution* (Chicago: University of Chicago Press, 1996).

32. Céline Spector, "Les lumières avant les Lumières: Tribunal de la raison et opinion publique," *Révolution française.net*, March 2009, http://revolution-francaise.net/2009/03/01/299-les-lumieres-avant-les-lumieres-tribunal-de-la-raison-et-opinion-publique. The thesis of this article, which the author kindly shared with me after I had finished a first draft of this study, is remarkably similar to the one presented here.

33. On this point, see Lilti, "Comment écrit-on l'histoire intellectuelle des Lumières?" 202–3.

34. Josiah Ober, "Postscript: Culture, Thin Coherence, and the Persistence of Politics," in *The Cultures within Ancient Greek Culture*, ed. Carol Dougherty and Leslie Kurke (Cambridge: Cambridge University Press, 2003), 237–56; and William Sewell, "The Concept(s) of Culture" (1999), reprinted in *Logics of History: Social Theory and Social Transformation* (Chicago: University of Chicago Press, 2005), 152–74. The notion of "thin cultural coherence" is of course an alternative to Clifford Geertz's theory of "thick description," as set forth in "Thick Description: Toward an Interpretive Theory of Culture," in *The Interpretation of Cultures: Selected Essays* (1973; New York: Basic Books, 2005), 3–30.

35. See, e.g., Roland Mortier, "'Lumière' et 'Lumières': Histoire d'une image et d'une idée au XVIIe et au XVIIIe siècle," in *Clartés et ombres du siècle des Lumières: Etudes sur le XVIIIe siècle littéraire* (Geneva: Droz, 1969), 13–59; Michel Delon, "Les Lumières: Travail d'une métaphore," *Studies on Voltaire and the Eighteenth Century* 152 (1976): 527–41;

and Diego Venturino, "Appendice sur la genèse de l'expression 'siècle des Lumières' (XVIIIe–XXe siècles)," in *Historiographie et usages des Lumières*, ed. Giuseppe Ricuperati (Berlin: Berlin Verlag, 2002), 59–83. On the German side, see Horst Stuke, "Aufklärung," in *Geschichtliche Grundbegriffe: Historisches Lexikon zur politisch-sozialen Sprache in Deutschland*, ed. Otto Brunner, Werner Conze, and Reinhart Koselleck, 9 vols. (Stuttgart: E. Klett, 1972–95), 1:243–342; and Hans Ulrich Gumbrecht, "Who Were the *Philosophes?*" in *Making Sense in Life and Literature*, trans. Glen Burns (Minneapolis: University of Minnesota Press, 1992), 133–77. More recently, see Jin Lu, *Qui sont les philosophes?* (Quebec City: Presses de l'Université Laval, 2005); and Spector, "Les lumières avant les Lumières." For a related approach in Anglo-American studies, see Raymond Williams, *Keywords: A Vocabulary of Culture and Society*, rev. ed. (New York: Oxford University Press, 1983).

36. Siep Stuurman, *François Poulain de la Barre and the Invention of Modern Equality* (Cambridge, MA: Harvard University Press, 2004), 272. See also James Schmidt, "Inventing the Enlightenment: British Hegelians, Anti-Jacobins, and the *Oxford English Dictionary,*" *Journal of the History of Ideas* 64, no. 3 (2004): 421–43. Roger Chartier even suggested that the Enlightenment became a recognizable category only at the time of the French Revolution; see *The Cultural Origins of the French Revolution*, trans. Lydia G. Cochrane (Durham, NC: Duke University Press, 1991), 5.

37. Venturino, "Sur la genèse de l'expression 'siècle des Lumières,'" 60–76.

38. See, e.g., John Pocock, "The Concept of a Language and the *Métier d'Historien*: Some Considerations on Practice," in *The Languages of Political Theory in Early-Modern Europe*, ed. Anthony Pagden (Cambridge: Cambridge University Press, 1987), 19–38. For an earlier methodological statement, see Quentin Skinner, "Meaning and Understanding in the History of Ideas," *History and Theory* 8 (1969): 3–53; and, more recently, by the same author, *Visions of Politics*, 3 vols. (Cambridge: Cambridge University Press, 2002), vol. 1.

39. Keith Baker, *Inventing the French Revolution* (Cambridge: Cambridge University Press, 1990), 5–27.

40. There is, of course, a whole school of literary theory inspired by structuralism (and, before that, formalism), known as "narratology." But with a few exceptions—the most important being Hayden White's *Metahistory: The Historical Imagination in Nineteenth-Century Europe*

(Baltimore, MD: Johns Hopkins University Press, 1975)—this theoretical approach has not made much of a mark on historiography.

41. Jean Dagen hinted at this historicist understanding of the Enlightenment in *L'histoire de l'esprit humain dans la pensée française de Fontenelle à Condorcet* (Paris: Klincksieck, 1977). It is only more recently that this conception has entered Anglo-American studies: in a very brief article published in 1992, John Pocock noted how he considered "Enlightenment as a phenomenon in historical consciousness"; see "The Dutch Republican Tradition," in *The Dutch Republic in the Eighteenth Century*, ed. Jacob and Mijnhardt, 191. He has since examined the constitutive role of historical narratives in Enlightenment thought in *Narratives of Civil Government*, vol. 2 of *Barbarism and Religion* (Cambridge: Cambridge University Press, 2001). Daniel Brewer, in *The Enlightenment Past: Reconstructing Eighteenth-Century French Thought* (Cambridge: Cambridge University Press, 2008), further develops this historical definition of the Enlightenment, as does Shank in *Newton Wars*.

42. Hannah Arendt, *Between Past and Future: Eight Exercises in Political Thought* (1961; New York: Penguin Classics, 1993); Reinhart Koselleck, *Futures Past: On the Semantics of Historical Time*, trans. Keith Tribe (1979; New York: Columbia University Press, 2004). See also Anthony Kemp, *The Estrangement of the Past: A Study in the Origins of Modern Historical Consciousness* (New York: Oxford University Press, 1991).

43. François Hartog, *Régimes d'historicité: Présentisme et expériences du temps* (Paris: Seuil, 2003). Brewer draws on this notion in *Enlightenment Past*, 2.

44. J. David Velleman, "Narrative Explanation," *Philosophical Review* 112 (2003): 1–25.

45. Darrin McMahon, "What Are Enlightenments?" *Modern Intellectual History* 4, no. 3 (2007): 601–16 (quotation on 602).

46. See, e.g., Claude Lévi-Strauss, "La structure des mythes," in *Anthropologie structurale* (1958; Paris: Plon, 1974), 227–55.

47. Lorraine Daston and Katharine Park make this point in *Wonders and the Order of Nature, 1150–1750* (New York: Zone Books, 2001), 329–30.

48. Dorinda Outram, *The Enlightenment* (Cambridge: Cambridge University Press, 1995), 113. This is not to say that there was no Jewish Enlightenment, but the more obvious candidate would be the Haskalah, centered in Prussia around the figure of Moses Mendelssohn;

see Michael A. Meyer, *The Origins of the Modern Jew: Jewish Identity and European Culture in Germany, 1749–1824* (Detroit, MI: Wayne State University Press, 1972).

49. Edward Andrew, "Samuel Johnson and the Question of Enlightenment in England," in *Patrons of Enlightenment* (Toronto: University of Toronto Press, 2006), 155. Andrew is referring to Roy Porter's *Creation of the Modern World.* For a similar criticism, see Robertson, *Case for the Enlightenment*, 16.

CHAPTER TWO

1. Allan Bloom, *The Closing of the American Mind* (New York: Simon and Schuster, 1987), 153.

2. Peter Gay, *The Rise of Modern Paganism*, vol. 1 of *The Enlightenment: An Interpretation* (New York: Knopf, 1966), 17.

3. Margaret Jacob, *The Radical Enlightenment: Pantheists, Freemasons and Republicans* (London: George Allen, 1981), quotation on 84; see also Roy Porter, *The Creation of the Modern World: The Untold Story of the British Enlightenment* (New York: Norton, 2001). For a more general treatment of space and ideas during this period, see Charles W. J. Withers, *Placing the Enlightenment: Thinking Geographically about the Age of Reason* (Chicago: University of Chicago Press, 2007).

4. See esp. Jacob, *Radical Enlightenment*; John Pocock, *The Enlightenments of Edward Gibbon*, vol. 1 of *Barbarism and Religion* (Cambridge: Cambridge University Press, 1999); and John Marshall, *John Locke, Toleration, and Early Enlightenment Culture: Religious Intolerance and Arguments for Religious Toleration in Early Modern and "Early Enlightenment" Europe* (Cambridge: Cambridge University Press, 2006).

5. Jonathan Israel, *Radical Enlightenment: Philosophy and the Making of Modernity, 1650–1750* (Oxford: Oxford University Press, 2002).

6. John Robertson, *The Case for the Enlightenment: Scotland and Naples, 1680–1760* (Cambridge: Cambridge University Press, 2005).

7. Jonathan Israel, *Enlightenment Contested: Philosophy, Modernity, and the Emancipation of Man, 1670–1752* (Oxford: Oxford University Press, 2006).

8. Gustave Lanson, *Origines et premières manifestations de l'esprit philosophique dans la littérature française de 1675 à 1748* (1908–10; New York: B. Franklin, 1973). Even today, it is unusual to find any discussion of English or Dutch influences in the French scholarship on the Enlightenment.

9. For instance, nearly every contributor to the recent volume *The Atlantic Enlightenment*, ed. Susan Manning and Francis D. Cogliano (Aldershot: Ashgate Publishing, 2008), is a scholar of American or British studies.

10. In the earlier literature, the place of the Quarrel in the genealogy of the Enlightenment was commonly acknowledged; see, e.g., Ira Wade, *The Intellectual Origins of the French Enlightenment* (Princeton, NJ: Princeton University Press, 1971), 624–31. See also Céline Spector, "Les lumières avant les Lumières: Tribunal de la raison et opinion publique," *Révolution française.net*, March 2009, http://revolution-francaise .net/2009/03/01/299-les-lumieres-avant-les-lumieres-tribunal-de-la-raison-et-opinion-publique. For additional secondary sources on the Quarrel, see below.

11. Daniel Mornet already argued in 1926: "Almost all the ideas that are dear to the 'philosophers' of the eighteenth century had been outlined or suggested as early as the beginning of the seventeenth." See his *French Thought in the Eighteenth Century*, trans. Lawrence Levin (New York: Archon Books, 1969), 42; much of this work is also dedicated to the question of the diffusion of (pre-)Enlightenment ideas. More recently, see Peter Hanns Reill, "The Legacy of the 'Scientific Revolution': Science and the Enlightenment," in *The Cambridge History of Science*, ed. Roy Porter (Cambridge: Cambridge University Press, 2003), 23–43.

12. Israel, *Enlightenment Contested*, 6; see also J. B. Shank, *The Newton Wars and the Beginning of the French Enlightenment* (Chicago: University of Chicago Press, 2008), 35.

13. My account of how the Quarrel of the Ancients and the Moderns fits into the genealogy of the Enlightenment departs in this respect from the standard account, which usually traces the views of the *philosophes* back to the Modern camp. See most recently Siep Stuurman, *François Poulain de la Barre and the Invention of Modern Equality* (Cambridge, MA: Harvard University Press, 2004). On the *philosophes'* indebtedness to antiquity, see esp. Gay, *Rise of Modern Paganism*.

14. The following paragraph was prompted by an exchange with John Pocock during a seminar at Johns Hopkins University. I am grateful for his challenging questions. Pocock's views on this matter and his examples were most recently expressed in his article "Historiography and Enlightenment: A View of Their History," *Modern Intellectual History* 5, no. 1 (2008): 83–96.

15. For a history of the light metaphor, see Roland Mortier, "'Lumière' et 'Lumières': Histoire d'une image et d'une idée au XVIIe et au XVIIIe siècle," in *Clartés et ombres du siècle des Lumières: Etudes sur le XVIIIe siècle littéraire* (Geneva: Droz, 1969), 13–59. On the different incarnations of *philosophes*, see Hans Ulrich Gumbrecht, "Who Were the *Philosophes?*" in *Making Sense in Life and Literature*, trans. Glen Burns (Minneapolis: University of Minnesota Press, 1992), 133–77.

16. James Swenson, "Critique, Progress, Autonomy," *Studies in Eighteenth-Century Culture* 36, no. 1 (2007): 1–11.

CHAPTER THREE

1. Jean-Baptiste Dubos (sometimes spelled Du Bos), *Réflexions critiques sur la poésie et la peinture*, 2 vols. (Paris: Mariette, 1719). I will also provide page references for the 1733 edition (same publisher), which is much more commonly available, notably in full-text digital form on both ARTFL and GALLICA. For convenience, I have cited from electronic editions where available. On Dubos's life, see the entry in Louis Gabriel Michaud's *Biographie universelle*, 45 vols. (Paris: A. Thoisnier Desplaces, 1843–65), 11:366–67 [GALLICA]. See also Alfred Lombard, *La Querelle des Anciens et des Modernes: L'abbé Du Bos* (1908; Geneva: Slatkine, 1969); Ernst Cassirer, *The Philosophy of the Enlightenment*, trans. James P. Pettegrove and Fritz C. A. Koelin (1932; Princeton, NJ: Princeton University Press, 1968); René Pomeau and Jean Ehrard, *De Fénelon à Voltaire* (Paris: Flammarion, 1988), 97–101; Joseph M. Donohue, "The Paradox of Passion in the Abbé Du Bos's *Réflexions Critiques,*" *Studies on Voltaire and the Eighteenth Century*, no. 12 (2001): 417–21; Dominique Désirat, "Le sixième sens de l'abbé Dubos," *La licorne* 23 (2005), http://edel.univ-poitiers.fr/licorne/document.php?id=280; and Thomas M. Kavanaugh, *Enlightened Pleasures: Eighteenth-Century France and the New Epicureanism* (New Haven, CT: Yale University Press, 2010). On Diderot's debt to Dubos, see Rémy G. Saisselin, "Genius," in *The Rule of Reason and the Ruses of the Heart: A Philosophical Dictionary of Classical French Criticism, Critics, and Aesthetic Issues* (Cleveland: Case Western Reserve University, 1970), 89–96.

2. Voltaire, *Siècle de Louis XIV*, "Catalogue des écrivains" [VOLTAIRE]. Voltaire later defended Dubos against Montesquieu's attacks on Dubos's *Histoire critique de l'établissement de la monarchie française dans les Gaules* (Paris: Osmont, 1734); see his *Questions sur l'"Encyclopédie,"* s.v. "Lois." Voltaire initiated a brief correspondence with Dubos in 1738 on

the subject of his *Siècle*; their exchange, laced with flatteries, contains some illuminating remarks on both sides about historiography.

3. These results were obtained using the PAIR search engine developed by the ARTFL Project at the University of Chicago, which finds matching passages through sequence alignment (the same kind of program used in plagiarism software): http://artfl-project.uchicago.edu/node/54.

4. Dubos, *Réflexions critiques*, 2:446 (2:478 in 1733 ed.); of course, Dubos may have been employing the authorial *nous* in this passage ("cette supériorité de raison, que nous appelons esprit philosophique").

5. Fontenelle wrote, "One can tell that Mr. Leibniz disdained nothing in his vast reading; and it is astonishing how many mediocre or nearly ignored books he was gracious enough to read; but what is even more so is that he could place so much philosophical spirit [*mettre autant d'esprit philosophique*] in such unphilosophical matter," in *Eloges des académiciens de l'académie royale des sciences, morts depuis l'an 1699* (Paris: Librairie Arthème Fayard, 1989–97), 382 [CORPUS]. On Fréret's *Réflexion générale*, see below.

6. Dubos, *Réflexions critiques*, 2:454 (2:487 in 1733 ed.).

7. Ibid., 2:424 (2:455 in 1733 ed.) (emphasis added).

8. I return below to the tension between Ancients and Moderns in Dubos's *Réflexions critiques*.

9. For a typical example, see Abraham Keller's assessment that "the moral licence which characterized the last years of Louis XIV's reign and the period of the Regency naturally encouraged irreverent thoughts [and] there was a general receptiveness which militated in favour of new standards," in *Prelude to Enlightenment: French Literature, 1690–1740* (Seattle: University of Washington Press, 1970), 11.

10. J. B. Shank, "'There Was No Such Thing as the "Newtonian Revolution," and the French Initiated It': Eighteenth-Century Mechanics in France before Maupertuis," *Early Science and Medicine* 9, no. 3 (2004): 257–92; and J. B. Shank, *The Newton Wars and the Beginning of the French Enlightenment* (Chicago: University of Chicago Press, 2008), pt. 1.

11. Shank, *Newton Wars*, 55.

12. Ibid., 112, 231, and passim.

13. Leonard M. Marsak, *Bernard de Fontenelle: The Idea of Science in the French Enlightenment* (Philadelphia: Transactions of the American Philosophical Society, 1959). More generally, see Alain Niderst, *Fontenelle à la recherche de lui-même (1657–1702)* (Paris: Nizet, 1972); Jean

Dagen, *L'histoire de l'esprit humain dans la pensée française de Fontenelle à Condorcet* (Paris: Klincksieck, 1977); and Roger Marchal, *Fontenelle à l'aube des Lumières* (Paris: Champion, 1997). On Fréret and Newton, see Frank Manuel, *The Eighteenth Century Confronts the Gods* (Cambridge, MA: Harvard University Press, 1959). For Dubos's comparison of Newton and Archimedes, see *Réflexions critiques*, 2:448 (2:481 in 1733 ed.).

14. Margaret Jacob, *The Radical Enlightenment: Pantheists, Freemasons, and Republicans* (London: George Allen, 1981), quotation on 197; see also 146. Montesquieu mentions Newton's experiments on optics in his 1716 *Discours de réception a l'Académie des sciences de Bordeaux* [ARTFL].

15. Robert Shackleton, *Montesquieu: A Critical Biography* (Oxford: Oxford University Press, 1970), 10–11. Montesquieu also knew Dubos, who frequented Madame de Lambert's salon (ibid., 56, 303). He would of course later criticize Dubos's history of the French monarchy at length in *De l'esprit des lois* (see esp. 6.30.12).

16. Pomeau and Ehrard, *Fénelon à Voltaire*, 98.

17. Ross Hutchinson, *Locke in France, 1688–1734*, Studies on Voltaire and the Eighteenth Century, vol. 290 (Oxford: Voltaire Foundation, 1991), 86–88. Locke is never mentioned in the *Réflexions critiques*. D'Alembert similarly regards the empiricist postulate as a "principle of the first [i.e., Ancient] Philosophers"; see the "Discours préliminaire des éditeurs," *Encyclopédie*, 1:ii. A similar opinion was held by Fontenelle; see Niderst, *Fontenelle à la recherche de lui-même*, 54. The "Lockean" adage *nihil in intellectu nisi prius in sensu* was also a staple of Scholasticism, featuring notably in Aquinas's *Summa*.

18. Emmanuel Bury, *Littérature et politesse: L'invention de l'honnête homme, 1580–1750* (Paris: Presses Universitaires de France, 1996), 217. On Malebranche, Dubos, and sentiment, see also Katherine J. Hamerton, "Malebranche, Taste, and Sensibility: The Origins of Sensitive Taste and a Reconsideration of Cartesianism's Feminist Potential," *Journal of the History of Ideas* 69 (2008): 533–58. My thanks to J. B. Shank for supplying this reference.

19. On Fontenelle's debt to Bayle's *Pensées diverses sur la comète*, see Daniel Mornet, *French Thought in the Eighteenth Century*, trans. Lawrence Levin (New York: Archon Books, 1969), 47. Renée Simon debunked the myth that Fréret read Bayle's *Dictionnaire historique et critique* while locked up in the Bastille; see her *Nicolas Fréret, académicien*, Studies on Voltaire and the Eighteenth Century, vol. 17 (Oxford: Vol-

taire Foundation, 1961), 173. See also Pierre Rétat, *Le "Dictionnaire" de Bayle et la lutte philosophique au XVIIIe siècle* (Paris: Belles Lettres, 1971), 228.

20. Joseph Dedieu, *Montesquieu et la tradition politique anglaise en France: Les sources anglaises de "l'Esprit des lois"* (1909; Manchester: Ayer Publishing, 1969), 139–40. According to Dedieu, it was during his travels to Rome and the Dutch provinces that Montesquieu shook off his youthful republican sympathies, evident in many of his *Persian Letters*.

21. Dubos, *Histoire critique de l'établissement de la monarchie française dans les Gaules*; and Thomas E. Kaiser, "The Abbé Dubos and the Historical Defence of Monarchy in Early Eighteenth Century France," *Studies on Voltaire and the Eighteenth Century* 267 (1989): 77–102. On Boulainvilliers, see Harold Ellis, *Boulainvilliers and the French Monarchy: Aristocratic Politics in Early Eighteenth-Century France* (Ithaca, NY: Cornell University Press, 1988).

22. Jonathan Israel, *Radical Enlightenment: Philosophy and the Making of Modernity, 1650–1750* (Oxford: Oxford University Press, 2002), 361; and Marsak, *Bernard de Fontenelle*, 56. See also Marchal, *Fontenelle à l'aube des Lumières*, 138–45. On the "Radical Enlightenment," see below.

23. Niderst, *Fontenelle à la recherche de lui-même*, 187–201.

24. Most scholars doubt this attribution; see Simon, *Nicolas Fréret*, 173ff. Rétat notes, "The attribution is so uncertain that in the absence of formal proofs, we must doubt it"; *"Dictionnaire" de Bayle*, 229. More recently, see Miguel Benítez's close analysis of this attribution and his conclusion that "Fréret may perhaps have developed in his youth the early kernel of the work. But others no doubt gave it the form under which it commonly circulated"; "La composition de la *Lettre de Thrasybule à Leucippe*: Une conjecture raisonnable," in *Nicolas Fréret: Légende et vérité*, ed. Chantal Grell and Catherine Volphilac-Auger (Oxford: Voltaire Foundation, 1994), 192. Israel calls Fréret the "reputed author" of this work in *Radical Enlightenment* (373n104), but in his subsequent *Enlightenment Contested: Philosophy, Modernity, and the Emancipation of Man, 1670–1752* (Oxford: Oxford University Press, 2006), Fréret is identified without any qualifications as a member of a "'determinist,' anti-scriptural and *matérialiste* grouping" (365) and is unambiguously stated to be the author of the *Lettre de Thrasybule* (728).

25. Dubos, *Réflexions critiques*, 2:443 (2:475 in 1733 ed.). For a similar chronological revision, cf. 2:432 (2:464 in 1733 ed.).

26. Ibid., 2:439–40; in the 1733 edition, the date is revised to "soixante

ou quatre-vingt ans" (2:471). Dubos himself warned about relying ex-
cessively on this chronological marker: "Cette date de soixante ans
[increased to "soixante et dix ans" in 1733] qu'on donne pour époque
à ce renouvellement prétendu des esprits est mal choisie" (2:424 [and
2:454]).

27. Ibid., 2:323 for Bacon and 2:430 for Descartes (2:343 and 2:461 in
1733 ed.).

28. Bernard Le Bovier de Fontenelle, *Digression sur les Anciens et les
Modernes* (1688), in *La Querelle des Anciens et des Modernes*, ed. Anne-
Marie Lecoq (Paris: Gallimard, 2001), 302. In his critical *Voyage au
monde de Descartes* (Paris: Vve S. Bernard, 1690), the Jesuit priest Gabriel Daniel used the expression "*la nouvelle philosophie*" on at least ten
occasions in reference to Descartes's system.

29. Nicolas Fréret, *Réflexion générale sur l'étude des anciennes histoires*
(Paris, 1724), 9–10 [CORPUS].

30. Voltaire, *Lettres philosophiques* (Paris: Garnier-Flammarion,
1964), 94, letter 14.

31. Ibid. Fréret had described Scholastic philosophy very similarly
as "this monstrous assembly of fantasy beings, accidents, qualities, and
occult virtues of attraction, sympathy, antipathy, and other feelings that
are attributed to the most passive and inanimate beings or, in a word,
this heap of *chimeras* that the Peripatetics of the last centuries called
Aristotle's system" (*Réflexion générale*, 9, emphasis added).

32. On Bacon's and Descartes's status as "the great propagandists
of science," see Peter Gay, *The Rise of Modern Paganism*, vol. 1 of *The
Enlightenment: An Interpretation* (New York: Knopf, 1966), 310–14. According to Voltaire, Bacon "had disdained from a young age what the
universities called philosophy" in order to become himself "the father of
experimental philosophy" (*Lettres philosophiques*, 78, letter 12).

33. Jean-le-Rond d'Alembert's "Discours préliminaire" and his later
Essai sur les éléments de philosophie (1759). On the differences between the
epistemologies of Bacon and the *Encyclopédie*, see Martine Groult, "Le
système figuré des connaissances humaines ou le projet philosophique
de l'*Encyclopédie*," http://www.lib.uchicago.edu/efts/ARTFL/projects/
encyc/groult/.

34. Paul Hazard, *La crise de la conscience européene* (Paris: Livre de
Poche, 1935), 26. For an example of this tendency, see most recently
John Robertson, who focuses on "the encounter between the Augus-
tinian rigorism of Pascal and Port Royal and the revived, supposedly

Christianised Epicureanism championed by Gassendi and his follow-ers" as the intellectual crucible of the Enlightenment; *The Case for the Enlightenment: Scotland and Naples, 1680–1760* (Cambridge: Cambridge University Press, 2005), 32–33. See also, in a similar vein, Israel, *Radical Enlightenment*, in which part of the introduction is entitled "The 'Crisis of the European Mind'" and which, as many critics have noted, grants an inordinate importance to Spinoza. See esp. Margaret Jacob's review of this work in *Journal of Modern History* 75 (2003): 387–89; and An-toine Lilti, "Comment écrit-on l'histoire intellectuelle des Lumières? Spinozisme, radicalisme, et philosophie," *Annales HSS* 64 (2009): 171–206.

35. Hazard's thesis sparked a lively critical debate that lasted until the 1970s. For an overview of this literature, see Ira Wade, *The Intel-lectual Origins of the French Enlightenment* (Princeton, NJ: Princeton University Press, 1971), 43–52. For another criticism of Hazard, see Peter Gay, *The Party of Humanity: Essays in the French Enlightenment* (New York: Knopf, 1964), 120.

36. Dubos, *Réflexions critiques*, 2:440–43 on "Harvée" and 2:444 on Copernicus (2:472–74 and 2:477 in 1733 ed.).

37. Thomas Sprat, "To the Royal Society," in his *The History of the Royal Society of London*, 3rd ed. (London, 1722). My thanks to John Mar-shall for calling this text to my attention.

38. Sprat, *History of the Royal Society of London*, 327. Interestingly, Sprat insists that only natural philosophy will be affected by the new science: "we find nothing will be indanger'd [among "the chief Parts of Education"] but only the *Physics* of *Antiquity*" (328); the *esprit phi-losophique* diagnosed by Dubos and others, by contrast, affects all areas of learning, science, and the arts.

CHAPTER FOUR

1. On these "parallel histories of nature, man, and God," see Anthony Grafton, *What Was History? The Art of History in Early Modern Europe* (Cambridge: Cambridge University Press, 2007), 27.

2. See also Ernst Breisach, *Historiography: Ancient, Medieval, and Modern*, 3rd ed. (Chicago: University of Chicago Press, 2007), esp. chap. 12 (notably on Walter Raleigh's 1614 *History of the World*).

3. Thomas Sprat, "To the Royal Society," in *History of the Royal So-ciety of London*, 3rd ed. (London, 1722). As Margaret Jacob has shown, later defenses of Newtonianism presented him under a Latitudinarian

light; see *The Newtonians and the English Revolution, 1689–1720* (Ithaca, NY: Cornell University Press, 1976).

4. For Dubos, the role of the public was particularly evident in aesthetic matters; see Céline Spector, "Les lumières avant les Lumières: Tribunal de la raison et opinion publique," *Révolution française. net*, March 2009, http://revolution-francaise.net/2009/03/01/299-les-lumieres-avant-les-lumieres-tribunal-de-la-raison-et-opinion-publique.

5. Voltaire, *Siècle de Louis XIV*, chap. 1 [VOLTAIRE].

6. D'Alembert, "Discours préliminaire des éditeurs," *Encyclopédie*, 1: xxxiv.

7. Keith Baker, "Enlightenment and the Institution of Society: Notes for a Conceptual History," in *Main Trends in Cultural History*, ed. Willem Melching and Wyger Velema (Amsterdam: Rodopi, 1994), 96; *Encyclopédie*, s.v. "Philosophe," 12:510.

8. In addition to Baker's "Enlightenment and the Institution of Society," see Daniel Gordon, *Citizens without Sovereignty: Equality and Sociability in French Thought, 1670–1789* (Princeton, NJ: Princeton University Press, 1994); and Yair Mintzker, "'A Word Newly Introduced into Language': The Appearance and Spread of 'Social' in French Enlightened Thought, 1745–1765," *History of European Ideas* 34 (2008): 500–513.

9. Céline Spector, *Montesquieu: Pouvoirs, richesses et sociétés* (Paris: Presses Universitaires de France, 2004), 151–66. Hobbes's 1642 *De Cive* was translated in 1649 by Samuel Sorbière as *Elémens philosophiques du citoyen, traicté politique où les fondemens de la société civile sont descouverts* (Amsterdam: J. Blaev, 1649). The expression "*société civile*" soon became common in French works; see, e.g., "si les hommes ne pouvoient jamais dire la verité, nous serions tous barbares les uns aux autres. . . . La société civilie se dissoudroit de soy-mesme"; Jean-Louis Guez de Balzac, *Dissertations chrestiennes et morales*, in his *Œuvres* (Paris: T. Jolly, 1665), 298 [ARTFL]. Previously this expression had generally been synonymous in French with "polite society."

10. See, e.g., the long passage on natural equality, which Etienne de La Boétie presents as proof that nature "a cherché, par toutes sortes de moyens à former et resserer le nœud de notre alliance, les liens de notre société"; *Discours de la servitude volontaire* (Paris: Payot, 1993), 12 [ARTFL]. Montaigne speaks on three occasions of the "société des hommes" (in the *Essais*), an expression that denotes a very similar concept.

11. Pierre Bayle, "Conjectures sur les mœurs d'une société qui seroit sans religion," in *Pensées diverses sur la comète*, 2 vols. (Rotterdam: Reinier Leers, 1683), §161: "Il me semble qu'à l'égard des mœurs & des actions civiles, elle seroit toute semblable à une Société de Payens. Il y faudroit à la vérité des loix fort sévères. . . . Mais n'en faut-il pas par tout?" (491). On the repercussions of this thesis, see John Robertson, *The Case for the Enlightenment: Scotland and Naples, 1680–1760* (Cambridge: Cambridge University Press, 2005), 130, 220, and passim.

12. Nicolas Fréret, *Réflexions sur les principes généraux de l'art d'écrire* (Paris, 1718), 40 [CORPUS].

13. Robertson, *Case for the Enlightenment*, 32.

14. Jean-Baptiste Dubos, *Réflexions critiques sur la poésie et la peinture*, 2 vols. (Paris: Mariette, 1719), 1:148–49 (1:157 in 1733 ed.).

15. "Quand on dit que la tragédie purge les passions, on entend parler seulement des passions vitieuses et préjudiciables à la société"; ibid., 1:632 (1:441 in 1733 ed.).

16. "Un art necessaire et même simplement utile dans la societé, n'en doit pas être banni, parce qu'il peut devenir un art nuisible entre les mains de ceux qui en abuseroient"; ibid., 1:44 (1:47 in 1733 ed.).

17. "Ils ont été une société naissante avant que d'être une nation polie"; ibid., 2:502 (2:539 in 1733 ed.)

18. Ibid., 2:131 (2:149 in 1733 ed.).

19. John Locke, *An Essay concerning Human Understanding* (1690), bk. 3, chap. 10, §9. Keith Baker makes this argument in *Condorcet: From Natural Philosophy to Social Mathematics* (Chicago: University of Chicago Press, 1975), 87–95, 129–38.

20. Montesquieu, *Persian Letters*, trans. Mr. Flloyd, 2 vols. (London: J. and R. Tonson, 1762), 1:212, letter 69. On the modest epistemology of the Enlightenment, see, e.g., Robert Darnton, "Philosophers Trim the Tree of Knowledge: The Epistemological Strategy of the *Encyclopédie*," in *The Great Cat Massacre and Other Episodes in French Cultural History* (New York: Basic Books, 1984), 191–214.

21. *Encyclopédie*, s.v. "Encyclopédie," 5:642.

22. Keith Baker, "Epistémologie et politique: Pourquoi l'*Encyclopédie* est-elle un dictionnaire?" in *L'"Encyclopédie": Du réseau au livre et du livre au réseau*, ed. Robert Morrissey and Philippe Roger (Paris: Champion, 2001), 51–58. Kant had famously proposed *aude sapere* as the motto of the Enlightenment in his essay "Was ist Aufklärung?" On the *philosophes'* difficulties of staying within "the limits of human understanding,"

see the introduction to *The Super-Enlightenment: Daring to Know Too Much*, ed. Dan Edelstein, Studies on Voltaire and the Eighteenth Century, vol. 2010:01 (Oxford: Voltaire Foundation, 2010).

23. This point is emphasized by David A. Bell, *The Cult of the Nation in France: Inventing Nationalism, 1680–1800* (Cambridge, MA: Harvard University Press, 2001), 27–32. I am indebted to the author, as well as to Keith Baker, for many of the arguments in this chapter.

24. See esp. Marcel Gauchet, *The Disenchantment of the World: A Political History of Religion*, trans. Oscar Burge (Princeton, NJ: Princeton University Press, 1999). See also Baker, "Enlightenment and the Institution of Society," 110–14; Dale Van Kley, *The Religious Origins of the French Revolution: From Calvin to the Civil Constitution, 1560–1791* (New Haven, CT: Yale University Press, 1996); and Bell, *Cult of the Nation*, chap. 1.

25. See esp. Emmanuel Bury, *Littérature et politesse: L'invention de l'honnête homme, 1580–1750* (Paris: Presses Universitaires de France, 1996), 195–203. See also Norbert Elias, *The Civilizing Process: Sociogenetic and Psychogenetic Investigations*, trans. Edmund Jephcott (1939; Oxford: Blackwell, 2000); Carolyn Lougee Chapell, *Le Paradis des Femmes: Women, Salons, and Social Stratification in Seventeenth-Century France* (Princeton, NJ: Princeton University Press, 1976); Joan DeJean, *Tender Geographies: Women and the Origins of the Novel in France* (New York: Columbia University Press, 1991); and Benedetta Craveri, *The Age of Conversation*, trans. Teresa Waugh (New York: New York Review of Books, 2005).

26. As a search in ARTFL's FRANTEXT database reveals, this expression begins to be commonly employed in the late seventeenth century: six instances can be found in the correspondence of Madame de Sévigné alone.

27. The "*philosophe très-galant*" of Montesquieu's letter 38 is widely recognized as a reference to Fontenelle.

28. César Dumarsais, *Le philosophe*, in anon., *Nouvelles libertés de penser* (Amsterdam: Piget, 1734), 200 [GALLICA]; this passage would be included in Diderot's abridgement of this text for the article "Philosophe" in the *Encyclopédie*, 12:510. For a critical edition of this work, see Herbert Dieckmann, *"Le Philosophe": Text and Interpretation* (St. Louis, MO: Washington University, 1948).

29. Alain Viala, *La France galante: Essai historique sur une catégorie*

culturelle, de ses origines jusqu'à la Révolution (Paris: Presses Universitaires de France, 2008), 172–73.

30. James Collins, *The State in Early-Modern France* (Cambridge: Cambridge University Press, 1995).

31. Reinhart Koselleck, *Critique and Crisis: Enlightenment and the Pathogenesis of Modern Society* (1959; Cambridge, MA: MIT Press, 1988), esp. chaps. 1, 2, and 4.

32. Quoted in Margaret Jacob, *Strangers Nowhere in the World: The Rise of Cosmopolitanism in Early Modern Europe* (Philadelphia: University of Pennsylvania Press, 2006), 58.

33. Simone Mazauric, *Fontenelle et l'invention de l'histoire des sciences à l'aube des Lumières* (Paris: Fayard, 2007).

34. Keith Baker, "Public Opinion as Political Invention," in his *Inventing the French Revolution* (Cambridge: Cambridge University Press, 1990), 167–99. Here as well, the argument in this paragraph owes a great deal to conversations with Keith Baker.

35. While it is true that these values were more established in England and the Netherlands at this time, the idea of religious toleration was not exactly new: Henry IV, after all, signed the Edict of Nantes in 1598.

36. Max Horkheimer and Theodor Adorno, *Dialectic of Enlightenment*, trans. Edmund Jephcott (Stanford, CA: Stanford University Press, 2002); and Noël Antoine Pluche, *Spectacle de la nature: or, nature display'd. Being discourses on such particulars of natural history as were thought most proper to excite . . .* , 2nd ed. (London, 1733), 287, 300. For a typical reaction to this work, see Voltaire's satirical comments in the entry "Bacon" in his *Questions sur l'"Encyclopédie."* See also Norman Hampson, *A Cultural History of the Enlightenment* (New York: Pantheon, 1968), 82.

CHAPTER FIVE

1. For an insightful introduction to the Quarrel, see Marc Fumaroli, "Les abeilles et les araignées," in *La Querelle des Anciens et des Modernes*, ed. Anne-Marie Lecoq (Paris: Gallimard, 2001), 8–218. See also, among many other works, Nicole Ferrier-Caverivière, *L'image de Louis XIV dans la littérature française de 1660 à 1715* (Paris: Presses Universitaires de France, 1981); Joan DeJean, *Ancients against Moderns: Culture Wars and the Making of a Fin de Siècle* (Chicago: University of Chicago

Press, 1997); Levent Yilmaz, *Le temps moderne: Variations sur les anciens et les contemporains* (Paris: Gallimard, 2004); and for a more *longue durée* study, François Hartog, *Anciens, modernes, sauvages* (Paris: Galaade, 2005). My own understanding of the Quarrel is greatly indebted to Larry F. Norman's forthcoming study, *The Shock of the Ancient.* My utmost thanks to the author for sharing his manuscript with me before its publication. On the English repercussions of the Quarrel, see Joseph Levine, *The Battle of the Books: History and Literature in the Augustan Age* (Ithaca, NY: Cornell University Press, 1991). Levine's title, borrowed from Swift, underscores the extent to which the Quarrel remained mostly confined to literary (rather than scientific, philosophical, and cultural) matters in England.

2. Jean-Baptiste Dubos, *Réflexions critiques sur la poésie et la peinture*, 2 vols. (Paris: Mariette, 1719), 2:33 (2:452 in 1733 ed.).

3. René Pomeau and Jean Ehrard, *Fénelon à Voltaire* (Paris: Flammarion, 1988), 98. I return to the importance of Dubos's work at the end of this chapter.

4. Dubos mentions Perrault fourteen times in his *Réflexions critiques*; although he is generally committed to opposing Perrault's thesis, he nonetheless describes his opponent honorably (3:188, only in 1733 ed.). For a reading of the Quarrel as culture war, see DeJean, *Ancients against Moderns.*

5. The poem is reprinted in Lecoq, *Querelle des Anciens et des Modernes*, 256–73; on the academy session, see Fumaroli, "Les abeilles et les araignées," 18–24.

6. Charles Perrault, *Parallèle des Anciens et des Modernes en ce qui regarde les arts et les sciences* (1688–97), ed. Hans Robert Jauss (Munich: Eidos Verlag, 1964). Apart from the preface (which is unpaginated in the original), page references are to the seventeenth-century edition (which Jauss reproduces).

7. Perrault's official title was *contrôleur général de la surintendance des bâtiments du roi.* This brief historical summary of the Quarrel is mostly drawn from Fumaroli, "Les abeilles et les araignées."

8. Jacob Soll, *The Information Master: Jean-Baptiste Colbert's Secret State Intelligence System* (Ann Arbor: University of Michigan Press, 2009).

9. DeJean, *Ancients against Moderns*, 17.

10. Francis Bacon, *The New Organon*, trans. and ed. Lisa Jardine and

Michael Silverthorne (Cambridge: Cambridge University Press, 2000), 2.7 (107).

11. Norman, *Shock of the Ancient*, pt. 1. For Boileau, see his *Arrêt burlesque* (1671), in *Œuvres complètes de Boileau-Despréaux*, ed. P.-C.-F. Daunou, 3 vols. (Paris: Dupont, 1825), 3:117 [GALLICA]; for Longepierre, see his *Discours sur les anciens*, excerpted in Lecoq, *Querelle des Anciens et des Modernes*, 279–93.

12. Yilmaz, *Temps moderne*, 29.

13. Perrault, *Parallèle*, 5:285.

14. Ibid., 5:96, 5:97, 1:54. Joan DeJean has argued that it was only around this time (and perhaps even thanks to Perrault) that "*siècle*" acquired its contemporary meaning of "one hundred years," as opposed to referring to a monarch's reign or general epoch (*Ancients against Moderns*, 19).

15. On medicine, see Perrault, *Parallèle*, 5:244–45; for the lengthy discussion of Descartes's philosophy, see 5:156–228. It is worth noting that Perrault is in fact quite critical of Cartesian physics, but like Fréret, Voltaire, d'Alembert, and many others after them, he credits Descartes for having shown a new, if not the right, way to explore nature (5:173).

16. Dubos, *Réflexions critiques*, 2:422 (2:453 in 1733 ed.).

17. Ibid., 2:426 (2:459 in 1733 ed.).

18. Dubos also imposed a starker distinction between the arts and sciences, arguing that since sentiment, not reason, determines the value of poetry, the passage of time and accumulation of experience do not confer any particular advantages to Modern writers (unlike in the sciences).

19. Ibid., 2:446 (2:478 in 1733 ed.). Dubos had commented previously on "the philosophical spirit . . . whose name only would have been new for the ancients"; 2:470 (2:504–5 in 1733 ed.).

20. Charles Perrault, *Parallèle*, 5:271.

21. Ibid., 2:452, 2:485.

22. Nicolas Fréret, *Réflexion générale sur l'étude des anciennes histoires* (Paris, 1724), 8 [CORPUS]. Anne-Robert-Jacques Turgot's *Philosophical Review of the Successive Advances of the Human Mind* (1750) similarly combines an admiration of the Ancients and a celebration of the Moderns; see Ronald Meek, ed. and trans., *Turgot on Progress, Sociology, and Economics* (Cambridge: Cambridge University Press, 1973).

23. Fumaroli, "Les abeilles et les araignées," 194–96.

24. François Fénelon, *Lettre à l'Académie, avec les versions primitives* (1714; Geneva: Droz, 1970), 122 [ARTFL]. Fénelon goes on to add that "one must be stubborn to judge a text by its date" (124). On this letter, which was written in 1714 and published the year after Fénelon's death in 1715, see Lecoq, *Querelle des Anciens et des Modernes*, 471–72. My thanks to Larry Norman for emphasizing Fénelon's dialectical stance.

25. Fénelon, *Lettre à l'Académie*, 125.

26. Voltaire, *Questions sur l'"Encyclopédie*," s.v. "Anciens et modernes."

27. Elena Russo, *Styles of Enlightenment: Taste, Politics, and Authorship in Eighteenth-Century France* (Baltimore, MD: Johns Hopkins University Press, 2007), 21.

28. Ibid., 261.

29. On Pierre Marivaux, the *bel esprit*, and the *philosophes*, see ibid., 62–63 and passim. Fontenelle was allegedly deeply insulted by the conclusion of Voltaire's *Micromégas*, in which the *secrétaire perpetuel* of the Académie des sciences (i.e., Fontenelle) is presented with a book containing the sum of all knowledge ("*le bout des choses*"), and when it transpires that the book's pages are blank, the witty *secrétaire* responds, "Ah! I knew it [*Je m'en étais bien douté*]." Jean de La Bruyère had already mocked Fontenelle as a "Cydias bel esprit" in *Les caractères ou les mœrs de ce siècle* (1688), in *Œuvres complètes*, ed. Julien Benda (Paris: Gallimard, 1951), 172 [ARTFL]; quoted in Fumaroli, "Les abeilles et les araignées," 185. See also Voltaire, *Encyclopédie*, s.v. "Gens de lettres," 7:600.

30. Montesquieu, *Persian Letters*, trans. Margaret Mauldon (Oxford: Oxford University Press, 2008), 194, letter 136 (letter 142 in standard French editions).

31. Ibid., 121, letter 87 (letter 89 in standard French editions). I return to the place of antiquity in Montesquieu's political thought in a subsequent chapter.

32. Voltaire, *Epître à l'auteur du livre des trois imposteurs*, in *Œuvres complètes de Voltaire*, ed. Louis Moland (Paris: Garnier, 1877–85), vol. 10 [VOLTAIRE]. In a note to the *Poème sur la loi naturelle*, he had already argued: "Tous les anciens, sans exception, ont cru l'éternité de la matière; c'est presque le seul point sur lequel ils convenaient." On Voltaire's use of tradition, see R. R. Palmer, *Catholics and Unbelievers in Eighteenth-Century France* (1939; New York: Cooper Square Publishers, 1961), chap. 3.

33. D'Alembert, "Discours préliminaire des éditeurs," *Encyclopédie,* 1:ii.

34. Ibid., xix.

CHAPTER SIX

1. For one of the most sustained and influential expressions of this opinion, see John Pocock, *The Enlightenments of Edward Gibbon,* vol. 1 of *Barbarism and Religion* (Cambridge: Cambridge University Press, 1999), discussed below.

2. Peter Gay, *The Rise of Modern Paganism,* vol. 1 of *The Enlightenment: An Interpretation* (New York: Knopf, 1966). Robert Darnton notably queried how Gay could convincingly distinguish between Renaissance and Enlightenment scholars on this basis, if both fashioned themselves so vividly on the Ancients; see "In Search of the Enlightenment: Recent Attempts to Create a Social History of Ideas," *Journal of Modern History* 43 (1971): 113–32.

3. For Diderot, see his *Essai sur la vie de Sénèque* (1778), in Seneca, *Œuvres,* vol. 7 (Paris: Frères de Bure, 1779), 31 [ARTFL].

4. Joscelyn Royé, "La littérature comique et la critique du latin au XVIIᵉ siècle," in *Tous vos gens à latin: Le latin, langue savante, langue mondaine (XIVᵉ–XVIIᵉ siècles),* ed. Emmanuel Bury (Geneva: Droz, 2005), 223–36. A century earlier, in fact, Montaigne had already penned an essay criticizing pedantry: "Du pédantisme," in *Essais,* vol. 1 (Paris: Gallimard, 1965), 203–16.

5. Blandine Barret-Kriegel, *La défaite de l'érudition* (Paris: Presses Universitaires de France, 1988). See also Henri Gouhier, *L'anti-humanisme au XVIIᵉ siècle* (Paris: Vrin, 1987); and Chantal Grell, *Le dix-huitième siècle et l'antiquité en France, 1680–1789,* 2 vols., Studies on Voltaire and the Eighteenth Century, vols. 330–31 (Oxford: Voltaire Foundation, 1995), 1:433–48.

6. Jean de La Bruyère, *Les caractères ou les mœurs de ce siècle* (1688), in *Œuvres complètes,* ed. Julien Benda (Paris: Gallimard, 1951), 431 [ARTFL]. This paragraph opens with the claim: "L'étude des textes ne peut jamais être assez recommandée; c'est le chemin le plus court, le plus sûr et le plus agréable pour tout genre d'érudition" (430). See also April Shelford's discussion of Pierre-Daniel Huet's ties to salon culture in her *Transforming the Republic of Letters: Pierre-Daniel Huet and European Intellectual Life, 1650–1720* (Rochester, NY: University of Rochester Press, 2007), chap. 3.

7. My thanks to Anthony Grafton for emphasizing this distinction. On Fréret, see notably Frank Manuel, *The Eighteenth Century Confronts the Gods* (Cambridge, MA: Harvard University Press, 1959); Renée Simon, *Nicolas Fréret, académicien*, Studies on Voltaire and the Eighteenth Century, vol. 17 (Geneva: Voltaire Foundation, 1961); and Chantall Grell and Catherine Volpilhac-Auger, eds., *Nicolas Fréret, légende et vérité* (Oxford: Voltaire Foundation, 1991).

8. See, in general, Anthony Grafton, *Defenders of the Text: The Traditions of Scholarship in an Age of Science, 1450–1800* (Cambridge, MA: Harvard University Press, 1991).

9. In the *Encyclopédie* article "Chronologie," written by d'Alembert, Fréret is held up as an exemplar of learning and knowledge: "we cannot let pass this opportunity to celebrate the memory of such a scholar, who combined immense erudition with a philosophical spirit, and who brandished this double torch deep into his studies of Antiquity" (3:392). The entries for "Dieu" (4:981) and "Etymologie" (6:111) also pay homage to Fréret.

10. This paper was Fréret's *Réflexion générale sur l'étude des anciennes histoires* (Paris, 1724), originally published in *Mémoires de littérature tirés des registres de l'Académie royale des inscriptions et belles-lettres* (The Hague, 1719–24). Fréret's commentary begins as follows: "The philosophical spirit is most opposed to the spirit of systems [*esprit de système*]; just as the former is necessary, the latter is dangerous"; *Réflexion générale* (Paris, 1724), 7–8. Fréret's opposition would be developed by Condillac in his *Traité des systèmes* (1749), before it was borrowed (without credit) by d'Alembert in the "Discours préliminaire des éditeurs," *Encyclopédie*, 1:xxxi. Pocock notes this parallel in *Enlightenments of Edward Gibbon*, 158.

11. Jean Seznec, "Le singe antiquaire," in *Essais sur Diderot et l'antiquité* (Oxford: Clarendon Press, 1957), 80–90.

12. François-Jean de Chastellux, *De la félicité publique*, 2 vols. (1772; Paris: A.-A. Renouard, 1822), 2:80. On Chastellux, see Alan Charles Kors, *D'Holbach's Coterie: An Enlightenment in Paris* (Princeton, NJ: Princeton University Press, 1976). Let us not forget that even Gibbon, the primary source for both Seznec and Pocock, found Caylus odd: "He rises early, runs through the artists' painting rooms all day long, comes home again at six o'clock in the evening, puts on his dressing-gown, and shuts himself up in his closet. Is this the way to see one's friends." Conversely, Gibbon seems to have mostly enjoyed the company of

d'Holbach: "The Baron possesses genius and learning, and, above all, he very often gives capital dinners. . . . In these symposia the pleasures of the table were improved by lively and liberal conversation"; *The Autobiography of Edward Gibbon* (New York: Buckland and Summer, 1846), 152 and 151.

13. Stéphane Baudens, "'Le fameux Linguet, cet avocat des Néron et des Caligula,'" in *L'histoire institutionnelle et juridique dans la pensée politique* (Aix-en-Provence: Presses Universitaires d'Aix-Marseille, 2006), 91–121.

14. The best introduction to the *Encyclopédie* remains Jacques Proust's *Diderot et l'"Encyclopédie"* (1967; Paris: A. Michel, 1995). See also John Lough, *Essays on the "Encyclopédie" of Diderot and d'Alembert* (Oxford: Oxford University Press, 1968).

15. See, e.g., Daniel Rosenberg, "An Eighteenth-Century Time Machine: The *Encyclopedia* of Denis Diderot," in *Postmodernism and the Enlightenment: New Perspectives in Eighteenth-Century French Intellectual History*, ed. Daniel Gordon (New York: Routledge, 2001), 45–66.

16. The full d'Alembert quotation reads as follows: "Hence, that crowd of Scholars [*Erudits*], versed in ancient languages to the point of dismissing their own, Scholars who, as a famous author wrote, were familiar with everything about the Ancients except their elegance and subtlety [*grâce et finesse*], and which a vain display of erudition made so prideful . . ." ("Discours préliminaire," 1:xx). Pocock argued that the *défaite de l'érudition* "consisted in the appearance and self-organisation of a class of *philosophes* who claimed not to need them [the *érudits*]" (*Enlightenments of Edward Gibbon*, 147).

17. D'Alembert, "Discours préliminaire," 1:xviii.

18. Ibid., xxiii.

19. *Encyclopédie*, s.v. "Critique" (Jean-François Marmontel), esp. 4:490–94. D'Alembert had already traced the origins of the process of critique back to erudition, in his article under the latter heading: "From the knowledge of history, languages, and books stems that important part of erudition known as *critique*" ("Erudition," 5:914).

20. "Previously, in the sixteenth century, and well before [in] the seventeenth, literary scholars spent a lot of their time on grammatical criticism of Greek and Latin authors; and it is to their labors that we owe the dictionaries, the accurate editions, the commentaries on the masterpieces of antiquity. Today this criticism is less necessary, and the

philosophical spirit has succeeded it. It is this philosophical spirit that seems to constitute the character of men of letters; and when it is combined with good taste, it forms an accomplished literary scholar" (*Encyclopédie*, "Gens de Lettres" [Voltaire], 7:599). This translation, by Dena Goodman, is from the University of Michigan collaborative translation project of the *Encyclopédie*.

21. Thanks to Keith Baker for this specific turn of phrase. The argument presented in the following paragraphs is developed further in my "Humanism, *l'Esprit Philosophique*, and the *Encyclopédie*," *Republics of Letters* 1, no. 1 (May 1, 2009), http://rofl.stanford.edu/node/27.

22. Sixteenth-century humanists also predominate: Scaliger is referenced more often (219 times) than Leibniz (211); and Charles Loyseau, a political jurist born in 1566, comes in ahead of Locke and Rousseau (127 vs. 116 each for the latter two).

23. Tournefort himself is something of an anomaly, as he was the favorite botanist of the chevalier de Jaucourt, the virtuoso author of no fewer than one quarter of all the articles in the *Encyclopédie*.

24. This sample data is gathered from hits 1–25 (from vol. 1), 1001–24 (vol. 11), 2001–24 (vol. 14), and 2856–80 (vol. 17) of a full-text search for "Pline."

25. D'Alembert, "Avertissement des éditeurs," *Encyclopédie*, 3:vii; see Muriel Brot, "Ecrire sans écrire: Les compilateurs au XVIIIᵉ siècle," in *Écriture, identité, anonymat au XVIIIᵉ siècle*, ed. Nicole Jacques-Lefèvre and Marie Leca-Tsiomis (Nanterre: Université Paris X–Nanterre, 2006), 87–104.

26. Diderot wrote that the goal of the *Encyclopédie* was to "gather knowledge that has been scattered across the globe; reveal its general system to our fellow men; and transmit it to posterity, so that the work of past centuries was not in vain for the centuries to come" (*Encyclopédie*, s.v. "Encyclopédie," 5:635).

27. Richard Yeo, *Encyclopedic Visions: Scientific Dictionaries and Enlightenment Culture* (Cambridge: Cambridge University Press, 2001); Alain Rey, *Miroirs du monde: Une histoire de l'encyclopédisme* (Paris: Fayard, 2007); and Ann Blair, *Too Much to Know: Managing Scholarly Information before the Modern Age* (forthcoming).

28. D'Alembert, "Avertissement des éditeurs," 3:vii.

29. See also the article "Abrégé": "One must say in favor of summaries [*abrégés*] that they are helpful for those people who do not have the time to consult original texts, nor the ability to procure them, nor the

talent to develop them, nor to unravel what a skilled and precise editor [*compilateur*] offers them all predigested"; "They are useful . . . when they are produced in such a way that they provide a full understanding of an object, as a miniature version of a larger portrait" (1:35). See Ann Blair, "Reading Strategies for Coping with Information Overload, ca. 1550–1700," *Journal of the History of Ideas* 64 (2003): 11–28.

CHAPTER SEVEN

1. Thomas E. Kaiser, "The Abbé Dubos and the Historical Defence of Monarchy in Early Eighteenth Century France," *Studies on Voltaire and the Eighteenth Century* 267 (1989): 95–102.

2. Peter Burke, *The Fabrication of Louis XIV* (New Haven, CT: Yale University Press, 1992).

3. See esp. Lionel Rothkrug, *Opposition to Louis XIV: The Political and Social Origins of the French Enlightenment* (Princeton, NJ: Princeton University Press, 1965). See also Harold Ellis, *Boulainvilliers and the French Monarchy: Aristocratic Politics in Early Eighteenth-Century France* (Ithaca, NY: Cornell University Press, 1988); and Margaret Jacob, *The Radical Enlightenment: Pantheists, Freemasons, and Republicans* (London: George Allen, 1981).

4. As Patrick Riley observes, "certainly some very characteristic Fénelon utterances seem more Greek, and more exactly Platonic, than 'Christian'"; see Riley's introduction to Fénelon's *Telemachus, Son of Ulysses*, ed. and trans. P. Riley (Cambridge: Cambridge University Press, 1994), xxvii–xxviii.

5. François Fénelon, *Lettre à l'Académie, avec les versions primitives* (Geneva: Droz, 1970), 138–42.

6. See esp. Albert Chérel, *Fénelon au 18ᵉ siècle en France (1715–1820): Son prestige, son influence* (1917; Geneva: Slatkine Reprints, 1970). I develop Fénelon's place in "natural republican" theory, as well as many of the other themes in this section, in *The Terror of Natural Right: Republicanism, the Cult of Nature, and the French Revolution* (Chicago: University of Chicago Press, 2009).

7. Thomas Kaiser, "Louis *le Bien-Aimé* and the Rhetoric of the Royal Body," in *From the Royal to the Republican Body: Incorporating the Political in Seventeenth- and Eighteenth-Century France*, ed. Sara E. Melzer and Kathryn Norberg (Berkeley and Los Angeles: University of California Press, 1998), 131–61. See also Joël Cornette, *Le roi de guerre: Essai sur la souveraineté dans la France du grand siècle* (Paris: Payot, 1993). It is

worth recalling that by 1691 Louis XIV had ceased to lead his army in person, preferring to conduct what became known as *"guerres de cabinet"*; see Christy Pichichero, "Battles of the Self: War and Subjectivity in Early Modern France" (PhD diss., Stanford University, 2008).

8. For a list of the dozen books he took with him to Paris, see Louis-Antoine Saint-Just, *Œuvres complètes*, ed. Anne Kupiec and Miguel Abensour (Paris: Gallimard, 2004), 1194–95.

9. On school syllabi in the eighteenth century, see L. W. B. Brockliss, *French Higher Education in the Seventeenth and Eighteenth Centuries: A Cultural History* (Oxford: Clarendon Press, 1987). On the place of antiquity in Enlightenment political thought more generally, see Claude Mossé, *L'antiquité dans la Révolution française* (Paris: Albin Michel, 1989), chap. 2; and François Hartog, *Anciens, modernes, sauvages* (Paris: Galaade, 2005), chap. 2.

10. Louis-Sebastien Mercier, *Tableau de Paris*, 12 vols. (Amsterdam: n.p., 1783–88), chap. 81, 1:254–55. I discuss the literary and educational contributions of *collèges* to eighteenth-century republicanism in *Terror of Natural Right*, chap. 1.

11. Catherine Volphilhac-Auger, *Tacite et Montesquieu*, Studies on Voltaire and the Eighteenth Century, vol. 232 (Oxford: Voltaire Foundation, 1985); and Catherine Volphilhac-Auger, *Tacite en France de Montesquieu à Chateaubriand*, Studies on Voltaire and the Eighteenth Century, vol. 313 (Oxford: Voltaire Foundation, 1993).

12. Jacob Soll, *Publishing "The Prince": History, Reading, and the Birth of Political Criticism* (Ann Arbor: University of Michigan Press, 2005). For Rousseau, see *Du contrat social*, 3.6, in *Œuvres complètes*, ed. Bernard Gagnebin and Marcel Raymond, 5 vols. (Paris: Gallimard/Pléiade, 1959–95), 3:409.

13. There was indeed nothing new with this infatuation with ancient republican texts: Hobbes had already warned against "the Reading of … Histories of the antient Greeks, and Romans; from which … men have undertaken to kill their Kings" (*Leviathan*, 2.29).

14. Quentin Skinner, "A Third Concept of Liberty," *Proceedings of the British Academy* 117 (2002): 237–68.

15. See esp. Elena Russo, "Virtuous Economies: Modernity and Noble Expenditure from Montesquieu to Caillois," in *Postmodernism and the Enlightenment: New Perspectives in Eighteenth-Century French Intellectual History*, ed. Daniel Gordon (New York: Routledge, 2001), 67–92 (quotation on 67).

16. In the earlier literature, classical republicanism was sometimes called "civic humanism"; see, e.g., Hans Baron, *The Crisis of the Early Italian Renaissance: Civic Humanism and Republican Liberty in an Age of Classicism and Tyranny* (1966; Princeton, NJ: Princeton University Press, 1993), who traced this discourse back to Leonardo Bruni's Florence. Quentin Skinner has extended its genealogy farther back, to twelfth-century authors; see Quentin Skinner, *The Renaissance*, vol. 1 of *Foundations of Modern Political Thought* (Cambridge: Cambridge University Press, 1978). A synthetic narrative of its modern history can be found in John Pocock, in *The Machiavellian Moment: Florentine Political Thought and the Atlantic Republican Tradition* (1975; Princeton, NJ: Princeton University Press, 2003). For the French side of this story, see esp. Keith Baker, "Transformations of Classical Republicanism in Eighteenth-Century France," *Journal of Modern History* 73 (2001): 32–53; and Johnson Kent Wright, *A Classical Republican in Eighteenth-Century France: The Political Thought of Mably* (Stanford, CA: Stanford University Press, 1997).

17. Hence, historians sometimes refer to Fénelon's "republican monarchism"; see esp. Patrick Riley, "Fénelon's 'Republican' Monarchism in *Telemachus*," in *Monarchisms in the Age of Enlightenment: Liberty, Patriotism, and the Common Good*, ed. Hans Blom, John Christian Laursen, and Luisa Simonutti (Toronto: University of Toronto Press, 2007). Even Rousseau acknowledged in the *Social Contract* that monarchy is not incompatible with his republican form of government.

18. Niccolò Machiavelli, *Discourses on Livy*, trans. Harvey C. Mansfield and Nathan Tarcov (Chicago: University of Chicago Press, 1998), 1.11.2, 35. Lycurgus, with whom Plutarch compared Numa (their lives are recounted in parallel), was also a contender for this prime billing.

19. See esp. Judith Shklar, *Men and Citizens: A Study of Rousseau's Social Theory* (Cambridge: Cambridge University Press, 1969). Michael Sonenscher has more recently made the case for a "Cynical" reading of Rousseau's thought; *Sans-Culottes: An Eighteenth-Century Emblem in the French Revolution* (Princeton, NJ: Princeton University Press, 2008).

20. Thomas Pangle, *Montesquieu's Philosophy of Liberalism: A Commentary on "The Spirit of the Laws"* (Chicago: University of Chicago Press, 1973), 217. See also Judith Shklar, "Montesquieu and the New Republicanism," in *Machiavelli and Republicanism*, ed. Gisele Bock, Quentin Skinner, and Maurizio Viroli (Cambridge: Cambridge University Press, 1990).

21. On Montesquieu's acceptance of the *esprit de commerce*, see notably Céline Spector, *Montesquieu: Pouvoirs, richesses et sociétés* (Paris: Presses Universitaires de France, 2004). It was of course in England, notably with Bernard de Mandeville, and later in Scotland, with David Hume and Adam Smith, that the Modern defense of commercial activity would be most strongly developed. See Istvan Hont, *Jealousy of Trade: International Competition and the Nation-State in Historical Perspective* (Cambridge, MA: Harvard University Press, 2005). On the debates around political economy in France, see most recently John Shovlin, *The Political Economy of Virtue: Luxury, Patriotism, and the Origins of the French Revolution* (Ithaca, NY: Cornell University Press, 2006); and Michael Sonenscher, *Before the Deluge: Public Debt, Inequality, and the Intellectual Origins of the French Revolution* (Princeton, NJ: Princeton University Press, 2007).

22. Benjamin Constant, "The Liberty of the Ancients Compared with That of the Moderns," in *Political Writings*, ed. Biancamaria Fontana (Cambridge: Cambridge University Press, 1988), 313.

23. See esp. the essays collected in David W. Carrithers, Michael A. Mosher, and Paul A. Rahe, eds., *Montesquieu's Science of Politics: Essays on "The Spirit of the Laws"* (Lanham, MD: Rowman and Littlefield, 2001); and David W. Carrithers and Patrick Coleman, eds., *Montesquieu and the Spirit of Modernity*, Studies on Voltaire and the Eighteenth Century, vol. 2002:09 (Oxford: Voltaire Foundation, 2002).

24. Paul Rahe, *Soft Despotism, Democracy's Drift: Montesquieu, Rousseau, Tocqueville, and the Modern Prospect* (New Haven, CT: Yale University Press, 2009), 75–95. On Montesquieu's ambiguous attitude toward commerce, see also Robert Morrissey, *Napoléon et l'héritage de la gloire* (Paris: PUF, 2010).

25. Andrew Jainchill, *Rethinking Politics after the Terror: The Republican Origins of French Liberalism* (Ithaca, NY: Cornell University Press, 2008), 249.

26. I discuss the voluminous scholarship on Rousseau's *Social Contract* in *Terror of Natural Right*, chap. 1.

27. M. J. C. Vile, *Constitutionalism and the Separation of Powers* (1967; Indianapolis: Liberty Fund, 1998); my thanks to Kent Wright for this reference and for insightful discussions on Montesquieu.

28. John Adams, *A Defence of the Constitutions of Government of the United States of America* (London: C. Dilly, 1787). My thanks to Caroline Winterer for pointing out the importance of antiquarianism in

American political thought. See her *The Culture of Classicism: Ancient Greece and Rome in American Intellectual Life, 1780–1910* (Baltimore, MD: Johns Hopkins University Press, 2004). For Voltaire, see *Lettres philosophiques* (Paris: Garnier-Flammarion, 1964), 21.

29. See, e.g., Robert Darnton, "In Search of the Enlightenment: Recent Attempts to Create a Social History of Ideas," *Journal of Modern History* 43 (1971): 120. The following discussion draws on my previous study, *Terror of Natural Right*. On liberalism and natural right, see notably Louis Hartz, *The Liberal Tradition in America: An Interpretation of American Political Thought since the Revolution* (New York: Harcourt, Brace, 1955). John Dunn has challenged this liberal reading of Locke; see his *The Political Thought of John Locke* (Cambridge: Cambridge University Press, 1969).

30. See Jean Barbeyrac's translation of Samuel von Pufendorf's *Les devoirs de l'homme et du citoyen* (Amsterdam: H. Schelte, 1707) and of Hugo Grotius's *Le droit de la guerre et de la paix* (Amsterdam: P. de Coup, 1724). For Jean-Jacques Burlamaqui, see his *Principes du droit naturel* (Geneva: Barrillot et Fils, 1747) and its companion *Principes du droit politique* (Amsterdam: Zacharie Chatelain, 1751). On these works, see Robert Derathé, *Jean-Jacques Rousseau et la science politique de son temps*, 2nd ed. (Paris: Vrin, 1992).

31. Helena Rosenblatt, *Rousseau and Geneva: From the First "Discourse" to "The Social Contract," 1749–1762* (Cambridge: Cambridge University Press, 1997).

32. For the description of legal despotism, see Pierre-Paul Le Mercier de la Rivière's 1767 *L'ordre naturel et essentiel des sociétés politiques*, ed. Edgard Depitre (Paris: Paul Geuthner, 1910) [GALLICA]. See more generally Elizabeth Fox-Genovese, *The Origins of Physiocracy: Economic Revolution and Social Order in Eighteenth-Century France* (Ithaca, NY: Cornell University Press, 1976); Michael Sonenscher, "Physiocracy as Theodicy," *History of Political Thought* 23, no. 2 (2002): 326–39; and Liana Vardi, *The Necessary Arts: The Physiocrats and Their World* (Cambridge: Cambridge University Press, forthcoming).

33. See my *Terror of Natural Right*, chap. 2. For Leo Strauss, see esp. his *Natural Right and History* (Chicago: University of Chicago, 1947).

34. Denis Diderot, *A Supplement to the Voyage of Bougainville* (1772), in *Political Writings*, ed. and trans. John Hope Mason and Robert Wokler (New York: Cambridge University Press, 1992), 71.

35. Paul Friedland, *Political Actors: Representative Bodies and Theatricality in the Age of the French Revolution* (Ithaca, NY: Cornell University Press, 2002). See also Keith Baker, "Representation Redefined," in *Inventing the French Revolution* (Cambridge: Cambridge University Press, 1990), 224–51.

36. Montesquieu highlights the benefits of political representation in *De l'esprit des lois*, but only in the idiosyncratic case of England (see bk. 11, chap. 6); Diderot similarly praises the English model (albeit in a "purged" form) in his *Observations on the Nakaz*, in *Political Writings*, 92; and Voltaire speaks favorably of representatives in his *Idées républicaines par un membre du corps*, written in the voice of a Genevan citizen. But these isolated comments—the first two of which concern constitutional monarchies—are quite exceptional.

37. Anne-Robert-Jacques Turgot, *Mémoire au roi sur les municipalités* (1775), in *Œuvres de Turgot*, ed. Eugène Daire and Hippolyte Dussard, 2 vols. (repr., Osnabrück: O. Zeller, 1966), 2:502–50 [GALLICA].

38. See, e.g., François Robert, *Le républicanisme adapté à la France* (1790), vol. 2 of *Aux origines de la République, 1789–1792* (Paris: EDHIS, 1991).

39. Montesquieu, *De l'esprit des lois*, 2.9.1, 2.9.3. Claude Adrien Helvétius praised republican government in *De l'homme* (posthumously published in 1773). See also David Warner Smith, *Helvétius: A Study in Persecution* (Oxford: Clarendon Press, 1965). Writers in other countries, particularly England and Scotland, were more willing to consider representational forms of government. Hume, for instance, proposed a federative model of republics loosely based on Harrington's *Oceana*; Hume, "Idea of a Perfect Commonwealth," in *Selected Essays*, ed. Stephen Copley and Andrew Edgar (Oxford: Oxford University Press, 1998).

40. See, e.g., Lynn Hunt, *Inventing Human Rights: A History* (New York: Norton, 2007).

41. Jean-Baptiste Dubos, *Réflexions critiques sur la poésie et la peinture*, 2 vols. (Paris: Mariette, 1719), 2:316 (2:334 in 1733 ed.); quoted by Joan DeJean, *Ancients against Moderns: Culture Wars and the Making of a Fin de Siècle* (Chicago: University of Chicago Press, 1997), 64.

42. Habermas had already noted the place of theatrical judgment in the development of a public sphere; Jürgen Habermas, *The Structural Transformation of the Public Sphere: An Inquiry into a Category of Bourgeois Society*, trans. Thomas Burger (Cambridge, MA: MIT Press, 1992),

38–41. DeJean argues that literary debates, particularly in the French press, played an equally important role; "The Invention of a Public for Literature," in *Ancients against Moderns*, 31–76.

43. Habermas, *Structural Transformation*. See also, among numerous others, Keith Baker, "Public Opinion as Political Invention," in his *Inventing the French Revolution* (Cambridge: Cambridge University Press, 1990), 167–99; and James van Horn Melton, *Rise of the Public in Enlightenment Europe* (Cambridge: Cambridge University Press, 2001).

CHAPTER EIGHT

1. On the "feminism" of the Moderns (esp. Perrault, Poulain de la Barre, and Fontenelle), see esp. Joan DeJean, *Ancients against Moderns: Culture Wars and the Making of a Fin de Siècle* (Chicago: University of Chicago Press, 1997), 67–68; and Siep Stuurman, *François Poulain de la Barre and the Invention of Modern Equality* (Cambridge, MA: Harvard University Press, 2004).

2. Anne-Marie Lecoq, ed., *La Querelle des Anciens et des Modernes* (Paris: Gallimard, 2001), 273.

3. On Modern religious intolerance, see Larry F. Norman, *The Shock of the Ancient* (forthcoming), pt. 2.

4. Voltaire, *Discours de l'empereur Julien contre les chrétiens*, esp. the opening section, "Portrait de l'empereur Julien" [VOLTAIRE]; and his *Traité sur la tolérance*, chap. 4. His discussion of English tolerance can be found in the opening letters of the *Lettres philosophiques*. As I note below, antiquity plays an equally important role for English Deists.

5. Michael Hickson, "The Message of Bayle's Last Title: Providence and Toleration in the 'Entretiens de Maxime et de Thémiste,'" *Journal of the History of Ideas* (forthcoming).

6. On this topic as well, see Norman, *Shock of the Ancient*. For a sample of this discourse, see Charles Perrault, *Siècle de Louis le Grand*, in *Querelle des Anciens et des Modernes*, ed. Lecoq, 260–62.

7. Lecoq, *Querelle des Anciens et des Modernes*, 296–97; and the discussion in DeJean, *Ancients against Moderns*, 125–26.

8. Norman, *Shock of the Ancient*, pt. 2.

9. This account is discussed and largely disputed in S. J. Barnett, *The Enlightenment and Religion: The Myths of Modernity* (Manchester: Manchester University Press, 2003). See also C. J. Betts, *Early Deism in France: From the So-called "Déistes" of Lyon (1564) to Voltaire's "Lettres philosophiques" (1734)* (The Hague: Martinus Nijhoff, 1984); and

James A. Herrick, *The Radical Rhetoric of the English Deists: The Discourse of Skepticism, 1680–1750* (Columbia: University of South Carolina Press, 1997).

10. See the classic works by René Pintard, *Le libertinage érudit dans la première moitié du XVIIᵉ siècle* (Paris: Boivin, 1943), and Richard Popkin, *The History of Scepticism: From Savonarola to Bayle* (1960; Oxford: Oxford University Press, 2003).

11. Alain Niderst, *Fontenelle à la recherche de lui-même (1657–1702)* (Paris: Nizet, 1972), conclusion.

12. See esp. Pintard, *Libertinage érudit*; Peter Gay, *Rise of Modern Paganism*, vol. 1 of *The Enlightenment: An Interpretation* (New York: Knopf, 1966); Alan Charles Kors, *Atheism in France, 1650–1729* (Princeton, NJ: Princeton University Press, 1990); and Michael Hunter and David Wootton, eds., *Atheism from the Reformation to the Enlightenment* (Oxford: Oxford University Press, 1992).

13. On the University of Padua and Pomponazzi's unorthodox interpretation of Aristotle, see Pintard, *Libertinage érudit*; Ira Wade, *The Intellectual Origins of the French Enlightenment* (Princeton, NJ: Princeton University Press, 1971); and Nicholas Davidson, "Unbelief and Atheism in Italy, 1500–1700," in *Atheism*, ed. Hunter and Wootton, 55–86.

14. On Bruno, see esp. Frances Yates, *Giordano Bruno and the Hermetic Tradition* (Florence, KY: Routledge, 1964). On Sarpi, see David Wootton, *Paolo Sarpi: Between Renaissance and Enlightenment* (Cambridge: Cambridge University Press, 1983).

15. Jonathan Israel, *Radical Enlightenment: Philosophy and the Making of Modernity, 1650–1750* (Oxford: Oxford University Press, 2002), 15. Curiously, Israel does not refer to Pintard's study. Margaret Jacob, on the other hand, has stressed the continuity between early and late-seventeenth-century freethinkers, pointing, for instance, to the influence of Giordano Bruno on John Toland; Margaret Jacob, *The Radical Enlightenment: Pantheists, Freemasons, and Republicans* (London: George Allen, 1981), 35–39.

16. Nicolas Fréret, *Réflexion générale sur l'étude des anciennes histoires* (Paris, 1724), 7–8. Dubos had similarly opposed earlier attempts to build a "general system of physics" with the Baconian emphasis on empirical inquiry; Jean-Baptiste Dubos, *Réflexions critiques sur la poésie et la peinture*, 2 vols. (Paris: Mariette, 1719), 2:323 (2:343 in 1733 ed.). On the success of this opposition during the Enlightenment, see above.

17. Simone Mazauric notes that "a certain methodological skepti-

cism, metaphysically grounded in a dogmatic refusal of systems," underpinned the epistemological outlook of the Académie des sciences and the editorial policy of the *Histoire de l'Académie royale des sciences*; Simone Mazauric, *Fontenelle et l'invention de l'histoire des sciences à l'aube des Lumières* (Paris: Fayard, 2007), 105. J. B. Shank discusses the French Jesuits' marked preference for empiricism over rationalism in *The Newton Wars and the Beginning of the French Enlightenment* (Chicago: University of Chicago Press, 2008), 198.

18. Antoine Lilti, "Comment écrit-on l'histoire intellectuelle des Lumières? Spinozisme, radicalisme, et philosophie," *Annales HSS* 64 (2009): 171–206.

19. Alan Charles Kors, *D'Holbach's Coterie: An Enlightenment in Paris* (Princeton, NJ: Princeton University Press, 1976), chaps. 2–3. According to Kors, only three members of the *coterie* proper can accurately be classified as atheists—Diderot, d'Holbach, Naigeon—and "the latter two, and they alone, correspond to the traditional stereotype of the proselytizing atheists" (49).

20. Roy Porter, *The Creation of the Modern World: The Untold Story of the British Enlightenment* (New York: Norton, 2001), chap. 5; and Kors, *Atheism in France.*

21. Roger Pearson, *Voltaire Almighty: A Life in Pursuit of Freedom* (London: Bloomsbury, 2005), 31, 132. For the quotation, see René Pomeau, *La religion de Voltaire* (Paris: Nizet, 1969), 40. As other students of Voltaire's professor (the père Porée) at the Collège Louis-le-Grand, Pomeau lists the d'Argenson brothers, the duc de Richelieu, Helvétius, Malesherbes, the duc de Choiseul, the chancellor Maupéou, Daniel-Charles Trudaine, and Diderot. The duc de Nivernais, Gresset, and Turgot also attended this same *collège*. Fontenelle was educated by the Jesuits at Rouen.

22. Robert Palmer, *Catholics and Unbelievers in Eighteenth-Century France* (Princeton, NJ: Princeton University Press, 1939), chaps. 2 and 9. More recently, see Catherine Northeast, *The Parisian Jesuits and the Enlightenment, 1700–1762,* Studies on Voltaire and the Eighteenth Century, vol. 288 (Oxford: Voltaire Foundation, 1991).

23. Palmer, *Catholics and Unbelievers,* 31.

24. Jean Porter, *Nature as Reason: A Thomistic Theory of the Natural Law* (Grand Rapids, MI: Wm. B. Eerdmans Publishing, 2005), 385.

25. David A. Bell, *The Cult of the Nation in France: Inventing Nationalism, 1680–1800* (Cambridge, MA: Harvard University Press, 2001).

26. Yves Citton, *L'envers de la liberté: L'invention d'un imaginaire spinoziste dans la France des Lumières* (Paris: Amsterdam, 2006).

27. "Le sistême de Spinosa, et de quelques autres athées, dont je t'ai fait voir la fausseté et l'horreur"; marquis Boyer d'Argens, *Lettres juives* (The Hague: P. Paupie, 1738), 292 [ARTFL].

28. Frank Manuel, *The Eighteenth Century Confronts the Gods* (Cambridge, MA: Harvard University Press, 1959).

29. See esp. Porter, *Creation of the Modern World*, 96–129. Jonathan Sheehan has reminded us that many Enlightenment thinkers in fact remained fascinated with religious thought and sought to resituate it on more credible grounds; see his "Enlightenment, Religion, and the Enigma of Secularization: A Review Essay," *American Historical Review* 108, no. 4 (2003): 1061–80; and, more recently, *The Enlightenment Bible: Translation, Scholarship, Culture* (Princeton, NJ: Princeton University Press, 2005).

30. John Toland, *Letters to Serena* (London, 1704) [ECCO], 130 (emphasis added).

31. Voltaire, *Dictionnaire philosophique*, s.v. "Théiste" (emphasis added). See also *Essai sur les mœurs et l'esprit des nations*, ed. René Pomeau (Paris: Bordas, 1990), on "le culte pur d'un Etre suprême dégagé de toute superstition et de tout fanatisme" that "les premiers brachmanes avaient fondé." Voltaire adds: "Il est si naturel de croire un Dieu unique, de l'adorer, et de sentir dans le fond de son cœur qu'il faut être juste" (237).

32. Voltaire, *Epitre à l'auteur du livre des trois imposteurs*, in *Œuvres complètes de Voltaire*, ed. Louis Moland (Paris: Garnier, 1877–85), vol. 10 [VOLTAIRE].

CHAPTER NINE

1. Denis Diderot, *Lettre sur les aveugles* (1749; Geneva: Droz, 1963), 13 [ARTFL]; Voltaire, *Dictionnaire philosophique*, s.v. "Catéchisme du curé"; and Jean-Jacques Rousseau, *Rousseau juge de Jean-Jacques* (1776; Paris: Armand Colin, 1962), third dialogue, 275 [ARTFL].

2. Charles Bonnet, *La palingénésie philosophique* (Geneva: Philibert and Chirol, 1769), 194 [ARTFL].

3. Antoine-Léonard Thomas, *Essai sur les éloges* (1773), in *Œuvres complètes*, vol. 3 (Paris: Desessarts, 1802), 116 [ARTFL]. Friedrich Melchior Grimm offered a nearly identical assessment in 1757; see Leonard M. Marsak, *Bernard de Fontenelle: The Idea of Science in the French Enlight-*

enment (Philadelphia: Transactions of the American Philosophical Society, 1959), 6.

4. Jean-Baptiste Dubos, *Réflexions critiques sur la poésie et la peinture*, 2 vols. (Paris: Mariette, 1719), 2:446 (2:478 in 1733 ed.). Elsewhere, Dubos adds a more empirical twist to this definition, stating that "L'Esprit Philosophique . . . n'est autre chose que la raison fortifiée par la réflexion & par l'expérience" (2:470 [2:504 in 1733 ed.]).

5. César Dumarsais, *Le philosophe*, in anon., *Nouvelles libertés de penser* (Amsterdam: Piget, 1743), 184–85 [GALLICA].

6. Nicolas Fréret, *Réflexion générale sur l'étude des anciennes histoires* (Paris, 1724), 10–11.

7. *Encyclopédie*, s.v. "Gens de lettres," 7:599.

8. The term "*esprit philosophique*" is used to define a positive aesthetic quality in the articles "Fiction," "Grammarien," and "Philosophique, esprit" (where it is described as "the rule of truth and beauty" by Jaucourt), but a negative one in the "Discours préliminaire des éditeurs" and the article "Minotaure." It designates rational, systematic inquiry in the "Eloge de M. du Marsais," as well as in the articles "Goût," "Logomachie," and "Philosophie" (where it is opposed, interestingly, to the "systematic spirit [*esprit systématique*]," i.e., the precise expression that d'Alembert had championed in the "Discours préliminaire"), and it designates empirical observation in "Observation" (some articles, such as "Goût" and "Philosophie" in fact use it in both senses). Finally, it designates an antisuperstitious attitude in the articles "Fondation," "Hongrie," "Jésuite," "Richesse," and "Subside." Other eighteenth-century texts employ the expression in yet different senses: for the marquis de Chastellux, the term is synonymous with "whoever, concerning himself with politics and morality, keeps human happiness in mind"; see François-Jean de Chastellux, *De la félicité publique*, 2 vols. (1772; Paris: A.-A. Renouard, 1822), 2:86 [GALLICA]. This passage is quoted in Alan Charles Kors, *D'Holbach's Coterie: An Enlightenment in Paris* (Princeton, NJ: Princeton University Press, 1976), 132.

9. Two authors who do discuss the "*esprit philosophique*" are Gustave Lanson, *Origines et premières manifestations de l'esprit philosophique dans la littérature française de 1675 à 1748* (1908–10; New York: B. Franklin, 1973); and Ira Wade, *Structure and Form of the French Enlightenment*, vol. 1 (Princeton, NJ: Princeton University Press, 1977); yet neither provides a history of the term or examines it at all "philologically." On *Begriffsgeschichte* studies of the Enlightenment, see the introduction.

10. "From mid-century—at the very moment at which the Enlightenment project seemed to be gaining intellectual hegemony—key terms such as 'reason,' 'nature,' 'civilization,' and, indeed, 'enlightenment' (*'lumières'*) were vigorously contested. And as the century wore on, there was a growing sense of the fragility of the optimism prevalent at the *Encyclopédie* moment." Jones goes on to note later how "the field of reason . . . began to fragment and fissure along a number of divergent tracks. Politics felt different after mid-century because of the growing influence of men of letters and writers who subscribed to the light of reason. But that influence was thrown behind a wide range of scenarios and strategies and pointed in no single direction." Colin Jones, *The Great Nation: France from Louis XV to Napoleon* (London: Penguin, 2002), 212, 223.

11. Robert Darnton, *The Forbidden Best-Sellers of Pre-Revolutionary France* (New York: Norton, 1996), esp. chap. 2.

12. Charles Duclos, *Considérations sur les mœurs de ce siècle* (Amsterdam: Aux dépens de la Compagnie, 1751), 17 [ARTFL].

13. The expression "floating signifier" was coined by Claude Lévi-Strauss in his *Introduction to the Work of Marcel Mauss*, trans. Felicity Baker (1950; London: Routledge, 1987), 63. Lévi-Strauss's prime example of a floating signifier was the Polynesian concept of *mana*, a sacred force that could exist in a variety of disparate objects.

14. Dan Edelstein, ed., *The Super-Enlightenment: Daring to Know Too Much*, Studies on Voltaire and the Eighteenth Century, vol. 2010:01 (Oxford: Voltaire Foundation, 2010).

15. Darrin McMahon, *Enemies of the Enlightenment: The French Counter-Enlightenment and the Making of Modernity* (New York: Oxford University Press, 2001).

16. "I discuss in brief the mind, common sense, / Passions, laws, and governments; / Virtue, morals, climates, customs, / Policed and savage peoples; / Apparent disorder and universal order, / Ideal and real happiness. / I carefully study the first principles of things, / The secret chain of cause and effect." Charles Palissot, *Les philosophes* (Paris: Duchesne, 1760), I, V; 26–27.

17. Ibid., II, V; 52.

18. Robert Gildea, *Children of the Revolution: The French, 1799–1914* (London: Allen Lane, 2008).

19. Daniel Brewer, *The Enlightenment Past: Reconstructing Eighteenth-

Century French Thought (Cambridge: Cambridge University Press, 2008), 2, 203, in reference to Hartog's *Régimes d'historicité*.

20. Jean Le Rond d'Alembert, *Essai sur les éléments de philosophie* (1759; Paris: Fayard, 1986), 3 [CORPUS].

21. Duclos, *Considérations sur les mœurs*, 34.

22. Abbé Sieyès, *Qu'est-ce que le Tiers Etat?* ed. Edme Champion (1789; Paris: Société de l'Histoire de la Révolution Française, 1888), 54 [ARTFL].

23. Brewer, *Enlightenment Past*, 78. Michel Foucault made a similar point in his essay "What Is Enlightenment?" in *The Foucault Reader*, ed. Paul Rabinow (New York: Pantheon, 1984), 32–50.

24. Margaret Jacob, *Living the Enlightenment: Freemasonry and Politics in Eighteenth-Century Europe* (Oxford: Oxford University Press, 1991), 146 and passim.

25. Condorcet, *Esquisse d'un tableau . . .* (1794; Paris: Boivin, 1933), 204 [ARTFL]. For another typical expression of this sentiment, see Baron d'Holbach, *Système de la nature, ou, des loix du monde physique et du monde moral* (London, 1771), 426 (2.13) [ARTFL]: "le tems, aidé des lumières progressives des siècles, peut un jour éclairer ces princes mêmes que nous voyons si déchaînés contre la vérité, si ennemis de la justice et de la liberté des hommes."

26. Immanuel Kant, "An Answer to the Question: 'What Is Enlightenment?'" in *Political Writings*, trans. and ed. Hugh Barr Nisbet and Hans Reiss (Cambridge: Cambridge University Press, 1970), 58.

27. See, among others, Ernst Cassirer, *Philosophy of the Enlightenment*, trans. James P. Pettegrove and Fritz C. A. Koelin (1932; Princeton, NJ: Princeton University Press, 1968), 9; and James Swenson, "Critique, Progress, Autonomy," *Studies in Eighteenth-Century Culture* 36, no. 1 (2007): 1–11. Kors discusses the grimmer views held by certain *philosophes*—including, in fact, Grimm himself—in *D'Holbach's Coterie*, 139–46.

28. D'Alembert, *Essai sur les éléments de philosophie*, 6.

29. Bernard Le Bovier de Fontenelle, *Digression sur les Anciens et les Modernes* (1688), in *La Querelle des Anciens et des Modernes*, ed. Anne-Marie Lecoq (Paris: Gallimard, 2001), 305. See also Fréret's observation that the *esprit philosophique* (defined in this instance as "true criticism") "renders intelligible what the great men who lived before us said and thought [and] thus enables philosophers to extend the breadth of

their minds, by adding to their own knowledge what the ancients had learned"; *Réflexion générale*, 11. See also Dubos on how "the knowledge [*lumières*] resulting from the preceding inventions, having been developed independently, began to combine"; *Réflexions critiques*, 2:439 (2:471 in 1733 ed.). On Perrault, see below.

30. I discuss the notion of a return to nature during the French Revolution in *The Terror of Natural Right: Republicanism, the Cult of Nature, and the French Revolution* (Chicago: University of Chicago Press, 2009). More generally, this account of the Enlightenment further confirms Reinhart Koselleck's hypothesis that a radical change in historical consciousness occurred at the turn of the eighteenth century; see his "Modernity and the Planes of Historicity," in *Futures Past: On the Semantics of Historical Time*, trans. Keith Tribe (1979; New York: Columbia University Press, 2004), 9–25; see also Hannah Arendt, *Between Past and Future* (London: Faber and Faber, 1961).

CHAPTER TEN

1. The quotations are from d'Alembert's "Tableau de l'esprit humain au milieu du dix-huitième siècle," which constitutes the opening chapter of his *Essai sur les éléments de philosophie* (1759; Paris: Fayard, 1986), 2–9 [CORPUS]. Ernst Cassirer discusses this work in his *Philosophy of Enlightenment*, trans. James P. Pettegrove and Fritz C. A. Koelin (1932; Princeton, NJ: Princeton University Press, 1968), 4. D'Alembert's history in the "Tableau" essentially recapitulates the intellectual history outlined in his earlier "Discours préliminaire des éditeurs" to the *Encyclopédie*; similar accounts can be found in the first chapter of Voltaire's *Siècle de Louis XIV*, the beginning of Rousseau's first *Discourse*, Turgot's *Philosophical Review of the Successive Advances of the Human Mind*, Chastellux's *De la félicité publique*, and Condorcet's *Esquisse d'un tableau historique des progrès de l'esprit humain*, among numerous other works. See also Jean Dagen, *L'histoire de l'esprit humain dans la pensée française de Fontenelle à Condorcet* (Paris: Klincksieck, 1977).

2. Hilaire-Bernard de Longepierre, *Discours sur les Anciens* (1687), in *La Querelle des Anciens et des Modernes*, ed. Anne-Marie Lecoq (Paris: Gallimard, 2001), 284. It is unclear when exactly this narrative was established. Nancy Bisaha claimed that "as many [Greek] scholars arrived in Italy fleeing the Turkish advance, the connection was readily apparent [at the time]" between the fall of Constantinople and the revival of Greek learning, but she does not provide any documentary evidence that

this connection was actually made; she herself demonstrates how the initial reactions were more focused on recovering Constantinople from the "barbarians"; see her *Creating East and West: Renaissance Humanists and the Ottoman Turks* (Philadelphia: University of Pennsylvania Press, 2006), 108. In a much earlier study, Wallace F. Ferguson argued that in fact "it was only at a much later time [after 1490] that the Greek revival was dated from the fall of Constantinople"; see his *The Renaissance in Historical Thought: Five Centuries of Interpretation* (Boston: Houghton Mifflin, 1948), 24. Ferguson points to Théodore de Bèze as one of the first authors to explicitly link these two events (57), yet Bèze only refers in passing to the presence in Florence of "certains grands personnages fugitifs de Grèce," and not to the fall of Constantinople per se; see Théodore de Bèze, *Histoire ecclésiastique des églises réformées au royaume de France*, ed. T.-A. Marzials (1580; Lille: Leleux, 1841), 2 [GALLICA]. It does seem probable, however, that this narrative was of Protestant origin: in a 1524 exhortation "To the Councilmen of All Cities in Germany That They Establish and Maintain Christian Schools," Luther wrote, "Formerly no one knew why God had the [Greek and Latin] languages revived, but now for the first time we see that it was done for the sake of the gospel, which he intended to bring to light and use in exposing and destroying the kingdom of Antichrist. To this end he gave over Greece to the Turk in order that the Greeks, driven out and scattered, might disseminate their language and provide an incentive to the study of other languages as well"; *Selected Writings of Martin Luther*, ed. and trans. Theodore G. Tappert, 4 vols. (Minneapolis, MN: Fortress Press, 1967), 2:51. This text is discussed in Bard Thompson, *Humanists and Reformers: A History of the Renaissance and Reformation* (Cambridge: Wm. B. Eerdmans, 1996), 373. Ferguson also suggests that this "Northern protestant" narrative became firmly established with Pierre Bayle, who indeed wrote that "la plupart des Beaux-Esprits, & des savans Humanistes, qui brillèrent en Italie, lors que les Belles-Lettres commencèrent à renaitre, après la prise de Constantinople, n'avoient guere de Religion," in *Dictionnaire historique et critique*, s.v. "Takiddin," 315 [ARTFL]. Bayle's explicit source, however, is an earlier text by the abbé Jacques de Clavigny de Sainte Honorine, *Le discernement et l'usage que le prince doit faire des livres suspects* (Paris, 1672). The earliest French version of this narrative that I was able to locate can be found in Gabriel Naudé, who spoke in 1625 of "la derniere prise de Constantinople, apres lequel tout le monde a commencé de changer de face, le ciel à rouler sur des nouvelles hypotheses . . . et les sciences à *reprendre* leur premier lustre . . . en Italie par Hermolaus, Politian, Picus, et tous les [g]recs qui s'y estoient refugiez de Constantinople"; *Apologie pour tous les grand hommes qui ont esté accusez de magie* (Paris: Eschart, 1669), 82–83 (emphasis added) [ARTFL]. Special thanks to Paula Findlen and Giovanna Ceserani for helping me research this question.

3. See, e.g., Rabelais's description of the "clarity [*la lumière*] and dignity that were restored in my age [*mon âge*] to Letters"; *Pantagruel,* ed. Abel Lefranc (Paris: Champion, 1931), 102 [ARTFL].

4. Voltaire, *Siècle de Louis XIV,* chap. 1 [VOLTAIRE]; d'Alembert, "Discours préliminaire des éditeurs," *Encyclopédie;* and Condorcet, *Esquisse d'un tableau historique des progrès de l'esprit humain,* seventh and eighth epochs. Ferguson discusses the Enlightenment conception of the Renaissance in *Renaissance in Historical Thought,* 78–112. Fontenelle had similarly incorporated an ancient narrative into his history of the French Académie des sciences: "When after a long period of barbarism, the sciences and arts were slowly reborn [*commencèrenet à renaître*] in Europe, eloquence, poetry, painting, and architecture first emerged from the darkness [*ténèbres*]; and during the last [e.g., sixteenth] century, they shone forth again. But the sciences requiring greater meditation, such as mathematics and physics, returned to the world only much later. . . . It is only to the current century that we can date the renewal of mathematics and physics"; preface to the *Histoire de l'Académie des sciences depuis 1666 jusqu'en 1699* (Paris: Fayard, 1989) [CORPUS], 1. This text is discussed in Simone Mazauric, *Fontenelle et l'invention de l'histoire des sciences à l'aube des Lumières* (Paris: Fayard, 2007), 221.

5. On the reciprocity between the narratives of the Ancients and the Moderns, see Larry F. Norman, *The Shock of the Ancient* (forthcoming).

6. Charles Perrault, *Siècle de Louis le Grand,* in *La Querelle des Anciens et des Modernes,* ed. Anne-Marie Lecoq (Paris: Gallimard, 2001), 259 (emphasis added).

7. Ibid., 272. Fontenelle had already asked, "do we not find both wise and ignorant centuries?" in his 1683 *Nouveaux dialogues des morts;* quoted in Marc Fumaroli, "Les abeilles et les araignées," in *Querelle des Anciens et des Modernes,* ed. Lecoq, 190.

8. Voltaire, *Siècle de Louis XIV,* chap. 1.

9. "L'étude des *Sciences* doit tirer beaucoup de lumières de la lecture des anciens"; *Encyclopédie,* s.v. "Erudition," 5:918 (emphasis added). The following quotations are from the same source.

10. Steven Shapin, *The Scientific Revolution* (Chicago: University of Chicago Press, 1996), 68–69.

11. On the medieval history of this trope, see Ernst Robert Curtius, *European Literature and the Latin Middle Ages*, trans. Willard Ropes Trask (1952; Princeton, NJ: Princeton University Press, 1990), 29, 384–85; and Margaret Hogden, *Early Anthropology in the Sixteenth and Seventeenth Centuries* (Philadelphia: University of Pennsylvania Press, 1964), 462.

12. Jean-Sylvain Bailly, *Histoire de l'astronomie ancienne, depuis son origine jusqu'à l'établissement de l'école d'Alexandrie* (Paris: Debure, 1775), 3.

13. Ibid.

14. Voltaire, *Essai sur les mœurs et l'esprit des nations*, ed. René Pomeau (Paris: Bordas, 1990), 197. Voltaire repeated a similar assertion in a letter to Bailly: "je suis convaincu que tout nous vient des bords du Gange, astronomie, astrologie, métempsycose, &c"; *Lettres sur l'origine des sciences et sur celle des peuples d'Asie: adressées à M. de Voltaire par M. Bailly & précédées de quelques lettres de M. de Voltaire à l'Auteur* (Paris: Debure, 1777), 4. On Voltaire's "Orientalism," see esp. Raymond Schwab, *La renaissance orientale* (Paris: Payot, 1950); and, more recently, Dorothy Figueira, *Aryans, Jews, Brahims: Theorizing Authority through Myths of Identity* (Albany: State University of New York Press, 2002). For a slightly earlier period, see Nicolas Dew, *Orientalism in Louis XIV's France* (Oxford: Oxford University Press, 2009).

15. On cultural diffusionism, see notably Marvin Harris, *The Rise of Anthropological Theory: A History of Theories of Culture* (New York: Crowell, 1968), 373–92. On the Egyptian version of this story, see notably Erik Iversen, *The Myth of Egypt and Its Hieroglyphs in the European Tradition* (Copenhagen: Gec Gad, 1961), 99–123; Margaret Jacob, *Living the Enlightenment: Freemasonry and Politics in Eighteenth-Century Europe* (Oxford: Oxford University Press, 1991); Chantal Grell, ed., *L'Egypte imaginaire de la Renaissance à Champollion* (Paris: Presses de l'Université de Paris-Sorbonne, 2001); and Brian Curran, *The Egyptian Renaissance: The Afterlife of Ancient Egypt in Early Modern Italy* (Chicago: University of Chicago Press, 2007). I discuss the place of Egypt in Enlightenment France in "The Egyptian French Revolution: Antiquarianism, Freemasonry, and the Mythology of Nature," in *The Super-Enlightenment: Daring to Know Too Much*, ed. Dan Edelstein, Studies on Voltaire and the Eighteenth Century, vol. 2010:01 (Oxford: Voltaire Foundation, 2010).

16. *Encyclopédie*, s.v. "Egypte," 5:434. Eleven years later (in 1766), when the entry on "Inde" appeared, the author expressed greater reservations: "Les Sciences étoient peut-être plus anciennes dans l'*Inde* que dans l'Egypte" (8:661).

17. Bailly, *Lettres sur l'origine des sciences*, 207. The notion of a highly civilized primitive world owed a great deal to Masonic-inspired literature on the special status of ancient Egypt: the chevalier Ramsay, for instance, describes how the first Egyptians "avoient plusieurs connoissances traditionnelles que nous avons perdues . . . tout ce qui est du ressort de l'imagination, ne sont que des jeux d'esprit en comparaison des hautes sciences, connues des premiers hommes"; Andrew Michael Ramsay, *Les voyages de Cyrus* (Paris: G. F. Quillau, 1727), 185.

18. Antoine Court de Gébelin, *Monde primitif considéré dans son génie allégorique et dans les allégories auxquelles conduisit ce génie . . .* , 9 vols. (Paris: n.p., 1773–81). On this work, see esp. Anne-Marie Mercier-Faivre, *Un supplément à l'"Encyclopédie": Le "Monde primitif" d'Antoine Court de Gébelin* (Paris: Champion, 1999). I discuss Court's "ancient and eternal order" in *The Terror of Natural Right: Republicanism, the Cult of Nature, and the French Revolution* (Chicago: University of Chicago Press, 2009). These examples confirm David Bell's observation that "new constructions" in eighteenth-century French thought "tend to be presented as acts of reconstruction, recovery, and regeneration"; *The Cult of the Nation in France: Inventing Nationalism, 1680–1800* (Cambridge, MA: Harvard University Press, 2001), 5.

CHAPTER ELEVEN

1. Larry Stewart, *The Rise of Public Science: Rhetoric, Technology, and Natural Philosophy in Newtonian Britain, 1600–1750* (Cambridge: Cambridge University Press, 1993); and G. L'E. Turner, "Eighteenth-Century Scientific Instruments and Their Makers," in *The Cambridge History of Science*, ed. Roy Porter (Cambridge: Cambridge University Press, 2003), 511–35. John Keill delivered public lectures at Oxford between 1700 and 1709; his successor, John Desaguilers, continued the practice in London.

2. "A philosophical spirit has been spreading for some time, a light that did not illuminate our ancestors"; Fontenelle, *Réponse à l'évêque de Luçon* (1732), 8 [CORPUS]. This text is in fact an *éloge* for Houdar de la Motte, who had died the previous year. See also Diderot's 1750 Prospectus for the *Encyclopédie* on "the general clarity [*lumières*] that has been

spreading in our society, and the kernel of science that unnoticeably leads minds toward greater knowledge" [ARTFL].

3. The quotation begins, "I shall be ambitious to have it said of me, that I have brought Philosophy out of the closets and libraries"; *Spectator* 10 (March 12, 1711). Addison is quoted by Martin Fitzpatrick in his introduction to *Enlightenment World*, ed. Martin Fitzpatrick, Peter Jones, Christa Knellwolf, and Iain McCalman (New York: Routledge, 2004), 83 (emphasis added).

4. Montesquieu, *Persian Letters*, trans. Margaret Mauldon (Oxford: Oxford University Press, 2008), 86, letter 64 (letter 66 in standard French editions). I return to the fashionableness of philosophy in the last chapter.

5. Jean-Baptiste Dubos, *Réflexions critiques sur la poésie et la peinture*, 2 vols. (Paris: Mariette, 1719), 2:417 (2:448 in 1733 ed.).

6. Erica Harth, *Cartesian Women: Versions and Subversions of Rational Discourse in the Old Regime* (Ithaca, NY: Cornell University Press, 1992), 64.

7. Bernard Le Bovier de Fontenelle, *Entretiens sur la pluralité des mondes* (Paris: M. Guerout, 1687), 2 [ARTFL].

8. Gabriel Daniel, *Voyage au monde de Descartes* (Paris: Vve S. Bernard, 1690), 285. Louis de Jaucourt would criticize this seventeenth-century fascination with the "new philosophy" in similar terms: "One can only conclude that in this nation [France] the love of sciences under Louis XIV was only a new fashion." See *Encyclopédie*, s.v. "Sciences," 14:789. For a less critical description of philosophical fashion, see the following comment in Simon Tyssot de Patot's 1710 novel: "Je fus d'autant plus excité à cela, que la philosophie et les mathématiques sembloient être devenuës à la mode: tout ce qu'il y avoit d'honnêtes gens s'y apliquoient, de quelqu'âge et condition qu'ils fussent"; *Voyages et avantures de Jaques Massé* (L'Utopie: Chez Jacques l'Aveugle, 1760), 12 [ARTFL]. See also, in a different context, Anne Kraatz, *Mode et philosophie ou le néoplatonisme en silhouette, 1470–1500* (Paris: Les Belles Lettres, 2005).

9. François Azouvi, *Descartes et la France: Histoire d'une passion nationale* (Paris: Fayard, 2002).

10. Antoine Lilti, *Le monde des salons: Sociabilité et mondanité à Paris au XVIIIᵉ siècle* (Paris: Fayard, 2005), 260–72 (quotation on 261). On public experimentation in France, see J. B. Shank, *The Newton Wars and the Beginning of the French Enlightenment* (Chicago: University of Chicago Press, 2008), 155.

11. The marquis de Vauvenargues is quoted in Charles Augustin Sainte-Beuve, ed., *Les moralistes français* (Paris: Garnier Frères, n.d.), 663, §219 [GALLICA]. See also the posthumous maxim "Philosophy is an old fashion [*une vieille mode*] that some people still put on, just as others wear red stockings, to stick it to the public"; Vauvenargues, *Réflexions et maximes* (1747), in *Œuvres*, ed. D. L. Gilbert (Paris: Furne, 1857), 446, §492 [ARTFL].

12. The *Encyclopédie* quotation is from d'Alembert, "Discours préliminaire des éditeurs," 1:xxxi. Colin Jones drew attention to how commercial efforts in the eighteenth century employed the vocabulary and imagery of Enlightenment in "The Great Chain of Buying: Medical Advertisement, the Bourgeois Public Sphere, and the Origins of the French Revolution," *American Historical Review* 101 (1996): 13–40 (esp. 24–25). As Joan DeJean noted, it was during Louis XIV's reign that the modern concept of fashion emerged; *The Essence of Style: How the French Invented High Fashion, Fine Food, Chic Cafés, Style, Sophistication, and Glamour* (New York: Free Press, 2005).

13. Dubos praises the Royal Society and the Académie des sciences as "the two most illustrious philosophical societies [*compagnies de Philosophes*] that exist in Europe"; *Réflexions critiques*, 2:323 (2:343 in 1733 ed.). Fréret offers a similar assessment in his *Réflexion générale sur l'étude des anciennes histoires* (Paris, 1724), 7. Charles Perrault had already celebrated "the establishment of the Academies of France and England" as an unsurpassed modern achievement in his *Parallèle des Anciens et des Modernes en ce qui regarde les arts et les sciences* (1688–97), ed. Hans Robert Jauss (Munich: Eidos Verlag, 1964), preface, 97. Voltaire would also point to the creation of the academies as a crucial step in the cultivation of French glory under Louis XIV; *Siècle de Louis XIV*, chap. 1 [VOLTAIRE].

14. H. F. Cohen, *The Scientific Revolution: A Historiographical Inquiry* (Chicago: University of Chicago Press, 1994); and more specifically Roger Hahn, *The Anatomy of a Scientific Institution: The Paris Academy of Sciences, 1666–1803* (Berkeley and Los Angeles: University of California Press, 1971). As Margaret Jacob observed, the Académie des sciences was chiefly preoccupied with the study of alchemy until 1685 and became a "modern" scientific body only around 1699; see her *Strangers Nowhere in the World: The Rise of Cosmopolitanism in Early Modern Europe* (Philadelphia: University of Pennsylvania Press, 2006), 57–63.

15. Marc Fumaroli, "Les abeilles et les araignées," in *La Querelle des Anciens et des Modernes*, ed. Anne-Marie Lecoq (Paris: Gallimard, 2001), 198–200; Daniel Roche, *France in the Enlightenment*, trans. Arthur Goldhammer (Cambridge, MA: Harvard University Press, 1998), 665; and, for an earlier study, Lucien Brunel, *Les philosophes et l'Académie française au dix-huitième siècle* (1884; Geneva: Slatkine, 1967).

16. Martin Fitzpatrick, "The Age of Louis XIV and Early Enlightenment in France," in *Enlightenment World*, ed. Fitzpatrick et al., 134–55. On secrecy in the Académie des sciences, see Jacob, *Strangers Nowhere in the World*, chap. 2. As Peter Burke reminds us, the Royal Society, despite its name, was not patronized by the king, unlike its French correspondent; *The Fabrication of Louis XIV* (New Haven, CT: Yale University Press, 1992), 53.

17. *Encyclopédie*, s.v. "Fondation" (Anne-Robert-Jacques Turgot), 7:75.

18. Diderot writes, "If the government were involved in such a project, it would never be completed. The government should only seek to facilitate its completion [*favoriser l'exécution*]"; *Encyclopédie*, s.v. "Encyclopédie," 5:636.

19. See esp. John Marshall, *John Locke, Toleration, and Early Enlightenment Culture: Religious Intolerance and Arguments for Religious Toleration in Early Modern and "Early Enlightenment" Europe* (Cambridge: Cambridge University Press, 2006), chap. 20. See also John Pocock, *Enlightenments of Edward Gibbon*, vol. 1 of *Barbarism and Religion* (Cambridge: Cambridge University Press, 1999), 85–86.

20. Marshall, *John Locke, Toleration, and Early Enlightenment Culture*, esp. 501–22 (quotation on 518). As Anthony Grafton recently commented, the geography of the Republic of Letters was mostly imaginary: "it had no borders, no government, no capital"; "A Sketch Map of a Lost Continent: The Republic of Letters," *Republics of Letters* 1 (2009), http://rofl.stanford.edu/node/34.

21. Stéphane Van Damme, *Paris, capitale philosophique: De la Fronde à la Révolution* (Paris: Odile Jacob, 2005).

22. The portrait of the scholar is drawn from the image described by Marshall in *John Locke, Toleration, and Early Enlightenment Culture*, 511–14, found in Jean Le Clerc's *Bibliothèque universelle et historique* (Amsterdam, 1686–93). This ideal portrait of the *philosophe* is a composite of, respectively, Van Loo's portrait of Diderot, the frontispiece of

Raynal's *Histoire philosophique et politique* (3rd ed.), and Houdon's statue of Voltaire, now in Saint Petersburg.

23. Peter N. Miller, *Peiresc's Europe: Learning and Virtue in the Seventeenth Century* (New Haven, CT: Yale University Press, 2000), 101. See also Grafton, "Sketch Map of a Lost Continent"; and Deborah Harkness, *The Jewel House: Elizabethan London and the Scientific Revolution* (New Haven, CT: Yale University Press, 2007), 28–31.

24. Jacob Soll, *The Information Master: Jean-Baptiste Colbert's Secret State Intelligence System* (Ann Arbor: University of Michigan Press, 2009).

25. Pocock, *Enlightenments of Edward Gibbon*, 86.

26. See, e.g., Guez de Balzac's comment about "nostre incomparable Saumaise, qui se joüe des gryphes et des enigmes; qui ne trouva jamais de lieu difficile, en quelque part de la republique des lettres qu'il ait mis le pied"; *Le barbon* (1648), in *Œuvres* (Paris: T. Jolly, 1665), 2:694 [ARTFL]. For a genealogy of this expression (in its Latin and vernacular forms), which became common in scholarly discourse in the early sixteenth century, see Hans Bots and Françoise Waquet, *La république des lettres* (Paris: Belin, 1997), 11–13. In eighteenth-century French, the expression was predominantly used simply to designate the intellectual world of books and authors, without any thought given to its political or ideological ramifications. Charles Duclos, for instance, defined the Republic of Letters in terms of three classes: scholars dedicated to erudite pursuits, scholars interested in science, and literary authors; *Considérations sur les mœurs de ce siècle* (Amsterdam: Aux dépens de la Compagnie, 1751), 246–48 [ARTFL].

27. Dena Goodman, *The Republic of Letters: A Cultural History of the French Enlightenment* (Ithaca, NY: Cornell University Press, 1994), 1.

28. Anne Goldgar, *Impolite Learning: Conduct and Community in the Republic of Letters, 1680–1750* (New Haven, CT: Yale University Press, 1995), 239. See also Antoine Lilti, "The Kingdom of Politesse: Salons and the Republic of Letters in Eighteenth-Century Paris," *Republics of Letters* 1 (2009), http://rofl.stanford.edu/node/38.

29. Montesquieu, *Persian Letters*, 221, supplementary letter 7 (letter 145 in standard French editions). I discuss Montesquieu's satires in more depth in "Humanism, *l'Esprit Philosophique*, and the Encyclopédie," *Republics of Letters* 1, no. 1 (May 1, 2009), http://rofl.stanford.edu/node/27.

30. *Encyclopédie*, s.v. "Encyclopédie," 5:644.

31. Lawrence Brockliss, *Calvet's Web: Enlightenment and the Republic of Letters in Eighteenth-Century France* (Oxford: Oxford University Press, 2002), 5–19, 396–411. See also April Shelford, *Transforming the Republic of Letters: Pierre-Daniel Huet and European Intellectual Life, 1650–1720* (Rochester, NY: University of Rochester Press, 2007).

CHAPTER TWELVE

1. Jean-Baptiste Dubos, *Réflexions critiques sur la poésie et la peinture*, 2 vols. (Paris: Mariette, 1719), 2:444 (2:477 in 1733 ed.).

2. L. W. B. Brockliss, *French Higher Education in the Seventeenth and Eighteenth Centuries: A Cultural History* (Oxford: Clarendon Press, 1987), 350–70; and, by the same author, "Science, the Universities, and Other Public Spaces: Teaching Science in Europe and the Americas," in *The Cambridge History of Science*, ed. Roy Porter (Cambridge: Cambridge University Press, 2003), 43–86. Newtonianism would begin to be taught in French universities only in the 1740s. Raymond Birn, in his study of royal censorship in France (discussed below), notes that the academies and universities constituted the two primary institutional affiliations of Malesherbes's censors; see his *La censure royale des livres dans la France des Lumières* (Paris: Odile Jacob, 2007), 105–6.

3. Alan Charles Kors, *D'Holbach's Coterie: An Enlightenment in Paris* (Princeton, NJ: Princeton University Press, 1976), 180–82.

4. Brockliss, *French Higher Education*, 454.

5. Notker Hammerstein, "Epilogue: The Enlightenment," in *Universities in Early Modern Europe (1500–1800)*, ed. Hilde de Ridder-Symoens, vol. 4 of *A History of the University in Europe* (Cambridge: Cambridge University Press, 1996), 621–38 (quotation on 631). See, by comparison, in the same volume, Roy Porter, "The Scientific Revolution and the Universities," 531–64.

6. Hammerstein, "Epilogue: The Enlightenment," 632.

7. *Encyclopédie*, s.v. "Collège," 3:636.

8. For an even more elegiac tribute by d'Alembert to Rollin, see the "Avertissement des éditeurs" to the third volume of the *Encyclopédie*, 3:vii.

9. For a comprehensive summary of the Prades affair, see John McManners, *Church and Society in Eighteenth-Century France* (Oxford: Oxford University Press, 1998), 666–67.

10. *Encyclopédie*, s.v. "Encyclopédie," 5:642 (emphasis added).

11. On the impact of Enlightenment ideas on less educated classes,

see Thomas Munck, *The Enlightenment: A Comparative Social History, 1721–1794* (London: Arnold, 2000).

12. Fontenelle, *De l'origine des fables*, 10 [CORPUS]. Voltaire similarly noted in his *Siècle de Louis XIV* how "this philosophical spirit . . . has affected almost every social condition except the lower class [*le bas peuple*]" (chap. 31 [VOLTAIRE]). See more generally Harry C. Payne, *The Philosophes and the People* (New Haven, CT: Yale University Press, 1976).

13. Birn, *Censure royale des livres*, esp. the second and third lectures.

14. Birn's study confirms Kors's suggestive arguments about state toleration of Enlightenment philosophy in *D'Holbach's Coterie*, chap. 7. Madame de Pompadour's portrait by Maurice-Quentin Delatour is held at the Louvre.

15. For a recent critique of the "pornographic interpretation" of the Old Regime's collapse, most closely associated with Robert Darnton, see Simon Burrows, *Blackmail, Scandal, and Revolution: London's French Libellistes, 1758–92* (Manchester: Manchester University Press, 2006), 218–23. On Marie-Antoinette at the Comédie, see Darrin McMahon, *Enemies of the Enlightenment: The French Counter-Enlightenment and the Making of Modernity* (New York: Oxford University Press, 2001), 5–7.

16. James Collins, *The State in Early-Modern France* (Cambridge: Cambridge University Press, 1995); and Jacob Soll, *The Information Master: Jean-Baptiste Colbert's Secret State Intelligence System* (Ann Arbor: University of Michigan Press, 2009).

17. Birn, *Censure royale des livres*.

18. Antoine Lilti, "The Writing of Paranoia: Jean-Jacques Rousseau and the Paradoxes of Celebrity," *Representations* 103 (2008): 53–83 (esp. 61).

19. See esp. Emmanuel Le Roy Ladurie, *The Ancien Régime: A History of France, 1610–1774*, trans. Mark Greengrass (1991; Oxford: Blackwell, 1998). See also Michel Antoine, *Louis XV* (Paris: Fayard, 1989); John Hardman, *Louis XVI* (New Haven, CT: Yale University Press, 1994); and the numerous works on the parlements, including Julian Swann, *Politics and the Parlement of Paris under Louis XV, 1754–1774* (Cambridge: Cambridge University Press, 1995). On the crisis surrounding the publication of the *Encyclopédie*, see Arthur M. Wilson, *Diderot: The Testing Years, 1713–1759* (New York: Oxford University Press, 1957).

20. McMahon, *Enemies of the Enlightenment*.

CHAPTER THIRTEEN

1. Charles Perrault, *Parallèle des Anciens et des Modernes en ce qui regarde les arts et les sciences* (1688–97), ed. Hans Robert Jauss (Munich: Eidos Verlag, 1964), 3.286. The central importance of *galanterie* in the Modern platform is discussed by Larry F. Norman in *The Shock of the Ancient* (forthcoming), pt. 2. See also Alain Viala, *La France galante: Essai historique sur une catégorie culturelle, de ses origines jusqu'à la Révolution* (Paris: Presses Universitaires de France, 2008).

2. Jean-Baptiste Dubos, *Réflexions critiques sur la poésie et la peinture*, 2 vols. (Paris: Mariette, 1719), 1:130 (1:137 in 1733 ed.).

3. Quotation from Voltaire, contrasting *gens de lettres* with *bel esprits*: "le bel esprit seul suppose moins de culture, moins d'étude, & n'exige nulle philosophie; il consiste principalement dans l'imagination brillante, dans les agrémens de la conversation, aidés d'une lecture commune"; see *Encyclopédie*, s.v. "Gens de lettres," 7:600. See more generally Antoine Lilti, *Le monde des salons: Sociabilité et mondanité à Paris au XVIIIᵉ siècle* (Paris: Fayard, 2005).

4. For Voltaire, it was precisely the fact that the *gens de lettres* were now "a necessary part" of *le monde* that made them "far superior to those who preceded them"; see *Encyclopédie*, s.v. "Gens de lettres," 7:599.

5. See esp. Alain Viala, *Naissance de l'écrivain: Sociologie de la littérature à l'âge classique* (Paris: Minuit, 1985); and Christian Jouhaud, *Les pouvoirs de la littérature: Histoire d'un paradoxe* (Paris: Gallimard, 2000).

6. Gregory Brown, *A Field of Honor: Writers, Court Culture, and Public Theater in French Literary Life from Racine to the Revolution* (New York: Columbia University Press, 2005). On the persistence of an aristocratic author model in the Enlightenment, see Geoffrey Turnovsky, *The Literary Market: Authorship and Modernity in the Old Regime* (Philadelphia: University of Pennsylvania Press, 2009).

7. Lilti, *Monde des salons*, esp. chap. 2.

8. Robert Darnton, "The High Enlightenment and the Low-Life of Literature in Pre-Revolutionary France," *The Literary Underground of the Old Regime* (Cambridge, MA: Harvard University Press, 1982), 1–40. See also Alan Charles Kors, *D'Holbach's Coterie: An Enlightenment in Paris* (Princeton, NJ: Princeton University Press, 1976).

9. Diderot published this text anonymously in the third edition of the abbé Raynal's *Histoire philosophique et politique des établissements et*

du commerce des Européens dans les deux Indes, 5 vols. (Geneva: Pellet, 1780); see Denis Diderot, *Political Writings*, ed. and trans. John Hope Mason and Robert Wokler (New York: Cambridge University Press, 1992), 171–73.

10. Jonathan Israel, *Radical Enlightenment: Philosophy and the Making of Modernity, 1650–1750* (Oxford: Oxford University Press, 2002); Jonathan Israel, *Enlightenment Contested: Philosophy, Modernity, and the Emancipation of Man, 1670–1752* (Oxford: Oxford University Press, 2006).

11. Lynn Hunt, Margaret Jacob, and Wijnand Mijnhardt, eds., *The Book That Changed Europe: Picart and Bernard's "Religious Ceremonies of the World"* (Cambridge, MA: Harvard University Press, 2010).

12. Israel, *Enlightenment Contested*, 849–50.

13. Results compiled with the assistance of Joseph St. Meyer, using the PAIR search engine: http://artfl-project.uchicago.edu/node/54.

14. Israel, *Enlightenment Contested*, x, 9, 11 (emphasis added). Needless to say, this interpretation of the origins of the French Revolution is shared by virtually no other historian today. Israel himself volunteers that he takes his lead from counterrevolutionary writers of the late eighteenth century, such as Barruel (vii–ix).

15. See, in general, Hamish M. Scott, *Enlightened Absolutism: Reform and Reformers in Later Eighteenth-Century Europe* (Ann Arbor: University of Michigan Press, 1990). On Tuscany and Grand Duke Leopold, see Peter Gay, *The Science of Freedom*, vol. 2 of *The Enlightenment: An Interpretation* (New York: Knopf, 1969), 499–501; and on the Tuscan Enlightenment, see Eric Cochrane, *Tradition and Enlightenment in the Tuscan Academies, 1690–1800* (Rome: Edizioni di Storia e Letteratura, 1961). On Austria and the Holy Roman Emperor Joseph II, see Franz A. J. Szabo, *Kaunitz and Enlightened Absolutism, 1753–1780* (Cambridge: Cambridge University Press, 1994); and Paul P. Bernard, *Jesuits and Jacobins: Enlightenment and Enlightened Despotism in Austria* (Urbana: University of Illinois Press, 1971). The French Crown passed an edict of toleration granting basic religious freedoms to Protestants in 1787; see Dale Van Kley, *The Religious Origins of the French Revolution: From Calvin to the Civil Constitution, 1560–1791* (New Haven, CT: Yale University Press, 1996), 12. On religious toleration more generally, see James Bradley and Dale Van Kley, eds., *Religion and Politics in Enlightened Europe* (Notre Dame, IN: University of Notre Dame Press, 2001). On Diderot's involvement in Catherine II's constitutional schemes (which

may have been no more than that), see Anthony Strugnell, *Diderot's Politics: A Study of the Evolution of Diderot's Political Thought after the "Encyclopédie"* (The Hague: Nijhoff, 1973); and Diderot's own *Observations on the Nakaz*, in his *Political Writings*, 77–164.

16. The first quotation can be found in Emma Rothschild, *Economic Sentiments: Condorcet, Adam Smith, and the Enlightenment* (Cambridge, MA: Harvard University Press, 2001), 241. Louis made the second declaration at a *lit de justice* in 1787; see Colin Jones, *The Great Nation: France from Louis XV to Napoleon* (London: Penguin, 2002), 387.

17. Robert D. Harris, *Necker, Reform Statesman of the Ancien Régime* (Berkeley and Los Angeles: University of California Press, 1979).

18. Vivan Gruder, *The Notables and the Nation: The Political Schooling of the French, 1787–1788* (Cambridge, MA: Harvard University Press, 2008), 11–88.

19. See the conclusion in Thomas Munck, *The Enlightenment: A Comparative Social History, 1721–1794* (London: Arnold, 2000), 220–23.

20. Robert Darnton, *The Forbidden Best-Sellers of Pre-Revolutionary France* (New York: Norton, 1996).

21. Kors, *D'Holbach's Coterie*, 208.

22. See d'Holbach's assessment: "L'athéisme, ainsi que la philosophie et toutes les sciences profondes et abstraites, n'est donc point fait pour le vulgaire, ni même pour le plus grand nombre des hommes"; in *Système de la nature, ou, des loix du monde physique et du monde moral* (London, 1771), 417, 420 (2.13) [ARTFL]. On the various publishing attitudes among the members of the *coterie* (not all of whom were atheists), see Kors, *D'Holbach's Coterie*, 94 and passim. On the "double doctrine," see Frank Manuel, *The Eighteenth Century Confronts the Gods* (Cambridge, MA: Harvard University Press, 1959), 59ff.

23. Peter Gay, *The Party of Humanity: Essays in the French Enlightenment* (New York: Knopf, 1964), 117. On the place of literature in the Enlightenment, see also Emmanuel Bury, *Littérature et politesse: L'invention de l'honnête homme, 1580–1750* (Paris: Presses Universitaires de France, 1996), 205–37.

24. Nicolas Fréret, *Réflexion générale sur l'étude des anciennes histoires* (Paris, 1724), 11–12.

CHAPTER FOURTEEN

1. Robert Darnton, *Mesmerism and the End of the Enlightenment in France* (Cambridge, MA: Harvard University Press, 1968).

2. Jessica Riskin, *Science in the Age of Sensibility* (Chicago: University of Chicago Press, 2002), chap. 6.

3. Edwin B. Smith, "Jean-Sylvain Bailly: Astronomer, Mystic, Revolutionary, 1736–1793," *Transactions of the American Philosophical Society* 44 (1954): 425–538.

4. For some forays into this topic, see notably Roger Chartier, *The Cultural Origins of the French Revolution*, trans. Lydia G. Cochrane (Durham, NC: Duke University Press, 1991); Peter R. Campbell, ed., *The Origins of the French Revolution* (New York: Palgrave Macmillan, 2006); and Keith Baker, "Enlightenment Idioms, Old Regime Discourses, and Revolutionary Improvisation" (forthcoming).

5. Keith Baker, *Condorcet: From Natural Philosophy to Social Mathematics* (Chicago: University of Chicago Press, 1975); and David Williams, *Condorcet and Modernity* (Cambridge: Cambridge University Press, 2004), chap. 8.

6. Guillaume-Thomas Raynal, *Révolution de l'Amérique* (London: L. Davis, 1781); *Adresse de Guillaume-Thomas Raynal* (Paris: Gattey, 1791).

7. Alan Charles Kors, *D'Holbach's Coterie: An Enlightenment in Paris* (Princeton, NJ: Princeton University Press, 1976), chaps. 8–9. Frank Kafker reaches a similar conclusion in his *The Encyclopedists as a Group: A Collective Biography of the Authors of the Encyclopédie*, Studies on Voltaire and the Eighteenth Century, vol. 345 (Oxford: Voltaire Foundation, 1996).

8. On the trials and tribulations of André Morellet, see Daniel Gordon, *Citizens without Sovereignty: Equality and Sociability in French Thought, 1670–1789* (Princeton, NJ: Princeton University Press, 1994). For Robespierre's indictment of the *gens de lettres*, see "Sur les rapports des idées religieuses et morales avec les principes républicains," in *Œuvres de Maximilien Robespierre*, ed. Société des études robespierristes, 10 vols. (Ivry: Phénix Editions, 2000), 10:460.

9. Quoted in Smith, "Jean-Sylvain Bailly," 510. All other biographical information in this paragraph is taken from this source.

10. Two helpful overviews of revolutionary politics can be found in Colin Jones, *The Great Nation: France from Louis XV to Napoleon* (London: Penguin, 2002); and William Doyle, *The Oxford History of the French Revolution* (Oxford: Oxford University Press, 2002).

11. On this event, see Timothy Tackett, *When the King Took Flight* (Cambridge, MA: Harvard University Press, 2003).

12. Kors, *D'Holbach's Coterie*, 307.

13. For instance, the Jacobins borrowed, but also transformed, Enlightenment notions of natural right and republicanism, as I discuss in *The Terror of Natural Right: Republicanism, the Cult of Nature, and the French Revolution* (Chicago: University of Chicago Press, 2009).

14. James Swenson, *On Jean-Jacques Rousseau Considered as One of the First Authors of the Revolution* (Stanford, CA: Stanford University Press, 2000); and Jean-Claude Bonnet, *Naissance du panthéon: Essai sur le culte des grands hommes* (Paris: Fayard, 1998).

15. See esp. Bronislaw Baczko, *Lumières de l'utopie* (Paris: Payot, 1978). See also Joseph Zizek, "The Politics and Poetics of History in the French Revolution, 1787–1794" (PhD diss., University of California at Berkeley, 1995).

16. Lynn Hunt, *Politics, Culture, and Class in the French Revolution* (Berkeley and Los Angeles: University of California Press, 1984), 27.

17. Maximilien Robespierre, "Sur les rapports des idées religieuses et morales avec les principes républicains," 444. Robert Darnton more generally discusses the "sense of boundless possibility" that characterized revolutionary sentiments in *The Kiss of Lamourette: Reflections in Cultural History* (New York: Norton, 1990), 3–20.

18. Baker, *Condorcet*, and above.

19. Keith Baker, "Toward a Revolutionary Lexicon," in his *Inventing the French Revolution* (Cambridge: Cambridge University Press, 1990), 218–23.

20. Karl Marx, *The Eighteenth Brumaire of Louis Bonaparte*, trans. Daniel de Leon (Chicago: Kerr, 1913), 10.

21. See esp. Harold Parker, *The Cult of Antiquity and the French Revolutionaries: A Study in the Development of the Revolutionary Spirit* (Chicago: University of Chicago Press, 1937); Jacques Bouineau, *Les toges du pouvoir, ou la révolution de droit antique, 1789–1799* (Toulouse: Editions Eché, 1986); and Mouza Raskolnikoff, "L'adoration des Romains sous la Révolution française et la réaction de Volney et des Idéologues," in *Des Anciens et des Modernes* (Paris: Publications de la Sorbonne, 1990). I also develop this idea further in *Terror of Natural Right*, chap. 5.

22. I discuss this episode in "The Egyptian French Revolution: Antiquarianism, Freemasonry, and the Mythology of Nature," in *The Super-Enlightenment: Daring to Know Too Much*, ed. Dan Edelstein, Studies on Voltaire and the Eighteenth Century, vol. 2010:01 (Oxford: Voltaire Foundation, 2010).

23. See, e.g., Hannah Arendt, *On Revolution* (1963; London: Penguin, 2006).

24. See esp. Edmund S. Morgan, *The Birth of the Republic, 1763–89* (Chicago: University of Chicago Press, 1992), 7.

25. Hans-Jürgen Lüsebrink and Rolf Reichardt, *The Bastille: A History of a Symbol of Despotism and Freedom*, trans. Norbert Schürer (Durham, NC: Duke University Press, 1997); Thomas Paine, "Thoughts on the Present State of American Affairs," *Common Sense*, in *Collected Writings* (New York: Library of America, 1995).

26. Louis-Antoine Saint-Just, "Rapport sur les factions de l'étranger," 23 ventôse an II (March 13, 1794), *SJ*, 736, in *Œuvres complètes*, ed. Michèle Duval (Paris: Lebovici, 1984).

CHAPTER FIFTEEN

1. For a case study of book distribution and the diffusion of ideas, see Richard B. Sher, *The Enlightenment and the Book: Scottish Authors and Their Publishers in Eighteenth-Century Britain, Ireland, and America* (Chicago: University of Chicago Press, 2006).

2. On the European dissemination of French Enlightenment texts, see Charles W. J. Withers, *Placing the Enlightenment: Thinking Geographically about the Age of Reason* (Chicago: University of Chicago Press, 2007), 50–57. See also Douglas Smith, "Freemasonry and the Public in Eighteenth-Century Russia," *Eighteenth-Century Studies* 29, no. 1 (1996): 25–44.

3. Louis Réau, *L'Europe française au siècle des Lumières* (1938; Paris: Albin Michel, 1951); Marc Fumaroli, *Quand l'Europe parlait français* (Paris: Fallois, 2001). See also Derek Beales, *Enlightenment and Reform in 18th-Century Europe* (London: I. B. Tauris, 2005), esp. chap. 3; and Robert Darnton, "The Unity of Europe: Culture and Politeness," *George Washington's False Teeth* (New York: Norton, 2003), 76–88.

4. Hamish Scott, "Diplomatic Culture in Old Regime Europe," in *Cultures of Power during the Long Eighteenth Century*, ed. Hamish Scott and Brendan Simms (Cambridge: Cambridge University Press, 2007), 65.

5. See esp. Timothy C. W. Blanning, *The Culture of Power and the Power of Culture: Old Regime Europe, 1660–1789* (Oxford: Oxford University Press, 2002), 49–52. As Blanning points out, claims about the universality of the French language (and French taste) were already being made by the late seventeenth century.

6. Voltaire, *Siècle de Louis XIV*, chap. 1 [VOLTAIRE].

7. See, e.g., Roy Porter, *The Creation of the Modern World: The Untold Story of the British Enlightenment* (New York: Norton, 2001).

8. Roger Emerson, "The Contexts of the Scottish Enlightenment," in *The Cambridge Companion to the Scottish Enlightenment*, ed. Alexander Broadie (Cambridge: Cambridge University Press, 2003), 18.

9. John Robertson, *The Case for the Enlightenment: Scotland and Naples, 1680–1760* (Cambridge: Cambridge University Press, 2005), 118.

10. E. C. Mossner, *The Life of David Hume* (Oxford: Oxford University Press, 1980), 100–104; see also Robertson, *Case for the Enlightenment*, 258.

11. See "My Own Life," in *The Cambridge Companion to Hume*, ed. David Fate Norton (Cambridge: Cambridge University Press, 1993), 356.

12. Aaron Garrett, "Anthropology: The 'Original' of Human Nature," in *Cambridge Companion to the Scottish Enlightenment*, 85.

13. David Hume, "Of the Rise and Progress of the Arts and Sciences," in *Selected Essays*, ed. Stephen Copley and Andrew Edgar (Oxford: Oxford University Press, 1998), 58.

14. Ibid., 72. It is worth noting that Jean-Baptiste Dubos's *Réflexions critiques sur la poésie et la peinture*, 2 vols. (Paris: Mariette, 1719), was republished in 1733, the year before Hume visited France. Hume cites the *Réflexions* in his essay on tragedy, first published in 1757; see *Four Dissertations: I. The Natural History of Religion, II. Of the Passions, III. Of Tragedy, IV. Of the Standard of Taste* (London: A. Millar, 1757), 186 [ECCO].

15. David Hume, "Of Refinement in the Arts" and "Of Civil Liberty," in *Selected Essays*, 175, 51. Hume goes on to note, in "Of Civil Liberty," that "the French are the only people, except the Greeks, who have been at once philosophers, poets, orators, historians, painters, architects, sculptors, and even musicians. . . . And, in common life, they have, in a great measure, perfected that art, the most useful and agreeable of any, *l'Art de Vivre*, the art of society and conversation" (51–52).

16. Hume, "Of Refinement in the Arts," 174.

17. Hume, "Of the Rise and Progress of the Arts and Sciences," 75, 77.

18. Jonathan Swift, *Gulliver's Travels*, ed. Claude Rawson (Oxford: Oxford University Press, 2005), pt. 3, chap. 5; and David Hume, "Of the Middle Station of Life," in *Selected Essays*, 9.

19. William Robertson, *The History of the Reign of the Emperor Charles*

V (Dublin: W. Smith [and twenty others], 1762–71), 305 (for the recognition of Voltaire) [ECCO].

20. Fania Oz-Salzberger, "The Political Theory of the Scottish Enlightenment," in *Cambridge Companion to the Scottish Enlightenment*, 170–171.

21. Adam Smith reviewed the second *Discourse* in 1756; see "Letter to the *Edinburgh Review*," in *Essays on Philosophical Subjects*, ed. W. P. D. Wightman, J. C. Bryce, and I. S. Ross, vol. 3 of *The Glasgow Edition of the Works and Correspondence of Adam Smith* (Oxford: Oxford University Press, 1980), 250. This characterization of Rousseau's influence on Smith is drawn from Pierre Force, *Self-Interest before Adam Smith: A Genealogy of Economic Science* (Cambridge: Cambridge University Press, 2003), 18–26 and passim.

22. See esp. R. H. Campbell and Andrew S. Skinner, *Adam Smith* (Beckenham: Routledge, 1982), 129 (on Voltaire) and 132–36 (on Quesnay).

23. Ian Hunter, *Rival Enlightenments: Civil and Metaphysical Philosophy in Early Modern Germany* (Cambridge: Cambridge University Press, 2001), 4.

24. Moses Mendelssohn, "On the Question: What Is Enlightenment?" (1784), in *What Is Enlightenment? Eighteenth-Century Answers and Twentieth-Century Questions*, ed. and trans. James Schmidt (Berkeley: University of California Press, 1996), 55. Despite its title, this book deals exclusively, on the eighteenth-century side, with German answers to the question.

25. See esp. Jonathan B. Knudsen, *Justus Möser and the German Enlightenment* (Cambridge: Cambridge University Press, 1986), 58.

26. As Norman Hampson noted, in almost all German states, "courtiers must have French literature and plays"; *A Cultural History of the Enlightenment* (New York: Pantheon, 1968), 61. See also Felicia Hardison Londré, *The History of World Theater* (New York: Continuum, 1991), 49.

27. Joseph R. Smiley, "The Subscribers of Grimm's *Correspondance Litteraire*," *Modern Language Notes* 62 (1947): 44–46.

28. Inna Gorbatov, *Catherine the Great and the French Philosophers of the Enlightenment* (Bethesda, MD: Academica Press, 2006), 65.

29. Giles MacDonogh, *Frederick the Great: A Life in Deed and Letters* (New York: Macmillan, 1999).

30. On the German reception of Rousseau, see Herbert Jaumann,

Rousseau in Deutschland: Neue Beiträge zur Erforschung seiner Rezeption (Berlin: de Gruyter, 1994), who compares Rousseau's place in German culture to that of a "media celebrity" (9).

31. Harold Mah, *Enlightenment Phantasies: Cultural Identity in France and Germany, 1750–1914* (Ithaca, NY: Cornell University Press, 2003), 35–36. See also Isaiah Berlin, *The Roots of Romanticism* (Princeton, NJ: Princeton University Press, 1999).

32. An incomplete list of these Francophile sovereigns would include, in addition to the ones listed above, Prince-Electors Maximilian III Joseph and Charles Theodore of Bavaria; Gustav III of Sweden; Joseph II of Austria; and his brother Leopold, Grand Duke of Tuscany. See esp. Robert Mandrou, *L'Europe "absolutiste": Raison et raison d'état, 1649–1775* (Paris: Fayard, 1977); and Hamish M. Scott, *Enlightened Absolutism: Reform and Reformers in Later Eighteenth-Century Europe* (Ann Arbor: University of Michigan Press, 1990). Some of these sovereigns' ministers also styled themselves as *philosophes*; see esp., for the Hapsburg case, Franz A. J. Szabo, *Kaunitz and Enlightened Absolutism, 1753–1780* (Cambridge: Cambridge University Press, 1994).

33. V. V. Zenkovsky, *A History of Russian Philosophy*, trans. George L. Kline, 3 vols. (London: Routledge, 1953), 1:73–75.

34. Natalie Bayer, "What Do You Seek from Us? Wisdom? Virtue? Enlightenment? Inventing a Masonic Science of Man in Russia," in *Super-Enlightenment*, ed. Edelstein, 169–90. Bayer further notes that "by the 1770s, Voltaire had become the dominant force in the intellectual and cultural life of the educated elite and the phenomenon of French intellectual influence was synthesized in the name of the most popular French *philosophe*" (173).

35. See esp. James Cracraft, *The Revolution of Peter the Great* (Cambridge, MA: Harvard University Press, 2006), 76–78; and Gorbatov, *Catherine the Great*.

36. Bayer, "What Do You Seek from Us?" n. 20; Gorbatov, *Catherine the Great*, 16.

37. As Dimitri Goutnov points out, 245 out of 527 articles in the *Nakaz* were borrowed from Montesquieu's work; see his "Montesquieu in Russia: Catherine II's Legal Reforms and Russian Cultural Tradition," in *La recherche dix-huitièmiste: Raison universelle et culture nationale au siècle des Lumières*, ed. David A. Bell, Ludmila Pimenova, and Stéphane Pujol (Paris: Champion, 1999), 61–69. Catherine enlisted other prominent Frenchmen to assist with her political reforms,

most notably Voltaire, with whom she began corresponding in 1763; the Physiocrat Pierre-Paul Le Mercier de la Rivière, author of *L'ordre naturel et essentiel des sociétés politiques* (1767), who traveled to Saint Petersburg at her request; and, of course, Diderot, who also made the trip to Russia and wrote a commentary on her political project, the 1774 *Observations sur le Nakaz* (with which Catherine was not particualrly pleased).

38. Voltaire, *Histoire de l'empire de Russie sous Pierre le Grand* (1761). The correspondence between Voltaire and Catherine II can be accessed through the *Electronic Enlightenment* database, http://www.e-enlightenment.com.

39. Piotr Stefan Wandycz, *The Price of Freedom: A History of East Central Europe from the Middle Ages to the Present* (London: Routledge, 2001), 109. On the influence of the French Enlightenment in Eastern Europe, see also Larry Wolff, *Inventing Eastern Europe: The Map of Civilization on the Mind of the Enlightenment* (Stanford, CA: Stanford University Press, 1994). Polish Francophilia was also encouraged from the top: King Stanisław Leszczyński, father-in-law to Louis XV, resided in France for the latter half of his life, engaging in debates with the *philosophes*. The connection between Poland and the *philosophes* extends to Rousseau and Mably, who were called upon by Polish nobles in 1770 to revise their government.

40. On Algarotti, see notably Robert Bufalini, "The Czarina's Russia through Mediterranean Eyes: Francesco Algarotti's Journey to Saint Petersburg," *Modern Language Notes* 121 (2006): 154–66. Voltaire himself was widely read and translated in Italy; see Réau, *L'Europe française*, 77–79. On the Italian reception of the French Enlightenment, see more generally Paolo Quintili, "Lumières de la France, de Paris à Rome; Voltaire, Galiani, Diderot: Arts, tolérance, droits de l'homme," in *Les Lumières en mouvement: La circulation des idées au XVIIIe siècle*, ed. Isabelle Moreau (Paris: ENS Editions, 2009), 45–64.

41. Quotes and references are from the French translation, *Le Newtonianisme pour les dames, ou Entretiens sur la lumière, sur les couleurs et sur l'attraction*, trans. Duperron de Castera, 2 vols. (Paris: Montalant, 1738), 1:17–29.

42. Paula Findlen, "Founding a Scientific Academy: Gender, Patronage, and Knowledge in Early Eighteenth-Century Milan," *Republics of Letters* 1 (2009), http://rofl.stanford.edu/node/33.

43. Beccaria also visited Paris very briefly in 1766, accompanied by

Pietro and Alessandro Verri. For Montesquieu's huge influence on *Dei delitti e delle pene*, see notably Frederick Rosen, "Utilitarianism and the Reform of the Criminal Law," in *The Cambridge History of Eighteenth-Century Political Thought*, ed. Mark Goldie and Robert Wokler (Cambridge: Cambridge University Press, 2006), 551. See also Franco Venturi, *Italy and the Enlightenment: Studies in a Cosmopolitan Century*, trans. Susan Corsi, ed. Stuart Woolf (London: Longman, 1972); and Owen Chadwick, *The Popes and European Revolution* (Oxford: Oxford University Press, 1981). Beccaria's work was translated into French by the *philosophe* Morellet in 1766; that same year, Voltaire himself published *Commentaire sur le livre des délits et des peines*.

44. Antonio Genovesi, *Spirito delle leggi del signore di Montesquieu, con le note dell'abate Antonio Genovesi*, 4 vols. (Naples: Domenico Terres, 1777). On Genovesi and Montesquieu, see Girolamo Imbruglia, "Enlightenment in Eighteenth-Century Naples," in *Naples in the Eighteenth Century*, ed. G. Imbruglia (Cambridge: Cambridge University Press, 2000), 74ff. For Montesquieu's influence on Neapolitan reformers, see also Robertson, *Case for Enlightenment*.

45. For Galiani, see esp. Francis Steegmuller, *A Woman, a Man, and Two Kingdoms: The Story of Madame d'Epinay and the Abbé Galiani* (New York: Knopf, 1991). Galiani's friend and fellow diplomat the marchese Domenico Caraccioli, who served as Neapolitan ambassador in Paris, is credited by Louis Réau as the author of another panegyric of France, *Paris, le modèle des nations étrangères, ou l'Europe française* (Paris: Vve Duchesne, 1777), but this work was in fact written by his distant (and French) cousin, Louis-Antoine Caraccioli. See Réau, *L'Europe française*, 1–2, 20.

46. Anthony Grafton, introduction to Giambattista Vico, *New Science*, 3rd ed., trans. David Marsh (London: Penguin, 1999), xii.

47. Isaiah Berlin, *Three Critics of the Enlightenment: Vico, Hamann, Herder*, ed. Henry Hardy (Princeton, NJ: Princeton University Press, 2000), 28–29.

48. Margaret Jacob, *The Radical Enlightenment: Pantheists, Freemasons, and Republicans* (London: George Allen, 1981); John Marshall, *John Locke, Toleration, and Early Enlightenment Culture: Religious Intolerance and Arguments for Religious Toleration in Early Modern and "Early Enlightenment" Europe* (Cambridge: Cambridge University Press, 2006); Jonathan Israel, *Radical Enlightenment: Philosophy and the Making of Modernity, 1650–1750* (Oxford: Oxford University Press, 2002).

49. Wijnand Mijnhardt, "The Dutch Enlightenment: Humanism, Nationalism, and Decline," in *The Dutch Republic in the Eighteenth Century: Decline, Enlightenment, and Revolution*, ed. Margaret C. Jacob and W. W. Mijnhardt (Ithaca, NY: Cornell University Press, 1992), 199–200.

50. Simon Schama, "The Enlightenment in the Netherlands," in *The Enlightenment in National Context*, ed. Roy Porter and Mikuláš Teich (Cambridge: Cambridge University Press, 1981), 61, 68–69; the Rey quote is also taken from this source. Schama's arguments are nuanced and criticized, if not fundamentally challenged, by the contributors to *The Dutch Republic in the Eighteenth Century*.

51. Hume, "Of the Rise of the Arts and Sciences," 58.

52. Franco Venturi, *The End of the Old Regime in Europe, 1776–1789*, trans. R. Burr Litchfield, 2 vols. (Princeton, NJ: Princeton University Press, 1991), 1:36.

53. Edmund Burke, *Reflections on the Revolution in France*, ed. L. G. Mitchell (New York: Oxford University Press, 1999), 89; my thanks to Jonathan Kramnick for this reference. Burke recognized that England had an older tradition of "freethinkers" but argued that "at present they repose in lasting oblivion." Porter dismisses this remark as a "*canard*" but does not address the initial point about the absence of a "philosophic . . . party in England" (*Creation of the Modern World*, 97).

54. John Seed, "'A Set of Men Powerful Enough in Many Things': Rational Dissent and Political Opposition in England, 1770–1790," in *Enlightenment and Religion: Rational Dissent in Eighteenth-Century Britain*, ed. Knud Haakonssen (Cambridge: Cambridge University Press, 1996), 140–68. My thanks to one of my anonymous reviewers for calling attention to the importance of this group.

55. Porter justifies using "the terms 'English' and 'British' somewhat interchangeably when referring to ideas and developments broadly shared by élites living in the British Isles," but the rest of this sentence complicates this claim: "practially all enlightened thinking was then actually coming out of English heads, especially during the first third of the eighteenth century" (*Creation of the Modern World*, xviii–xix). On English "Scottophobia," see notably Linda Colley, *Britons: Forging the Nation, 1707–1837* (New Haven, CT: Yale University Press, 2005), chap. 3. Scotland became part of Britain only in 1707, with the Acts of Union.

56. Jacob, *Radical Enlightenment*, esp. chap. 3. See also, by the same author, *The Newtonians and the English Revolution, 1689–1720* (Ithaca, NY: Cornell University Press, 1976), chap. 2.

57. Desaguliers writes, for instance, that "coerc'd by Laws, [the Sun] still leaves them [people/planets] free, / Directs but not Destroys, their Liberty . . . And reigning thus with limited Command, / He holds a lasting Scepter in his Hand"; *The Newtonian System of the World, the Best Model of Government: An Allegorical Poem* (Westminster, 1728), 24–26, 31 [ECCO]. On Desaguliers and on this poem, see Jacob, *Radical Enlightenment*, 122–24.

58. Colley, *Britons*, 19–22, 31.

59. Steve Pincus, *1688: The First Modern Revolution* (New Haven, CT: Yale University Press, 2009); on the eighteenth-century British reception of the Glorious Revolution, see 12–13.

60. John Wilkes, *The History of England from the Revolution to the Accession of the Brunswick Line* (London, 1768), 5 [ECCO]. On Wilkes, see esp. Peter D. G. Thomas, *John Wilkes: A Friend to Liberty* (Oxford: Oxford University Press, 1996).

61. See esp. Isaac Kramnick, *Bolingbroke and His Circle: The Politics of Nostalgia in the Age of Walpole* (Cambridge, MA: Harvard University Press, 1968).

62. Wilkes, *History of England*, 20.

63. Keith Baker, *Inventing the French Revolution* (Cambridge: Cambridge University Press, 1990), 173, in reference to Montesquieu's treatment of the British constitution in *The Spirit of the Laws* (bk. 11, chap. 6). I am indebted to David Bates's reading of this famous chapter in *States of War* (forthcoming).

CHAPTER SIXTEEN

1. See Jean-François Lyotard, *La condition postmoderne: Rapport sur le savoir* (Paris: Minuit, 1979). In a different vein, this account resembles Donald Kelley's description of how Renaissance humanists crafted their own "myth" of historical rupture; *Foundations of Modern Historical Scholarship: Language, Law, and History in the French Renaissance* (New York: Columbia University Press, 1970), 8; quoted in Larry F. Norman, *Shock of the Ancient* (forthcoming).

2. Georges Sorel, *Reflections on Violence*, ed. and trans. Jeremy Jennings (Cambridge: Cambridge University Press, 1999), 20.

3. Articles pertaining to anatomy, for example, provide detailed histories of discoveries stretching back to the sixteenth century.

4. Immanuel Kant, "An Answer to the Question: What Is Enlightenment?" in *What Is Enlightenment? Eighteenth-Century Answers and Twentieth-Century Questions*, ed. and trans. James Schmidt (Berkeley and Los Angeles: University of California Press, 1996), 58 (emphasis added).

5. *Encyclopédie*, s.v. "Gens de lettres" (Voltaire), 7:600 ("instruire & ... polir la nation").

6. Rousseau, letter to Jacob Vernes, April 2, 1755: "Des ouvrages graves et profonds peuvent nous honorer, tout le colifichet de cette petite philosophie à la mode nous va fort mal." In *Lettres de Jean-Jacques Rousseau (1728–1778)*, ed. Marcel Raymond (Lausanne: La Guilde du Livre, 1959), 64 [ARTFL].

7. Pascale Casanova employs this Bourdieusian concept in her discussion of the prestige that French literature, language, and writers enjoyed in the nineteenth and early twentieth centuries; *The World Republic of Letters*, trans. M. B. DeBevoise (Cambridge, MA: Harvard University Press, 2004). Her claim that Paris's unrivaled position at the top of the literary world was due to the French Revolution must be significantly revised, however. As Stéphane Van Damme argued, this position of privilege dates back at least to the seventeenth century; *Paris, capitale philosophique: De la Fronde à la Révolution* (Paris: Odile Jacob, 2005).

8. Michel Foucault, "What Is Enlightenment?" in *The Foucault Reader*, ed. Paul Rabinow (New York: Pantheon, 1984), 39–40.

Selected Bibliography
for the Enlightenment

PRIMARY SOURCES (LIMITED TO ONE EMBLEMATIC TEXT PER
AUTHOR, PREFERABLY IN TRANSLATION)

d'Alembert, Jean-le-Rond. "Preliminary Discourse to the *Encyclo-pédie*." 1751. Translated by Richard Schwab. Chicago: University of Chicago Press, 1995.

Algarotti, Francesco. *The Lady's Philosophy: or Sir Isaac Newton's Theory of Light and Colours, and His Principle of Attraction, Made Familiar to the Ladies in Several Entertainments.* 1738. London: F. Newbery, 1772.

Bayle, Pierre. *Miscellaneous Reflections, Occasion'd by the Comet which Appear'd in December 1680.* 1683. 2 vols. London: J. Morphew, 1708 [ECCO].

Beccaria, Cesare. *On Crimes and Punishments.* 1764. Translated by R. Davies and V. Cox. Cambridge: Cambridge University Press, 1995.

Condorcet. *Outlines of an Historical View of the Progress of the Human Mind.* 1794. London: J. Johnson, 1795.

Diderot, Denis. *A Supplement to the Voyage of Bougainville.* 1772. In *Political Writings*, edited and translated by John Hope Mason and Robert Wokler. New York: Cambridge University Press, 1992.

Dubos, Jean-Baptiste. *Critical Reflections on Poetry and Painting.* 1719. 3 vols. London: John Nourse, 1748 [ECCO].

Fénelon, François de Salignac de La Mothe. *Telemachus, Son of Ulysses.* 1699. Edited and translated by Patrick Riley. Cambridge: Cambridge University Press, 1994.

Fontenelle, Bernard Le Bovier de. *Conversations on the Plurality of Worlds.* 1687. Translated by Elizabeth Gunning. Richmond, UK: Tiger of the Stripe, 2008.

Franklin, Benjamin. *The Autobiography of Benjamin Franklin.* 1791. New Haven, CT: Yale University Press, 1964.

Fréret, Nicolas. *Réflexion générale sur l'étude des anciennes histoires.* Paris, 1724.

d'Holbach, Paul Henri Thiry. *The System of Nature; Or, the Laws of the Moral and Physical World.* 1770. London: G. Kearsley, 1797.

Hume, David. *Selected Essays.* Edited by Stephen Copley and Andrew Edgar. Oxford: Oxford University Press, 1998.

Kant, Immanuel. "An Answer to the Question: What Is Enlightenment?" In *Political Writings,* edited by H. S. Reiss. Cambridge: Cambridge University Press, 1991.

Montesquieu. *Persian Letters.* Translated by Margaret Mauldon. Oxford: Oxford University Press, 2008.

Raynal, Guillaume de. *A Philosophical and Political History of the Settlements and Trade of the Europeans in the East and West Indies.* Edinburgh: W. Gordon et al., 1782.

Rousseau, Jean-Jacques. *The "Discourses" and Other Early Political Writings.* Edited and translated by Victor Gourevitch. Cambridge: Cambridge University Press, 1997.

Smith, Adam. *The Theory of Moral Sentiments.* 1759. New York: Cosimo, 2007.

Voltaire, *Philosophical Letters.* 1734. Translated by P. L. Steiner. Indianapolis: Hackett Publishing, 2007.

INTELLECTUAL HISTORIES

Baker, Keith. "Enlightenment and the Institution of Society: Notes for a Conceptual History." In *Main Trends in Cultural History,* edited by Willem Melching and Wyger Velema. Amsterdam: Rodopi, 1994.

Brewer, Daniel. *The Enlightenment Past: Reconstructing Eighteenth-*

Century French Thought. Cambridge: Cambridge University Press, 2008.

Darnton, Robert. *The Forbidden Best-Sellers of Pre-Revolutionary France*. New York: Norton, 1996.

Fitzpatrick, Martin, Peter Jones, Christa Knellwolf, and Iain McCalman, eds. *The Enlightenment World*. New York: Routledge, 2004.

Gay, Peter. *The Enlightenment: An Interpretation*. 2 vols. New York: Knopf, 1966–69.

Gumbrecht, Hans Ulrich. "Who Were the *Philosophes?*" In *Making Sense in Life and Literature*, translated by Glen Burns. Minneapolis: University of Minnesota Press, 1992.

Israel, Jonathan. *Radical Enlightenment: Philosophy and the Making of Modernity, 1650–1750*. Oxford: Oxford University Press, 2002.

Jacob, Margaret. *The Radical Enlightenment: Pantheists, Freemasons, and Republicans*. London: George Allen, 1981.

Lilti, Antoine. "Comment écrit-on l'histoire intellectuelle des Lumières? Spinozisme, radicalisme, et philosophie." *Annales HSS* 64 (2009): 171–206.

Ricuperati, Giuseppe, ed. *Historiographie et usages des Lumières*. Berlin: Berlin Verlag, 2002.

Robertson, John. *The Case for the Enlightenment: Scotland and Naples, 1680–1760*. Cambridge: Cambridge University Press, 2005.

Rothkrug, Lionel. *Opposition to Louis XIV: The Political and Social Origins of the French Enlightenment*. Princeton, NJ: Princeton University Press, 1965.

Russo, Elena. *Styles of Enlightenment: Taste, Politics, and Authorship in Eighteenth-Century France*. Baltimore, MD: Johns Hopkins University Press, 2007.

Stuke, Horst. "Aufklärung." In *Geschichtliche Grundbegriffe: Historisches Lexikon zur politisch-sozialen Sprache in Deutschland*, edited by Otto Brunner, Werner Conze, and Reinhart Koselleck, 1:243–342. Stuttgart: E. Klett, 1972.

Venturi, Franco. *The End of the Old Regime in Europe, 1776–1789*. Translated by R. Burr Litchfield. 2 vols. Princeton, NJ: Princeton University Press, 1991.

———. *Utopia and Reform in the Enlightenment*. Cambridge: Cambridge University Press, 1971.

SOCIAL AND CULTURAL APPROACHES

Birn, Raymond. *La censure royale des livres dans la France des Lumières.*
Paris: Odile Jacob, 2007.

Bury, Emmanuel. *Littérature et politesse: L'invention de l'honnête
homme, 1580–1750.* Paris: Presses Universitaires de France, 1996.

Calhoun, Craig. *Habermas and the Public Sphere.* Cambridge, MA:
MIT Press, 1992.

Goodman, Dena. *The Republic of Letters: A Cultural History of the
French Enlightenment.* Ithaca, NY: Cornell University Press, 1994.

Habermas, Jürgen. *The Structural Transformation of the Public Sphere:
An Inquiry into a Category of Bourgeois Society.* Translated by
Thomas Burger. Cambridge, MA: MIT Press, 1992.

Hampson, Norman. *A Cultural History of the Enlightenment.* New
York: Pantheon, 1968.

Horn Melton, James van. *The Rise of the Public in Enlightenment
Europe.* Cambridge: Cambridge University Press, 2001.

Jacob, Margaret. *Living the Enlightenment: Freemasonry and Politics in
Eighteenth-Century Europe.* Oxford: Oxford University Press, 1991.

Lilti, Antoine. *Le monde des salons: Sociabilité et mondanité à Paris au
XVIIIe siècle.* Paris: Fayard, 2005.

Munck, Thomas. *The Enlightenment: A Comparative Social History,
1721–1719.* London: Arnold, 2000.

Roche, Daniel. *France in the Enlightenment.* Translated by Arthur
Goldhammer. Cambridge, MA: Harvard University Press, 1998.

SCIENTIFIC REVOLUTION AND ENLIGHTENMENT

Azouvi, François. *Descartes et la France: Histoire d'une passion nationale.*
Paris: Fayard, 2002.

Daston, Lorraine, and Katharine Park. *Wonders and the Order of
Nature, 1150–1750.* New York: Zone Books, 2001.

Hahn, Roger. *The Anatomy of a Scientific Institution: The Paris Academy
of Sciences, 1666–1803.* Berkeley and Los Angeles: University of
California Press, 1971.

Harth, Erica. *Cartesian Women: Versions and Subversions of Rational
Discourse in the Old Regime.* Ithaca, NY: Cornell University Press,
1992.

Mazauric, Simone. *Fontenelle et l'invention de l'histoire des sciences à l'aube des Lumières*. Paris: Fayard, 2007.

Reill, Peter Hanns. "The Legacy of the 'Scientific Revolution': Science and the Enlightenment." In *The Cambridge History of Science*, edited by Roy Porter. Cambridge: Cambridge University Press, 2003.

Riskin, Jessica. *Science in the Age of Sensibility*. Chicago: University of Chicago Press, 2002.

Shank, J. B. *The Newton Wars and the Beginning of the French Enlightenment*. Chicago: University of Chicago Press, 2008.

Shapin, Steven. *The Scientific Revolution*. Chicago: University of Chicago Press, 1996.

Van Damme, Stéphane. *Paris, capitale philosophique: De la Fronde à la Révolution*. Paris: Odile Jacob, 2005.

HUMANISM AND ENLIGHTENMENT

Blair, Ann. *Too Much to Know: Managing Scholarly Information before the Modern Age*. Forthcoming.

Bots, Hans, and Françoise Waquet. *La république des lettres*. Paris: Belin, 1997.

Brockliss, Lawrence. *Calvet's Web: Enlightenment and the Republic of Letters in Eighteenth-Century France*. Oxford: Oxford University Press, 2002.

Goldgar, Anne. *Impolite Learning: Conduct and Community in the Republic of Letters, 1680–1750*. New Haven, CT: Yale University Press, 1995.

Gouhier, Henri. *L'anti-humanisme au XVIIᵉ siècle*. Paris: Vrin, 1987.

Grafton, Anthony. *Defenders of the Text: The Traditions of Scholarship in an Age of Science, 1450–1800*. Cambridge, MA: Harvard University Press, 1991.

Grafton, Anthony, and Ann Blair, eds. *The Transmission of Culture in Early Modern Europe*. Philadelphia: University of Pennsylvania Press, 1999.

Grell, Chantal. *Le dix-huitième siècle et l'antiquité en France, 1680–1789*. 2 vols. Studies on Voltaire and the Eighteenth Century, vols. 330–31. Oxford: Voltaire Foundation, 1995.

Pintard, René. *Le libertinage érudit dans la première moitié du XVIIᵉ siècle*. Paris: Boivin, 1943.

Pocock, John. *The Enlightenments of Edward Gibbon.* Vol. 1 of *Barbarism and Religion.* Cambridge: Cambridge University Press, 1999.

Seznec, Jean. *Essais sur Diderot et l'antiquité.* Oxford: Clarendon Press, 1957.

Soll, Jacob. *Publishing "The Prince": History, Reading, and the Birth of Political Criticism.* Ann Arbor: University of Michigan Press, 2005.

Yeo, Richard. *Encyclopedic Visions: Scientific Dictionaries and Enlightenment Culture.* Cambridge: Cambridge University Press, 2001.

THE QUARREL OF THE ANCIENTS AND THE MODERNS

DeJean, Joan. *Ancients against Moderns: Culture Wars and the Making of a Fin de Siècle.* Chicago: University of Chicago Press, 1997.

Fumaroli, Marc. "Les abeilles et les araignées." In *La Querelle des Anciens et des Modernes,* edited by Anne-Marie Lecoq. Paris: Gallimard, 2001.

Hartog, François. *Anciens, modernes, sauvages.* Paris: Galaade, 2005.

Levine, Joseph. *The Battle of the Books: History and Literature in the Augustan Age.* Ithaca, NY: Cornell University Press, 1991.

Norman, Larry F. *The Shock of the Ancient.* Forthcoming.

Yilmaz, Levent. *Le temps moderne: Variations sur les anciens et les contemporains.* Paris: Gallimard, 2004.

ENLIGHTENMENT AND RELIGION

Bell, David A. *The Cult of the Nation in France: Inventing Nationalism, 1680–1800.* Cambridge, MA: Harvard University Press, 2001.

Hunter, Michael, and David Wootton, eds. *Atheism from the Reformation to the Enlightenment.* Oxford: Oxford University Press, 1992.

Kors, Alan Charles. *Atheism in France, 1650–1729.* Princeton, NJ: Princeton University Press, 1990.

Marshall, John. *John Locke, Toleration, and Early Enlightenment Culture: Religious Intolerance and Arguments for Religious Toleration in Early Modern and "Early Enlightenment" Europe.* Cambridge: Cambridge University Press, 2006.

McMahon, Darrin. *Enemies of the Enlightenment: The French Counter-Enlightenment and the Making of Modernity.* New York: Oxford University Press, 2001.

Northeast, Catherine. *The Parisian Jesuits and the Enlightenment, 1700–*

1762. Studies on Voltaire and the Eighteenth Century, vol. 288. Oxford: Voltaire Foundation, 1991.

Palmer, R. R. *Catholics and Unbelievers in Eighteenth-Century France.* 1939. New York: Cooper Square Publishers, 1961.

Sheehan, Jonathan. *The Enlightenment Bible: Translation, Scholarship, Culture.* Princeton, NJ: Princeton University Press, 2005.

NATIONAL STUDIES OF THE ENLIGHTENMENT

Beales, Derek. *Enlightenment and Reform in 18th-Century Europe.* London: I. B. Tauris, 2005.

Gorbatov, Inna. *Catherine the Great and the French Philosophers of the Enlightenment.* Betheseda, MD: Academica Press, 2006.

Hunter, Ian. *Rival Enlightenments: Civil and Metaphysical Philosophy in Early Modern Germany.* Cambridge: Cambridge University Press, 2001.

Imbruglia, Girolamo, ed. *Naples in the Eighteenth Century.* Cambridge: Cambridge University Press, 2000.

Jacob, Margaret C., and W. W. Mijnhardt, eds. *The Dutch Republic in the Eighteenth Century: Decline, Enlightenment, and Revolution.* Ithaca, NY: Cornell University Press, 1992.

Knudsen, Jonathan B. *Justus Möser and the German Enlightenment.* Cambridge: Cambridge University Press, 1986.

Porter, Roy. *The Creation of the Modern World: The Untold Story of the British Enlightenment.* New York: Norton, 2001.

Porter, Roy, and Mikuláš Teich, eds. *The Enlightenment in National Context.* Cambridge: Cambridge University Press, 1981.

Scott, Hamish M. *Enlightened Absolutism: Reform and Reformers in Later Eighteenth-Century Europe.* Ann Arbor: University of Michigan Press, 1990.

Szabo, Franz A. J. *Kaunitz and Enlightened Absolutism, 1753–1780.* Cambridge: Cambridge University Press, 1994.

Withers, Charles W. J. *Placing the Enlightenment: Thinking Geographically about the Age of Reason.* Chicago: University of Chicago Press, 2007.

Wolff, Larry. *Inventing Eastern Europe: The Map of Civilization on the Mind of the Enlightenment.* Stanford, CA: Stanford University Press, 1994.

CASE STUDIES OF ENLIGHTENMENT FIGURES

Carrithers, David W., and Patrick Coleman, eds. *Montesquieu and the Spirit of Modernity*. Studies on Voltaire and the Eighteenth Century, vol. 2002:09. Oxford: Voltaire Foundation, 2002.

Derathé, Robert. *Jean-Jacques Rousseau et la science politique de son temps*. 2nd ed. Paris: Vrin, 1992.

Ellis, Harold. *Boulainvilliers and the French Monarchy: Aristocratic Politics in Early Eighteenth-Century France*. Ithaca, NY: Cornell University Press, 1988.

Kors, Alan Charles. *D'Holbach's Coterie: An Enlightenment in Paris*. Princeton, NJ: Princeton University Press, 1976.

Lough, John. *Essays on the "Encyclopédie" of Diderot and d'Alembert*. Oxford: Oxford University Press, 1968.

Niderst, Alain. *Fontenelle à la recherche de lui-même (1657–1702)*. Paris: Nizet, 1972.

Pearson, Roger. *Voltaire Almighty: A Life in Pursuit of Freedom*. London: Bloomsbury, 2005.

Proust, Jacques. *Diderot et l'"Encyclopédie."* 1967. Paris: A. Michel, 1995.

Rétat, Pierre. *Le "Dictionnaire" de Bayle et la lutte philosophique au XVIIIe siècle*. Paris: Belles Lettres, 1971.

Rothschild, Emma. *Economic Sentiments: Condorcet, Adam Smith, and the Enlightenment*. Cambridge, MA: Harvard University Press, 2001.

Shackleton, Robert. *Montesquieu: A Critical Biography*. Oxford: Oxford University Press, 1970.

Smith, David Warner. *Helvétius: A Study in Persecution*. Oxford: Clarendon Press, 1965.

Spector, Céline. *Montesquieu: Pouvoirs, richesses et sociétés*. Paris: Presses Universitaires de France, 2004.

Starobinski, Jean. *Blessings in Disguise; or, The Morality of Evil*. Translated by Arthur Goldhammer. Cambridge, MA: Harvard University Press, 1993.

Wilson, Arthur M. *Diderot: The Testing Years, 1713–1759*. New York: Oxford University Press, 1957.

Index